It's More Than "Just Being In"

Ch 5, Ch 6
✓   ✓

Chapter 7, 8, 9

It's More Than "Just Being In"

Creating Authentic Inclusion for Students with Complex Support Needs

by

Cheryl M. Jorgensen, Ph.D.
South Acworth, New Hampshire

·P A U L·H·
BROOKES
PUBLISHING C⁰ ®

Baltimore • London • Sydney

Paul H. Brookes Publishing Co.
Post Office Box 10624
Baltimore, Maryland 21285-0624
USA

www.brookespublishing.com

Typeset by Progressive Publishing Services, York, Pennsylvania.
Manufactured in the United States of America by
Sheridan Books, Inc., Chelsea, Michigan.

The individuals described in this book are composites or real people whose situations are masked and are based on the author's experiences. In all instances, names and identifying details have been changed to protect confidentiality.

Case studies are real people or composites based on the authors' experiences. Real names and identifying details are used by permission.

Library of Congress Cataloging-in-Publication Data

Names: Jorgensen, Cheryl M., author.
Title: It's more than "just being in" : creating authentic inclusion for students with complex support
    needs / by Cheryl M. Jorgensen.
Description: Baltimore, Maryland : Paul H. Brookes Publishing Co., 2018. | Includes bibliographical
    references and index.
Identifiers: LCCN 2017051005 (print) | LCCN 2018005221 (ebook) | ISBN 9781681251738 (epub) |
    ISBN 9781681251752 (pdf) | ISBN 9781681250786 (paperback)
Subjects: LCSH: Inclusive education. | Children with disabilities—Education. | Classroom
    environment. | BISAC: EDUCATION / Special Education / General.
Classification: LCC LC1201 (ebook) | LCC LC1201 .J6699 2018 (print) | DDC 371.9/046—dc23
LC record available at https://lccn.loc.gov/2017051005

British Library Cataloguing in Publication data are available from the British Library.

2022   2021

10   9   8   7   6   5   4   3   2

Contents

About
the Downloads

Purchasers of this book may download, print, and/or photocopy the handouts and forms for educational use. These materials are included with the print book and are also available at **www.brookespublishing.com/jorgensen/materials** for both print and e-book buyers.

About the Author

Cheryl M. Jorgensen, Ph.D., is an inclusive education consultant in private practice after being a project director with the Institute on Disability at the University of New Hampshire (UNH) and an assistant research professor in UNH's Education Department from 1985 to 2011. During her tenure with the Institute on Disability, she was the director or coordinator of state and federally funded research, personnel preparation, model demonstration, alternate assessment, and in-service training grants totaling more than $12 million. She is a cofounder of the National Center on Inclusive Education and collaborated with the U.S. Department of Education's Schoolwide Integrated Framework for Transformation (SWIFT) Project.

Dr. Jorgensen works with parents, teachers, and administrators as part of the Vermont I-Team and in her private consultant role to increase their commitment to and capacity for including students with complex support needs in general education classes and to implement and sustain broad-based inclusive school reform.

Dr. Jorgensen has authored several books (including *The Inclusion Facilitator's Guide* and *The Beyond Access Model*) and research articles; presents at state, national, and international conferences; and provides student-specific consultation throughout the United States.

Dr. Jorgensen received an award from the National Down Syndrome Congress in 2008 for her contributions to inclusive education research.

Foreword

I was recently giving a presentation to a large group of educators. The talk went well, and the audience seemed receptive. A young teacher approached me as I was packing up to leave and asked a question I hear a lot. It seems like a simple question, but it is far from simple: "I really want to do this. I want to get students included in my school. How do I begin?"

I absolutely love this question, but I am often at a loss to answer it. It is hard to know what to share in this moment. I know enthusiastic educators do not want to hear all they need to learn, know, and do to successfully support students in inclusive environments. They want to know what step to take first and how to follow that successful step with another. I typically provide the people in these situations with a laundry list of recommended reading, web sites, and clips on YouTube because I am not sure how to give a pithy answer to such a big question. Unfortunately, this response can cause an interested advocate, teacher, or parent to feel totally overwhelmed and possibly to give up before they have even started.

I am so grateful that I can now provide a more helpful response to that teacher and others like her. My new response is, "You need to get a copy of *It's More Than 'Just Being In'* and read it cover to cover! This book will guide you on where to start, where to go next, and how to create big and small changes in your school and your district."

Believe me. There is not another book on the market like *It's More Than "Just Being In"* I have been a public school teacher and inclusion facilitator in both elementary and secondary schools. I have spent time planning with teachers in the role of inclusive education consultant. I have also worked as a university professor and teacher educator in inclusive schooling. Therefore, my sagging bookshelf is overflowing with books on this topic. I have books on universal design for instruction, teaching strategies, students with specific disabilities, positive behavior supports, collaboration and co-teaching, and school restructuring. So many of these resources are top-notch; so many are critical to my work; and so many are useful for broad audiences, but none will take you step-by-step through the process of supporting and including one, a few, or many students with identified needs in quite the way this book does.

The process I refer to begins with setting a vision. In this book, Cheryl Jorgensen examines the "why" and "how" of doing so and provides a pathway to realizing that vision via chapters that highlight positive practices that are critical to a high-quality inclusive experience today. Nothing is left to chance. No stone is left unturned. Every necessary detail is provided. Certainly, the book is filled with Cheryl's progressive values and ideology and it is—without question—centered on a broader agenda of social justice and democratic education. At the same time, however, the book is no nonsense and filled with the tips, reminders, and practical advice that busy educators, advocates, and families need. For example, she highlights the importance of focusing (and refocusing) on communication needs as a tool for support, connection, and learning; she examines the broad range of supplementary aids and services that learners might require in any inclusive environment; and she emphasizes the critical need to facilitate and honor authentic reciprocal social relationships.

Critically, these information-packed chapters are not filled with mere steps to follow and practices to put into place. You will find steps and practices, no doubt, but the pages of this book are also chockful of classroom stories and examples of how to implement the many ideas provided; these stories and examples are as real as they are varied, and readers will appreciate that they focus on students with a range of needs, abilities, skills, challenges, characteristics, and strengths. Research is also a centerpiece of these chapters. Studies relevant to each topic are explored to help readers understand every aspect of inclusive education and support the many practical recommendations offered throughout the book.

And if all of that is not enough reason to buy, read, and absorb the wisdom in this book, let me share one more point. The book you hold in your hands (or see on your screen) is written by a researcher, scholar, educator, and advocate who is, quite honestly and without exaggeration, second to none. No author is in a better position to share the most relevant research, offer guidance for change, highlight necessary values and practices, or provide tips and ideas that are both teacher and administrator tested. Cheryl has worked intimately with both families and educators and has served as a critical friend to both elementary and secondary schools. She has worked in teacher education for years and has inspired thousands of new K–12 educators to teach inclusively in her work at the university level. Furthermore, she not only knows the research on this topic inside and out, but she has also written several of the studies that matter the most to those of us seeking answers and guidance in this field.

For all these reasons, I hope that this book is used in your pursuit and study of inclusive education. I also hope that you pass it on to a teacher, parent, advocate, therapist, school board member, or student who needs some information, insight, or inspiration. I know I will be purchasing several copies. I definitely need one for my bulging bookshelf filled with inclusion-related titles, but I also need several others for those who will undoubtedly say, "I really want to do this! Where do I begin?"

Paula Kluth, Ph.D.
www.paulakluth.com

Foreword

Our son Samuel was diagnosed with a complex, lifelong disability when he was about a year old. My wife Betsy and I reacted with a web of emotions. Fear. Grief. Confusion. Uncertainty. We were overwhelmed, and we craved reassurance that Samuel could still have the fulfilling, happy life that we had envisioned for him and his older brother, Isaiah.

We were seeking a vision for Samuel's life. In that vision, Samuel would feel like he belonged—in our extended family, our neighborhood, our community and, most certainly, in our local schools.

Cheryl Jorgensen helped us find that vision.

One of Cheryl's many hats back in the early 2000s was serving as a facilitator for the New Hampshire Leadership Series, organized by the University of New Hampshire Institute on Disability (part of a national Partners in Policymaking model).

My wife and I participated in the Leadership Series before Samuel made it past preschool. At every juncture of this yearlong "boot camp for disability advocacy" as I called it, Cheryl assured us that Samuel could be fully included in general education with the proper supports and instruction. She backed up that assurance with extensive supporting research and practical strategies for schools and families.

When I graduated from the Leadership Series in 2003, I was inspired to begin work on a personal documentary project that would eventually become my 2008 film *Including Samuel*. Of course, Cheryl was among the very first people I turned to for guidance and interviews. One of my favorite lines in the film comes from Cheryl, who states plainly, "All kids, with the right support and the right technology and the right teaching, can learn the general education curriculum. And that's a pretty dramatic statement." It is a dramatic statement, and Cheryl lays out a compelling, practical case for support in this book.

It's More Than "Just Being In" is an essential and accessible tool for families and schools to develop a shared commitment to working in partnership for inclusion. The book is a blueprint for best educational practices, including

- Presuming competence
- Collaborative planning, teaching, and learning
- Administrative leadership
- Person-centered planning
- Communication strategies
- Self-advocacy and self-determination

- Standards-based individualized education programs

- Implementing adaptations, accommodations, and modifications with fidelity

- Facilitating social relationships

- Effective postsecondary transition

And much, much more.

It is important to understand that Cheryl is not an outlier. She is just outstanding at presenting comprehensive and cutting-edge information in an accessible, empowering manner.

As a national leader in inclusive education, Cheryl is plugged into the most current knowledge base for inclusive education, such as the Schoolwide Integrated Framework for Transformation (SWIFT). I have been involved as a filmmaker for the SWIFT technical assistance center throughout the life of this $25 million federally funded effort (based at the University of Kansas).

SWIFT is the best chance we have ever had to scale up inclusive education nationally. Research from SWIFT and other studies is persuasive—when students with different support needs learn together, they experience better academic and behavioral outcomes, social relationships, high school graduation rates, and post-school success.

Although we all want large-scale systems change such as SWIFT, Cheryl also recognizes that most parents need a road map to advocate for inclusion at every juncture. *It's More Than "Just Being In"* is that road map.

Oh, and I should mention that as I write this, Samuel is a high school senior, included in general education, on a track toward a regular diploma with an eye toward college, and surrounded by a wide circle of friends.

He belongs.

Thank you, Cheryl.

Dan Habib
Filmmaker and Project Director
University of New Hampshire Institute on Disability

Preface

Are you a general education teacher who will have a student with autism spectrum disorder (ASD) in your class next year and just do not know where to begin? Do you wonder how you will communicate with him or her? Have you heard rumors about his or her challenging behavior? Are you concerned that your teacher evaluation will be affected if you spend a disproportionate amount of time with this student and fall behind in your syllabus?

Perhaps you are a special education teacher who is responsible for facilitating the inclusion of several students with multiple disabilities but cannot imagine how you will manage this with all your other responsibilities. Are you concerned about meeting your students' individualized education program (IEP) goals within the general education curriculum and classroom?

Maybe you are a parent or guardian who desperately wants your child who has Down syndrome included with his or her classmates without disabilities, but you have not yet been able to convince the school that this is appropriate. Perhaps you have already tried the bit-by-bit approach suggested by the school but worry that at this rate your child will graduate before he or she gets the opportunity to be fully included. You want to be a collaborative team player and do not want to alienate those who are responsible for your child's safety and emotional well-being.

Are you a secondary school administrator who is getting more requests for inclusion from parents whose children were in general education in the lower grades? You have been to conferences and read a lot of articles about inclusive education, but few seem to address the unique needs of secondary school students and staff. Maybe you wish that there were a step-by-step guide so there is some consistency in students' educational programs and a shared understanding by staff about the purpose of inclusion.

This book was written to address these concerns and, more broadly, to help families and educators of students with intellectual and other developmental disabilities (IDD) to fully include those students in general education instruction within a general education classroom. Strategies are included for enhancing the participation of students who are already "in," as well as strategies for moving students from a self-contained or life skills class into general education.

This preface presents a little bit about my history in the field of inclusive education, provides alarming statistics about inclusion in the United States, introduces three students whose stories are featured in this book, and shows how this book can be used in your unique situation.

MY HISTORY

I was hired by the University of New Hampshire's (UNH) School of Health and Human Services in 1985 to coordinate a small in-service training project for teachers of "severely and profoundly handicapped" students. I spent the first couple of months of the project visiting the various programs in which these students were enrolled because I was new to the state and knew nothing about special education (I am a general educator by training and experience); some were in self-contained classrooms in public schools, some attended regional cooperative programs, and others attended classes housed in large residential facilities such as the now-closed Laconia State School. Two encounters during my tour of Laconia made a lasting impact on me.

I met Ronnie, who was lying naked on a gurney in the middle of a stark room that had no desks, books, or computers. The woman who was giving him a sponge bath said with a jolly laugh, "Don't worry about Ronnie. He doesn't mind. Come on in!" I was mortified, but I managed to say, "Oh, that's no problem. I'll just wait out here until you are finished." Ronnie had cerebral palsy, could not talk, and had no way to communicate. Neither he nor the other five students in the room appeared to be engaged in anything that could remotely be considered educational. Although the facility was clean and there appeared to be as many staff people as residents, there were vestiges of the institutional life that had existed there for almost 100 years. It was chilling to see, embedded in the concrete walls, the heavy iron rings used to restrain people while they were bathed with cold water sprayed from common garden hoses. I did not know what Laconia had been like in the past, but the attitude toward and treatment of Ronnie still seemed inhuman.

The second encounter I had was with a program director at Laconia. He proudly showed me the facility's "store." There were racks of clothing, and the residents could use tokens to "buy" one of the hundreds of identical navy blue T-shirts or khaki-colored pants.

I naively asked, "Why don't you just take people to K-Mart?"

The director said, "Well, we just don't have enough staff for that, and, besides, the residents don't have any money and all these clothes have been donated at no cost. It just wouldn't be fiscally possible."

I knew nothing about the disability rights movement at this point in my career. I had never heard of person-centered planning, community integration, or inclusive education. But I just felt in my gut that there was something drastically wrong with these situations, and I decided that I would do my best to ensure that no child was ever sent to a place like this again. I worked for the Institute on Disability at UNH for the next 26 years, supporting the inclusion of students with IDD through professional development, model demonstration projects, research, large-scale systems change efforts, reform of teacher certification and preparation, and dissemination of best practices. I retired from the university in 2011 and continue my work as an independent consultant and professional development trainer.

AND MILES TO GO

Much has changed since 1985, but much remains to be done.

- New Hampshire became the first state to close its public institution for people with IDD in 1991, and 11 additional states have since closed all of their state-run large institutional facilities. Although that is good news for people living in those states, more than 26,000 people in other states still live in developmental disability-specific institutional settings, and more than 29,000 live in nursing homes (National Council on Disability, n.d.).

- Most students with IDD are still largely segregated from their classmates without disabilities, despite the fact they are educated in public schools. For example, from 2002 to 2011, the percent of all students ages 6–21 served in special education who were educated inside the regular class 80% or more of the day increased from 48.2% to 61.1%. Yet, the 2012 average of all states' placement of students with intellectual disability (ID) at least 80% of the day in general education was only 17.1% (U.S. Department of Education, 2014).

- The average of all states' placement rates hides large state-to-state variation. According to the *36th Annual Report to Congress on the Implementation of IDEA* (U.S. Department of Education, 2014), the percent of students with ID educated at least 80% of the day in general education classes ranged from lows of 4.4% in Washington, 4.8% in New Jersey, and 5.5% in Nevada, to highs of 64% in Iowa, 48.6% in Puerto Rico, and 45.5% in Alabama.

- Approximately 62% of students with ID in the United States do not leave school with a regular high school diploma (Institute on Disability, 2015).

- The U.S. employment rate for people with ID (ages 21–64) is 26.1%, compared with 41.1% for people with disabilities overall and 79.1% for people without disabilities (Siperstein, Parker, & Drascher, 2013).

There are some good reasons to be hopeful that these statistics will change. More schools are adopting a multi-tiered system of supports (MTSS) instructional framework, which is a whole-school, data-driven, prevention-based framework for improving learning outcomes for every student through a layered continuum of evidence-based practices and systems. One principle of MTSS is that all students, including those with IDD, have access to high-quality core instruction based on the principles of universal design for learning (UDL).

The Schoolwide Integrated Framework for Transformation (SWIFT), another initiative funded by the U.S. Department of Education, was a kindergarten through eighth-grade technical assistance center that helped schools create academic and behavioral supports that promote inclusive learning and academic achievement of all students, including students with IDD (University of Kansas, 2016). Although the project ended in 2017, staff continue contracted work with school districts throughout the United States. SWIFT classrooms represent diverse learning communities in which all students are learning together and have the supports they need to fully participate in the general education curriculum. General educators, special educators, Title I tutors, other support staff, and family and community members work in tandem to differentiate instruction. For example, you may witness a parent volunteer practicing sight words with a student, a general educator and a special educator leading differentiated small reading groups, a speech-language pathologist working on reading vocabulary with another group of students, and classmates collaborating on a reading comprehension activity. Students are valued for their unique contributions to the learning community, and educators have the support they need to successfully teach all students.

A majority of schools are still at the very beginning stages of including students with IDD in general education classrooms, despite these promising initiatives. I typically see one of three common situations when I consult at a school.

1. A student is primarily a member of a self-contained classroom and is mainstreamed for morning meeting, lunch, music, and perhaps another nonacademic subject.

2. A student is primarily a member of a general education classroom but is pulled out of language arts and math lessons to receive instruction in a setting with other students with disabilities.

3. A student is a member of a general education classroom for most of the day but is not really participating with his or her classmates in the same general education instruction and is an "island in the mainstream" (Biklen, 1985, p. 18).

Even if your situation is slightly different from these, this book was written to enable you to use whichever chapters meet your needs.

THE PURPOSE OF THIS BOOK

The purpose of this book is to provide a step-by-step approach to the inclusion of students with IDD, such as Down syndrome, ASD, and multiple physical disabilities—all students with complex support needs. It is written for families, the school-based members of students' education teams, and administrators leading inclusion efforts in their schools. Although I am fully supportive of wholesale school restructuring to break down the barriers between general education, special education, Title I, and other categorical services, I know firsthand that most schools are not engaged in those efforts. And as my colleagues Barb McKenzie and Janet Sauer, parents of students with disabilities, say, "My child can't wait for systems change!"

The Students

This book describes a step-by-step approach to inclusion for students with IDD. Although these deficit-based definitions will not be used anywhere else in this book, nor do they reflect my own beliefs about students' capacity for learning, I share them here to let readers know that the strategies in this book are appropriate for students with the most complex support needs. A developmental disability

- Is attributable to a mental or physical impairment or a combination of those impairments

- Occurs before the individual reaches age 22

- Is likely to continue indefinitely

- Results in substantial functional limitations in three or more of the following areas of major life activity: 1) self-care, 2) receptive and expressive language, 3) learning, 4) mobility, 5) self-direction, 6) capacity for independent living, and 7) economic self-sufficiency

- Reflects the individual's need for a combination and sequence of special, interdisciplinary, or generic services, individualized supports, or other forms of assistance that are of lifelong or extended duration and are individually planned and coordinated

Some people with developmental disabilities are also diagnosed with an *intellectual disability,* which is defined (in the medical model of disability) as a significant limitation in both intellectual functioning and in adaptive behavior, which covers many everyday social and practical skills. Full disclosure here: I do not put any stock in the label of intellectual disability. All people have a variety of strengths and limitations and categories such as these are, in the opinion of many, wholly socially constructed (Biklen & Duchan, 1994).

The medical model definition of ASD includes deficits in social communication and social interaction across multiple contexts resulting in restricted, repetitive patterns of behavior, interests, or activities. In contrast to this deficit-based description, many people with ASD are constructing their own identities based on the idea of neurodiversity.

> The disability rights perspective within the Autistic community is represented in the neurodiversity movement, which promotes social acceptance of neurological difference as part of the broad landscape of human diversity and seeks to bring about a world in which Autistic people enjoy the same access, rights, and opportunities as all other citizens. Acceptance of difference is essential to understanding, accepting, and benefiting from the contributions of everyone in our society, thus allowing all people to live up to their potential. (Autistic Self Advocacy Network, 2018)

Composite Case Studies: Three Students

Examples from the educational programs of three students who represent composites of many students whom I have known since the late 1980s will be shared throughout the book. James is a second-grade student with multiple physical disabilities due to cerebral palsy and cortical visual impairment (CVI). I met him when I was asked to consult to his small elementary school in a rural school district. On the day that I first visited James I learned that his parents wanted him to be a member of a general education classroom, but his school believed that his disabilities were too significant for him to gain much benefit from either the general education curriculum or being around his typical classmates. James used a wheelchair and did not have any means of communication other than certain voice inflections or changes in his body posture. His forehead was supported by a strap attached to the back of his wheelchair so that he would not slump when his neck muscles got tired. He needed assistance moving his hands meaningfully, using the bathroom, and eating. I spent a little time reading to him and noticed that he perked up when there was dialogue or during an exciting part of the story. James spent his whole day in a self-contained classroom with three other students with multiple physical disabilities and was engaged primarily in hand-over-hand activities of daily living and various therapies. He had a seizure disorder that was well controlled by medication. He wore glasses and hearing aids, and orthotics on his lower legs. Students like James are often described as having profound disabilities, and they usually participate in their state's alternate assessment based on alternate achievement standards. I knew that there was much more to discover about James and was anxious to get to know his likes and dislikes, his personality, activities that aroused his attention, and, most important, what kind of communication supports would match his strengths and accommodate for his movement difficulties. James eventually became a fully participating member of a general education classroom through the advocacy of his parents and commitment of the other members of his education team. James now uses an iPad with the Compass app for communication.

Anna, a sixth-grade student with ASD, is the second student who is profiled in this book. I first met Anna at her home where she was the oldest child in a family of eight who were always on the go. She had just begun using an iPad, was a whiz at playing games, and could navigate through many different apps and web sites to find music and videos of her favorite singers. Anna's parents told me that they were certain that Anna knew more than she could demonstrate, and they wanted her to be enrolled in the full range of general education academic classes when she moved up to the middle school the following year. She participated in art, physical education, and science with her typical classmates when I met her, and she spent the rest of the time in a classroom with five other students with ASD. I spoke to Anna's case manager who was very concerned that Anna's behavior presented a barrier to her greater inclusion. She noted that Anna had only recently returned to the school district from an autism-only residential school, and she was unsure how the strict applied behavior analysis program currently being used in the self-contained classroom would work in a general education class. Anna was highly dependent on tangible rewards, and staff frequently used the promise of those rewards (or the threat that she would not receive them) as incentives. Anna spoke some very short phrases in a meaningful way but did not have the technology to enable her to meet the same communication needs as her typical classmates. She had mastered the pre-primer and primer level Dolch words in isolation but did not currently make sense of connected text (Dolch, 1936). Anna's eighth-grade year was fully inclusive of all core academic classes and electives after many professional development workshops and support from the districtwide inclusion facilitator. Anna currently uses an iPad with the TouchChat app for communication, and she participates in her state's general assessment with accommodations.

Selena is a tenth-grade student with Down syndrome. I learned that her educational program was comprised of half a day in a life skills classroom with 10 other students with disabilities and the other half of the day in three general education elective classes (e.g., culinary arts, early childhood development, pottery). Selena and her parents wanted her to go on to postsecondary education in the field of tourism or computer technology and wanted her to take a typical course load of classes to broaden her knowledge of literature, science, history, and mathematics. Selena's case manager expressed concern that her current academic skills were so far below those of the students in the high school's general education classes that she would be lost and could never meet the academic expectations. I found Selena's decoding skills to be quite good, but she struggled to demonstrate her comprehension when I spent a day observing her and working with her on some homework. Selena was often accompanied from class to class by a paraprofessional and would frequently glance behind her to see if the paraprofessional was still there. Through some restructuring of Selena's education team to include a special education resource teacher instead of the life skills teacher (who was already overwhelmed with the other students in her classroom), Selena added general education core academic classes to her schedule and joined a school club that was focused on civil rights and social justice and another club focused on technology.

HOW TO USE THIS BOOK

Unlike other books that present a variety of inclusive education topics in somewhat random order, this book is structured so that it can be used in a sequential, step-by-step manner. The titles of Chapters 2–10 begin with a verb—*imagine, construct, write, identify, describe, establish, facilitate,* and *develop.* This is quite intentional because I hope that you will be prepared to take action after reading each chapter. Each chapter begins with some background information about the topic, describes in detail the underlying rationale and detailed processes associated with the chapter topic, presents examples for one or more of the profiled students via the "student case study" boxes, and includes checklists that summarize the steps necessary to implement the suggested strategies. The book also features "best practices for inclusion" boxes to emphasize successful inclusion strategies.

Chapter 1 is titled "The Fundamentals of Inclusive Education." Even if you are knowledgeable about inclusive education, I recommend that you read it because it sets the stage for each of the following chapters. It begins with the values- and research-based rationale for inclusive education. The core elements of inclusion are then described, including presuming competence, welcome membership in general education, full participation in general education instruction, learning of general education academics and inclusive functional skills, collaborative teaming, and administrative leadership.

Chapter 2 is titled "Imagine an Inclusive Vision for Education and Adult Life." This chapter describes Making Action Plans (MAPS), a person-centered planning process that helps parents and schools establish inclusive visions for students' education and life after high school. I suggest that MAPS be used just prior to a student's very first day of public school (i.e., preschool, kindergarten) and then periodically until the student reaches about 10th grade. The best times to do revisions to the first plan are when there is a significant change in the student, in the composition of the student's IEP team, and prior to transition to a new school or school district (e.g., elementary to middle, middle to high school).

Chapter 3 is titled "Construct Learning and Communicative Competence." The fundamentals of presuming competence are taken to the next step—translating a belief in the student's competence to creating the conditions under which that competence is demonstrated. Specific strategies are described related to providing students with a way to communicate about all academic and social topics as well as strategies for promoting self-advocacy and self-determination, which are skills needed by self-actualized and competent people.

Chapter 4 is titled "Write an Inclusive Standards-Based Individualized Education Program." Sections from three inclusive standards-based IEPs are shared along with a step-by-step process for writing IEPs. Supplementary aids and services is addressed in a separate chapter because the topic is so extensive.

Chapter 5 is titled "Identify Supplementary Aids and Services as Part of an Inclusive Standards-Based IEP" and describes many possible supports, including adaptations, accommodations, and modifications, that a student might need for participation and learning. It also addresses a little-known aspect of supplementary aids and services, which are the supports needed by the team on behalf of the student, to enable him or her to make progress in the general education curriculum.

Chapter 6 is titled "Describe Inclusive Team Member Roles and Establish Collaborative Teaming Processes" and provides a guide for examining the current roles of all team members and restructuring those roles so that everyone is working toward the same goal—authentic inclusive education.

Chapter 7 is titled "Establish Valued Membership in General Education" and is based on the fundamentals of membership and belonging described in Chapter 1.

It presents a step-by-step guide to establishing a student's membership in a general education classroom, with specific examples from the profiled students' elementary, middle, and high school years.

Chapter 8 is titled "Facilitate Reciprocal Social Relationships" and describes what teams need to do and not do to make real friendships happen (Tashie, Shapiro-Barnard, & Rossetti, 2006). The importance of reducing barriers to authentic social relationships is presented along with strategies that parents and educators can use when more intentional facilitation is needed.

Chapter 9 is titled "Develop Learning and Participation Plans and Assess Their Fidelity of Implementation" and describes a collaborative planning process that identifies a student's priority learning objectives within a unit of instruction and the specific supports that are needed in the domains that are affected by the student's disability. A process for checking the fidelity of implementation of supports is also provided. Teams have greater confidence that the student's measured performance is reflective of his or her potential and not a lack of opportunity to learn or poor instruction when the fidelity of implementation of supports is highly rated. Sample learning and participation plans for each of the three profiled students are shared.

Moving from high school to adult life is one of the most important transitions that all students will experience. Person-centered planning is described in Chapter 10, which is titled "Plan and Prepare for an Inclusive Life After High School," as a strategy for planning and realizing students' postsecondary education, employment, and community living goals.

Chapter 11 is titled "Solutions to Common Problems and Challenges in Achieving Inclusive Education" and provides solutions to the most commonly asked questions about inclusive education posed by parents, administrators, educators, and related services providers.

Although you can pick up this book and read the chapter or chapters that address the topics that interest you the most, there are a few situations in which reading the book cover to cover and following all the implementation steps might make sense, including the following.

- A child is making the transition from preschool to kindergarten and his or her team is planning for his or her inclusion right from the start.

- A student is making the transition from one grade level and building to an entirely new situation (e.g., elementary to middle school, middle school to high school)

- A student is moving from being largely self-contained to being a full-time member of a general education class.

- A student is moving from one school district to another and the new team has no experience with inclusive education.

- A student has been partially integrated in some general education classes, but there is disagreement within the team concerning the rationale for and "doability" of fully including the student in an age-appropriate general education classroom.

REFERENCES

Autistic Self Advocacy Network. (2018). *Disability rights and neurodiversity: Acceptance of differ-ences.* Retrieved from http://autisticadvocacy.org/policy-advocacy/position-statements/

Biklen, D. (1985). *Achieving the complete school: Strategies for effective mainstreaming.* New York, NY: Teachers College Press.

Biklen, D., & Duchan, J. F. (1994). The social construction of mental retardation. *JASH, 19*(3), 173–184.

Dolch, E. W. (1936). A basic sight vocabulary. *Elementary School Journal, 36*(6), 456–460.

Institute on Disability, University of New Hampshire. (2015). *Annual disability statistics compendium.* Retrieved from https://disabilitycompendium.org/sites/default/files/user-uploads/Events/2015%20Annual%20Disability%20Statistics%20Compendium.pdf

Jorgensen, C. M., McKenzie, B., & Sauer, J. (2014, December). *My child can't wait for systems change!* Presentation at the TASH Conference, Washington, DC.

National Council on Disability. (n.d.). *Institutions in brief.* Retrieved from https://ncd.gov/publications/2012/DIToolkit/Institutions/inBrief

Siperstein, G. N., Parker, R. C., & Drascher, M. (2013). National snapshot of adults with intel-lectual disabilities in the labor force. *Journal of Vocational Rehabilitation, 39*(3), 157–165.

Tashie, C., Shapiro-Barnard, S., & Rossetti, Z. (2006). *Seeing the charade: What we need to do and undo to make friendships happen.* Nottingham, United Kingdom: Inclusive Solutions.

University of Kansas. (2016). *SWIFT education center.* Retrieved from http://www.swiftschools.org

U.S. Department of Education, Office of Special Education and Rehabilitative Services, Office of Special Education Programs. (2014). *Thirty-sixth annual report to Congress on the implementation of the Individuals with Disabilities Education Act, 2014.* Retrieved from http://www2.ed.gov/about/reports/annual/osep/2014/parts-b-c/36th-idea-arc.pdf

REFERENCES

With love to Byll, Katherine, Anne, Steve, Keith, Jason, Jordan, and Hugo

1

The Fundamentals
of Inclusive Education

DEFINITION OF INCLUSION

The term *inclusive education* was coined by Marsha Forest during a 1987 workshop for families and educators in New Hampshire (Forest, 1987). Since that time, people have used the term to describe a variety of educational practices that are not actually inclusion, such as part-time inclusion, reverse inclusion, inclusion classroom, or inclusion student. These terms lack one or more of the elements that make up authentic inclusion. The definition of *inclusion* states that all students

> are presumed competent, are welcomed as valued members of all general education classes and extra-curricular activities in their local schools, fully participate and learn alongside their same age peers in general education instruction based on the general education curriculum, and experience reciprocal social relationships. (TASH, n.d., para.1)

RATIONALE FOR INCLUSION

Research has shown a positive correlation between the time that students with disabilities spend in general education and the quality-of-life outcomes after high school. Research has also shown that students with and without disabilities perform better academically and socially when part of an inclusive classroom. Other rationales include social justice and civil rights, and legal and regulatory requirements. The second part of the chapter describes the core elements of inclusion and the rationale for each.

Social Justice and Civil Rights

Inclusive education has been justified on the basis of social justice and civil rights. For example, the introductory congressional findings of the Individuals with Disabilities Education Improvement Act (IDEA) of 2004 (PL 108-446) reflect the values- and evidence-based rationale for inclusive education.

> Disability is a natural part of the human experience and in no way diminishes the right of individuals to participate in or contribute to society. Almost 30 years of research and experience has demonstrated that the education of children with disabilities can be made more effective by having high expectations for such children and ensuring their access to the general education curriculum in the regular classroom, to the maximum extent possible. (pp. 2–3)

Least Restrictive Environment Mandate of IDEA

The term *least restrictive environment* (LRE), which is found in the final regulations that guide the implementation of IDEA 2004, is used to specify the meaning of access to the general education curriculum in the regular classroom.

> (1) To the maximum extent appropriate, handicapped children, including children in public or private institutions or other care facilities, are educated with children who are not handicapped, and (2) That special classes, separate schooling or other removal of handicapped children from the regular educational environment occurs only when the nature or severity of the handicap is such that education in regular classes with the use of supplementary aids and services cannot be achieved satisfactorily. (U.S. Department of Education, 2006, §§ 300.114–300.120)

Although the LRE mandate seems to give a very high priority to general education placement for students with disabilities, in reality, this is far from being achieved, especially for the 84% of students with intellectual and developmental disabilities (IDD) who still spend the majority of their day outside of a general education classroom (U.S. Department of Education, 2014).

Because of the vagueness of the LRE regulations, parents and schools have sought relief from various levels of the United States court system to define LRE for a particular student or class of students. Some of these cases have supported an individual student's inclusion and others have determined that a separate educational environment is the least restrictive. In reviewing these cases, there are only four reasons why students should not be placed in a general education class, with the burden placed on the individualized education program (IEP) team to justify removal from general education—lack of educational benefits, lack of nonacademic benefits, negative effect of the child on the teacher and other children, and unreasonable cost (Wright's Law, n.d., para. 15).

Unacceptable reasons for removing a student from a general education classroom, as described in a variety of guidance documents (South

Dakota Department of Education, 2013; Wright's Law, n.d., para. 15), include

- The number and intensity of needed services and supports
- Student's need for extensive curricular modifications
- Student's participation in a state's alternate assessment
- Student's need for behavioral support
- Student's reading level
- Student not having the prerequisite skills required by the curriculum being taught
- Student's use of communication or other assistive technologies (ATs)
- School's lack of experience with inclusion
- School's history of placing students in separate programs
- Location of skilled staff in other buildings or classrooms
- Class size
- Lack of knowledge or skills by staff

Better Outcomes in Inclusive Environments

Inclusive education is also supported by strong educational research. Jackson, Ryndak, and Wehmeyer (2008/2009) used theory, historical research, and empirical literature and made a case for inclusive education as a research-based practice and concluded:

> Placement in age- and grade-appropriate general education contexts and having special and general educators team to provide supports and modifications for all students are first-order research based practice, and the benefits of proven methods of instruction are realized in the long run only when this first step is implemented in the life of a child. (p. 190)

Findings from numerous research studies show a positive effect of inclusion for students with IDD, including

- Higher expectations for student learning (Jorgensen, McSheehan, & Sonnenmeier, 2007)
- Heightened engagement, affective demeanor, and participation in integrated social activities (Hunt, Farron-Davis, Beckstead, Curtis, & Goetz, 1994)
- Improved communication and social skills (Beukelman & Mirenda, 2013; Fisher & Meyer, 2002; McSheehan, Sonnenmeier, & Jorgensen, 2009; Soto, Muller, Hunt, & Goetz, 2001)

- More satisfying and diverse social relationships (Guralnick, Connor, Hammond, Gottman, & Kinnish, 1996)

- Optimal access to the general education curriculum (Jorgensen, McSheehan, & Sonnenmeier, 2010; Wehmeyer & Agran, 2006)

- Improved academic outcomes in the areas of literacy and mathematics (Cole, Waldron, & Majd, 2004; Cosier, Causton-Theoharis, & Theoharis, 2013; Dessemontet, Bless, & Morin, 2012; Kurth & Mastergeorge, 2010; Ryndak, Alper, Ward, Storch, & Montgomery, 2010; Ryndak, Morrison, & Sommerstein, 1999)

- Better quality IEPs (Hunt & Farron-Davis, 1992)

- Fewer absences from school and referrals for disruptive behavior (Helmstetter, Curry, Brennan, & Sampson-Saul, 1998)

- Achievement of more IEP goals (Brinker & Thorpe, 1984)

- Improved adult outcomes in the areas of postsecondary education, employment, and independence (White & Weiner, 2004)

Research on the impact of inclusion on the performance of students without disabilities has shown either a neutral or positive impact. Kalambouka, Farrell, Dyson, and Kaplan (2007) conducted a meta-analysis of research and found that 81% of the outcomes reported showed including students with disabilities resulted in either positive or neutral effects for students without disabilities. Theoharis and Causton-Theoharis (2010) found improved educational outcomes for students with and without disabilities when inclusion was the primary school reform.

Other positive effects of inclusion on students without disabilities include improved attitudes toward diversity (Finke, McNaughton, & Drager, 2009); unique opportunities for learning about prejudice and equity (Fisher, Sax, & Jorgensen, 1998); and increased academic achievement, assignment completion, and classroom participation by students providing peer supports (Cushing & Kennedy, 1997).

The rationale for inclusion is also supported by the fact that no studies conducted since the late 1970s have shown an academic advantage for students with IDD educated in separate settings (Falvey, 2004). In fact, studies have shown some negative effects of separate special education placement (Causton-Theoharis, Theoharis, Orsati, & Cosier, 2011; Fisher, Sax, Rodifer, & Pumpian, 1999; Hunt & Farron-Davis, 1992).

CORE ELEMENTS OF INCLUSIVE EDUCATION

The core elements of inclusive education are depicted in Figure 1.1 and include a foundation of effective team collaboration and strong administrative leadership, presuming students' competence, welcomed membership in a general education classroom, reciprocal social relationships, full

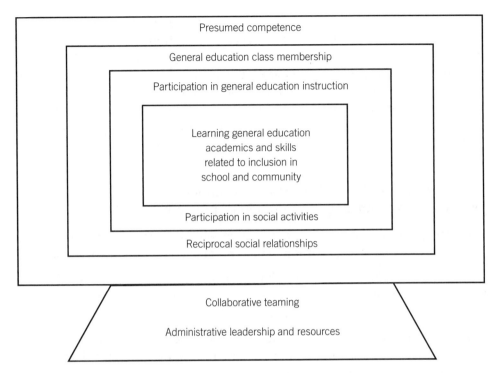

Figure 1.1. Core elements of inclusive education.

participation in general education instruction and social interactions in the classroom and school community, and learning general education academic content along with the skills necessary for participation in an inclusive school and community (Jorgensen et al., 2010).

Presuming Competence

Kim is a 16-year-old student who has an intellectual disability and will be attending high school next year. Recent assessments have determined that her IQ is 40, and she has a developmental age of 36 months. She has seizures and sensory processing difficulties. Her motor movements are jerky and uncoordinated, making it difficult for her to get around in small areas, write legibly, or use a computer. Kim is sensitive to certain environmental stimuli such as bright lights, loud noises, and rough textures. She has no conventional way to communicate; she uses facial expressions, body postures, and occasional vocalizations to express wants, needs, and emotions. She runs away or sometimes hits herself or others when she is frustrated by a task or situation. She does not appear to be able to read (Jorgensen et al., 2010).

How should this information affect Kim's educational program and future decisions about her life after high school? Should her team assume that these test results, labels, and observations are correct and accurately describe her current abilities as well as predict her future potential for learning? Will Kim's case manager suggest that her educational program reflect academic content from the general education curriculum or functional life skills? Should Kim be in classes alongside other students with significant disabilities, fully included in general education classes, or scheduled for a combination of both? It is important to take a step back and consider the history of education and treatment of people with Kim's profile, flawed assumptions about intelligence and intelligence testing, the meaning of the label of intellectual disability, and the vision that general society and schools, in particular, have for students like Kim.

Flawed Assumptions   Four flawed assumptions influence people's view of students like Kim and their educational programs.

1. Intelligence is something that can be reliably measured; therefore, significantly subaverage intelligence can also be reliably measured.

2. Students who are judged to have significantly subaverage intelligence cannot learn much of the general education curriculum, and even if they could, why would they need to?

3. Students who cannot learn much of the general education curriculum will not benefit from being in general education classes and should be taught functional life skills.

4. When students cannot effectively communicate, assumptions are based on what they currently know and what they might be able to learn on whatever communication abilities they may have or lack.

Students' educational programs often have the following characteristics when these assumptions are put into practice.

-   Students are not included in general education classes, or they are only included in classes such as music or art.

-   If students are included in any general education classes, then they are there only for the social interactions and not to learn academics.

-   Students are not provided with a way to communicate about age-appropriate academic or social topics.

-   Students who are included part time in a core academic class are working on skills that are far from the grade-level curriculum, or they are learning functional skills such as calling on the next student, washing the lab equipment, passing out papers, and so forth.

-   Students are given materials that are so different from their classmates that they find it difficult to work together.

-   People talk to students as if they are much younger than their chronological age.

- Students are not supported or are actively discouraged from participating in age-appropriate social activities.

- Planning for students' futures does not include the choice of postsecondary education.

- Career options are geared to lower skilled jobs or sheltered workshops rather than to jobs in integrated workplaces based on students' interests.

- Students are expected to live in congregate settings such as group homes rather than in integrated housing with supports.

A growing number of researchers, educators, parents, and self-advocates have argued that these educational program options are inappropriate for students with IDD, and the assumptions underlying such programs are seriously flawed.

Assumption 1: Intelligence Is Something That Can Be Reliably Measured; Therefore, Significantly Subaverage Intelligence Can Also Be Reliably Measured

French psychologist Alfred Binet developed a series of tests in the early 1900s to help identify students who were most likely to experience difficulties in school and need specialized assistance. When children's scores were computed, they were assigned a number to indicate their mental age versus their chronological age. Children whose mental age was less than their chronological age were then labeled, at that time, as "retarded." Binet (1909) cautioned against the overuse of the test, however, and said,

> Some recent philosophers seem to have given their moral approval to these deplorable verdicts that affirm that the intelligence of an individual is a fixed quantity, a quantity that cannot be augmented. We must protest and react against this brutal pessimism; we will try to demonstrate that it is founded on nothing. (p. 141)

Binet did not believe that his test or any other could or should be used to measure a single, permanent, and inborn level of intelligence. He felt that intelligence was far too broad a concept to quantify with a single number, insisting that intelligence was multifaceted, influenced by many factors other than innate ability, and could change over time with effective education. These tests were modified in the 1920s for use in the United States and they were termed *intelligence quotient* or *IQ tests*. And so began a history of using IQ testing not only for its original purpose but also for determining which immigrants would be let into the country ("feebleminded people" need not apply), which children were eligible for special education services and where they would be educated (low IQ resulted in being placed in segregated classrooms), and which adults would be placed in institutions (low IQ meant adults were a menace to society and unable to live and work safely or productively in the community).

Although the debate continues among psychologists, researchers, and others about whether there is such a thing as a general intelligence factor that can be accurately measured, the use of IQ testing has rarely served to help children gain access to high-quality educational services or help adults get the supports they need to live successfully in the community. Michael Wehmeyer, Professor of Special Education at the University of Kansas, said the following about IQ tests:

> I would argue that they have been used to determine a person's incapacities and incompetence to determine eligibility for the services and programs created, which of course have been primarily segregated settings. Short of qualifying for gifted and talented services in schools, there are few uses of IQ tests that I can come up with that determine capabilities and potential. (M. Wehmeyer, personal communication, June 30, 2014)

The results of research on how well IQ predicts student achievement is another rationale for extreme caution in using a number like a student's IQ to guide his or her education program. McGrew and Evans (2004) concluded

> Given the best available, theoretically and psychometrically sound, nationally standardized, individually administered intelligence test batteries, three statements hold true:
>
> • IQ test scores, under optimal test conditions, account for 40% to 50% of current expected achievement.
>
> • Thus, 50% to 60% of student achievement is related to variables "beyond intelligence."
>
> • For any given IQ test score, half of the students will obtain achievement scores at or below their IQ score. Conversely, and frequently not recognized, is that for any given IQ test score, half of the students will obtain achievement scores at or *above* their IQ score. (p. 6)

Assumption 2:   Students Who Are Judged to Have Significantly Subaverage Intelligence Cannot Learn Much of the General Education Curriculum, and Even If They Could, Why Would They Need To?

The first part of this assumption has been disproved by many researchers since the late 1970s. Browder and Spooner (2014) described a visit to a local high school and their observations of Lucas, a tenth-grade student labeled with an intellectual disability.

> When we arrive in his language arts class, Lucas has just finished a read-aloud with a peer from a chapter in the novel the class is reading. The teacher is asking about the main character, a young man who has to decide if he is going to be loyal to a friend who tries to manipulate him to do the wrong things. Along with his classmates, Lucas's goal is to form an opinion about whether the main character should trust this friend. Everyone must support their answers using facts from the text. For Lucas, writing will involve selecting some answers from a list of quotes from his chapter summary and dictating others. In math, Lucas is working on transformations on a coordinate plane. The content made no sense to him (or to a lot of his classmates) in the prior day's lesson. Today the teacher had the idea to show how characters in video games can be rotated, inverted, and so forth using the coordinates on a plane. The class had fun giving coordinates (e.g., –10, +2) and seeing what happened to their characters. Because Lucas can recognize numbers and understands that there can be both positive and negative numbers, he is able to do some of the transformations with his partner. (pp. 3–4)

The expectation that Lucas can and will learn some of the general education curriculum based on the general education standards is a cornerstone of IDEA 2004 and the Every Student Succeeds Act (ESSA) of 2015 (PL 114-95), which requires that students be involved in and make progress in the general education curriculum, the same curriculum that is taught to students without disabilities. Furthermore, schools are accountable for reporting on the progress of all students toward the achievement of general education curriculum standards, even those students who are judged to have the most significant cognitive disabilities. ESSA allows up to 1% of students in a state to participate in alternate assessments based on alternate achievement standards, which is a change from the previous allowance in the No Child Left Behind (NCLB) Act of 2001 (PL 107-110) that 1% of students' scores at the proficient level could be counted toward a state's annual report to Congress on student achievement. Alternate achievement standards must be "aligned with states' academic content standards, promote access to the general curriculum, and reflect professional judgment of the highest achievement standards possible" (Karger, 2004, p. 18).

If students judged to have a significant intellectual disability can learn the general education curriculum and two federal laws require schools to be accountable for such learning, then what is standing in the way of schools eagerly teaching students that curriculum? Parents of students with IDD are sometimes told it is more important for their children to learn functional life skills rather than academics. To weigh the merits of this argument, consider the functional life skills that students with IDD, particularly those in high school life skills classes, are commonly taught.

- Telling time and using money
- Brushing teeth and other personal hygiene tasks
- Getting dressed
- Recognizing safety signs
- Cooking
- Making beds
- Crossing streets
- Setting the table

Most people complete these tasks every day (well, perhaps not making one's bed), so they do seem like important skills to learn. But people without disabilities perform these skills to participate in the important things that make up their real lives—having satisfying relationships, earning a living, enjoying leisure time, and giving back to the community. These life skills do not, in and of themselves, make people's lives interesting and productive, yet they form the core of many self-contained educational programs. Life skills are important, but acquiring knowledge and passion for lifelong learning makes life interesting and enables people to develop relationships with others based on common interests. A student with IDD may not learn the whole periodic table of elements, but enjoying experimentation and discovery may mean a future job in a chemistry lab or at a science museum. A love of Shakespeare might inspire an actor or writer. Learning advanced math may lead to a job at a computer company. Mastering computer skills might lead to a job at Google or one of the many technology companies that are eager to hire individuals with disabilities.

Hundreds of inclusive opportunities are available to learn the functional skills that make life interesting and rewarding now and in the future, such as texting a friend, knowing how to throw a great party, or being part of a sports team and taking pride in victory while being gracious in defeat. The goal of an American education is to educate people to participate in democracy by understanding the lessons of history, the logic and magic of science and math, the joys of art and music, and the power of words to inspire and communicate. It is not equitable to deny those rights to a group of students who happen to have IDD.

Assumption 3: Students Who Cannot Learn Much of the General Education Curriculum, Including Those Participating in Alternate Assessments, Will Not Benefit From Being in General Education Classes

These faulty assumptions build on one another and form a seemingly airtight rationale for students to be segregated from their typical peers. Even if students cannot learn any of the general education curriculum, there are benefits to being in general education that are not available anywhere else. Where else do students learn the rules of social engagement than from being around a diverse group of peers? Adults may think that a social skills curriculum helps to teach those rules, but they need to hang out with a group of teenagers for an evening to see how kids communicate and interact with one another. They interrupt to talk about their own interests, often to the exclusion of others; swear and use slang and shorthand indecipherable to grown-ups; and are generally an unruly and sometimes rude bunch of developing human beings. If students with IDD want to really fit in inclusive environments, then an inclusive classroom in an inclusive school and in the related social activities pursued by all students is the best environment in which to learn social skills.

Assumption 4: When Students Cannot Effectively Communicate, Assumptions Are Made About What They Currently Know and What They Might Be Able to Learn on Whatever Communication Abilities They May Have or Lack

People associate being able to talk with being smart and the inability to talk with having an intellectual disability. This may be particularly true for some people with autism spectrum disorder (ASD) who do not speak and who have associated movement and sensory difficulties that make them very poor test takers. It surely cannot be very reliable to give a student with ASD an intelligence test if the student does not have an effective way to communicate, has difficulty with the physical movement of pointing, and who may not have had the opportunity to learn from a very young age because of the upfront assumption that he or she had an intellectual disability. This kind of circular reasoning is so harmful to students with IDD. Following is a scenario that shows the faulty nature of such reasoning.

> I think that you have an intellectual disability because of the way you talk and move and your past poor performance in school. Just to be sure, we need to give you a test that requires you to sit in an unfamiliar room, on an unfamiliar seat, with an unfamiliar person and answer a series of questions that you have never heard before that do not seem relevant to anything in your life and tests skills you have never been taught. When the result comes out that your IQ is under 70, I will base your entire educational career on that number and even influence your living and career options as you make the transition to adulthood. Because you cannot reliably show me that you know words such as *eat, break, yes,* and *no,* I will require you to be close to 100% accurate in handing me little cards on which those messages are printed day after day before I give you more complex vocabulary or a high-tech communication device.

The previous scenario does not exaggerate reality but is often heard in school after school when students are unable to communicate well. This assumption is flawed because a growing body of research shows that students can learn literacy skills when they have a means to communicate and are taught and supported well (Biklen & Cardinal, 1997; Broderick & Kasa-Hendrickson, 2001; Erickson, Koppenhaver, & Yoder, 2002; Erickson, Koppenhaver, Yoder, & Nance, 1997; Ryndak et al., 1999). ASD researchers who make pronouncements about students' intellectual shortcomings may not be as unbiased as they ought to be. Edelson (2006) reviewed 215 research articles published between 1937 and 2003 that proposed that the majority of students with ASD had an intellectual disability. She found that 74% of the claims in these papers came from nonempirical (nonscientific) sources, 53% of which never traced back to any empirical data. It seems that whole generations of children with ASD have been assumed to have an intellectual disability because researchers passed along unsubstantiated claims for more than seven decades.

New Assumptions If these four assumptions are faulty and have contributed to the current segregated educational programs for students with IDD, then what new assumptions can be made?

- Intelligence is not a single measurable characteristic.

- All students have different talents and skills.

- Students learn best when they feel valued, when people hold high expectations for them, and when they are taught and supported well.

- When students cannot currently communicate that they are smart (whatever that means), presume that they are and develop their educational programs based on that assumption.

Some people say, "How are these assumptions more accurate than the old ones?" A principle called *the least dangerous assumption* may help. Anne Donnellan (1984), a respected researcher in special education, wrote

> The criterion of least dangerous assumption holds that in the absence of conclusive data, educational decisions ought to be based on assumptions which, if incorrect, will have the least dangerous effect on the likelihood that students will be able to function independently as adults. (p. 142)

She also said, "We should assume that poor performance is due to instructional inadequacy rather than to student deficits" (Donnellan, 1984, p. 147). Consider how the least dangerous assumption might play out through three scenarios about Kim, the student introduced at the beginning of this section. Donnellan's principle of the least dangerous assumption is used at the end of each scenario to consider the potential harmfulness of each decision (Jorgensen et al., 2010).

Scenario 1:   It Is Presumed That Kim Is Competent to Communicate About and Learn the General Education Curriculum

The following decisions were implemented when Kim's educational program was developed.

- Kim is taught the general education curriculum in the general education class.

- Kim's IEP goals reflect general education curriculum content and learning functional skills within inclusive activities, such as belonging to clubs and extracurricular activities, working in the school store, having a summer job, and so forth.

- Kim is provided with an augmentative and alternative communication (AAC) system that includes age-appropriate social and subject-matter vocabulary.

- Kim's classroom materials reflect the same learning goals as students without disabilities.

- Teachers talk to Kim about current events and other age-appropriate subjects.

- Teachers support Kim to engage with classmates in typical social activities.

- Plans about Kim's transition to adult life will include postsecondary education, gainful employment, and living in an inclusive setting in the community.

Donnellan's (1984) least dangerous assumption principle will be used to evaluate whether these program decisions are appropriate or have caused harm. Envision a fictional time in the future when Kim's capacities and what she has learned is truly known. The least dangerous assumption principle requires considering the harm that might have been caused if the initial assumptions were wrong.

The newest brain imaging test in Kim's future shows that she is smart, she did learn the general education curriculum taught to her, and she does not have an intellectual disability. Did any harm come to her because of the educational decisions made based on the original assumption? No. The assumption was that she was competent, and it turned out to be correct and caused her no harm.

Scenario 2: It Is Presumed That Kim Is Competent to Communicate About and Learn the General Education Curriculum and Develop Her Educational Program Based on That Assumption

So far, this scenario is the same as Scenario 1. Again, Kim's educational program looks like it did in the first scenario.

- Kim is taught the general education curriculum in the general education class.

- Kim's IEP goals reflect general education curriculum content and learning functional skills within inclusive activities, such as belonging to clubs and extracurricular activities, working in the school store, having a summer job, and so forth.

- Kim is provided with an AAC system that includes age-appropriate social and subject-matter vocabulary.

- Kim's classroom materials reflect the same learning goals as students without disabilities.

- Teachers talk to Kim about current events and other age-appropriate subjects.

- Teachers support Kim to engage with her classmates in typical social activities.

- Plans about Kim's transition to adult life will include postsecondary education, gainful employment, and living in an inclusive setting in the community.

Donnellan's (1984) least dangerous assumption principle will be used to evaluate whether these program decisions caused harm. Envision a fictional time in the future when Kim's capacities and what she has learned are truly known.

This time the brain imaging test reveals that Kim did not learn much of the general education curriculum and does have an intellectual disability. Did any harm come to her because of the assumptions made based on educational decisions? Most people say no. Even though Kim did not learn much of the general education curriculum, she did learn functional skills that will help her in her adult life. She was exposed to a rich general education curriculum that may have helped her develop lifelong interests. Her communication skills flourished because she was around competent communicators all day. She had the opportunity to develop friendships with a diverse group of students, not just those with IDD. She had a typical high school experience.

Scenario 3:   The Accuracy of the IQ Test Results and the Judgments About Kim's Development Level Are Believable, and It Is Not Presumed That Kim Can Communicate About or Learn Much of the General Education Academic Content or Benefit From Being in General Education Classes

What might Kim's educational program look like under this scenario?

- Kim is not included in general education, or, if she is, then it is for the purpose of socialization and learning some functional skills.

- Kim's IEP goals primarily focus on communication, movement, self-regulation, self-determination, work skills, and social skills.

- Kim's communication supports have vocabulary and messages related to her perceived developmental level and enable her to communicate basic wants and needs but not academics.

- Kim is spoken to in a way that might be appropriate for a younger student at the same developmental level as the reports indicate.

- Kim is not supported or encouraged to engage with her classmates in social activities because it is perceived that she is too immature, too naïve, or is not interested in those activities.

- Kim's future plans might include working in a sheltered setting and living in a congregate facility with other people who have IDD.

Consider whether these decisions caused any harm if the assumption about Kim not being competent to learn the general education curriculum was wrong. This time, the future brain imaging test shows that Kim is smart, she could have learned the general education curriculum, and she would have benefitted from being included in inclusive social opportunities. Here is what most people say when asked if the incorrect assumptions and educational decisions were harmful.

- An opportunity was lost to teach Kim things she could have learned.

- Kim was not included as much as she should have been, and she did not develop a wide network of social relationships.

- Kim was not supported to develop communication skills beyond saying, "I am hungry," "I am thirsty," "I want a break," and so forth.

- Kim's self-esteem was negatively influenced by being treated as if she were not smart.

- Kim missed out on the typical high school experience.

- School personnel narrowed the possibilities for postsecondary education, her future career, and inclusive employment and living arrangements.

- Clearly, harm was done.

There are five reasons why the least dangerous assumption should be to presume all students' competence and promote their demonstration of that competence through an inclusive general education program.

First, expectations matter. In their classic book on the influence of teacher expectations on student performance, Rosenthal and Jacobson (1968) found that students' IQ scores significantly increased after a year of being in a classroom in which their teachers had been told that their students would blossom, even though there was no empirical evidence to suggest that they would.

Second, traditional assessments of people with disabilities are seriously flawed. Those that purport to measure students' intelligence and adaptive behavior usually measure what they cannot do, rather than what they might be able to do with the right supports. It simply is not ethical or good educational practice to use flawed assessment results when they might negatively influence a student's entire education career and future life options.

Third, research shows that a growing number of students and adults who were diagnosed with an intellectual disability have shown they are competent when they have a means to communicate, the opportunity to learn, and the right instructional and technology supports.

Fourth, to presume incompetence could result in harm to students if educators are wrong.

Fifth, even if educators are wrong about students' capacities to learn general education curriculum content, the consequences to students of that incorrect presumption are not as dangerous as the alternative.

Membership

High school encompasses many memories—the Pythagorean Theorem, converting grams to moles, the source of conflict in Act II of *Romeo and Juliet*, the pluperfect conjugation of the French irregular verb *prendre*. Although people might remember these academic facts, more people remember experiences, such as sitting with friends on the bus, reaching the state finals in basketball, getting in trouble for passing notes (or sending texts) in class, having a romantic crush, going to the junior prom, and having a great time on the senior trip. These memories are related to membership in a school community and whether people felt like they really fit in during high school. Fitting in marks the difference between people who fondly remember their school years and those who do not.

Being welcomed into an inclusive school community is often a battle for students with IDD and their families that must be fought year after year with no guarantee of success. Why is membership so important? Membership provides access to a rich general education classroom, a skilled general education teacher, typical students who are competent communicators, and a sense of unconditional belonging. Belonging that does not have any prerequisites.

Schnorr (1990) conducted a research project about Peter, a student with Down syndrome, who was primarily taught in a self-contained classroom and went into a first-grade general education class for activities such as morning meeting and one special subject (e.g., art, music, physical education, library) per day. This researcher was primarily interested in the perspectives of the students without disabilities. Here is what these students said when Schnorr interviewed them.

- Oh, that's Peter's desk. He comes here in the morning. He's not in our class. He doesn't ever stay. He comes in the morning when we have seat work. Then he leaves to go back to his room.
- He comes in the classroom when we get to school, and when it's after 9, then he goes up to his classroom. Sometimes he's in this class and the other time he goes down to his room.
- Peter gives a sticker book to his teacher, because if he behaves very well, she gives him a sticker, 'cause Peter's in Room 10.
- We do math, but he doesn't, he colors. (pp. 235–236)

Others who have studied the attitudes of typical students toward students with IDD have found a direct correlation between the amount of time that both student groups learn together and improved attitudes toward disability, specifically, and diversity, in general.

Several middle school students spoke about their friend Jocelyn, who had significant IDD, in the award-winning film, *Voices of Friendship* (Tashie & Martin, 1996). One remarked,

Jocelyn is a really good listener and you can sit and tell her any of your problems. One time we were at a school dance and one of our friends was sitting on the floor crying and Jocelyn reached out and put her arm on the girl's back. It just showed that she does understand how people feel and she is there for you as a friend.

Fisher (1999) interviewed typical students from an inclusive high school after some of their classmates with IDD enrolled in general education classes. They talked about the changes in two of their classmates with disabilities.

- He stays for the entire period, his Spanish has improved, and he has a great relationship with peers in his class.

- Julie's totally different now. She fits in, participates in the class, talks to her peers, raises her hand in class, and has some new clothes that are more appropriate for her age. (p. 462)

Students with IDD were fully included in a full range of general education classes at Souhegan High School, in southern New Hampshire, in the mid-1990s. They joined clubs and extracurricular activities and worked alongside their typical friends in summer jobs. Brad Fach (1994), one of the typical students, wrote about his friendship with one of these students.

> I feel that everyone has a special gift to share. Amro gave me his gift that year, and it was the gift of believing. I never would have thought that I would have the opportunity to become close friends with someone who talks to me through a keyboard but it happened. I am amazed at how our whole school accepts and respects these students who are different. I feel good because I know that I have given him something he has wanted for a long time, something that everyone needs, a sense of belonging and more importantly, friendship, But I know now that he has given me much more than I could ever give to him. (p. 9)

Reciprocal social relationships are the second aspect of this inclusion fundamental. Although special friends programs are popular, it needs to be determined if they are based on equal value of students with and without disabilities. Chapter 8 provides a specific example of this type of program. Unfortunately, special friends programs operate under a set of assumptions that can be harmful—not only to students with disabilities but also to typical students. They assume

- Students with disabilities have nothing in common with students without disabilities, therefore we have to set up special situations for them to come together.

- Students with disabilities deserve charity and benevolence because people should feel sorry for their plight.

- Students with disabilities do not really know that other students are not their real friends or that other kids have to be recruited to hang out with them.

- Students with disabilities are not seen as potential friends by students without disabilities.

- Students with disabilities should be friends with other students with disabilities.

Just like the harmful assumptions that often pervade views about the competence of students with IDD, these assumptions about students with disabilities and relationships can stand in the way of developing and maintaining authentic social connections. An alternate assumption about social relationships is not grounded in pity, charity, or benevolence. It is that all students can have real friends when the attitudinal and systemic barriers that keep students apart are addressed.

Participation in General Education Instruction

Full participation in general education instruction in a general education classroom marks the difference between students who are really included and those who are "islands in the mainstream" (Biklen, 1985, p. 18). Membership and participation go hand in hand; membership is necessary but not sufficient for learning, and that is where participation comes in to play. Participation means not only being there but also being an active learner in the same instructional routines as those experienced by typical students. It means everything from being called on in class, to having a meaningful role in small-group activities, to handing in homework, to singing in music class. Student engagement is one of the most powerful predictors of student learning, so it is vital that students with IDD are supported to participate in instruction by the general education teacher and are not sitting at the side or back of the room being taught by a paraprofessional. Engagement is ensured when students have the means to participate. Implementing the "try another way" approach in the general education classroom is needed instead of viewing students' disabilities as a reason why they cannot participate (Gold, 1980). Following are some examples of this approach.

- If a student does not use natural speech to communicate, then he or she needs AAC support to participate in class discussions or small-group activities.

- If a student cannot use a pencil or pen to write, then he or she needs a keyboard or other piece of AT to enable him or her to participate in notetaking or essay writing.

- If a student has difficulty walking from place to place, then he or she may need a wheelchair to enable him or her to move around a science lab to each of the experiment stations that need to be at a height that enables him or her to reach the top of the table.

- If a student cannot read, then he or she may need to have all text materials available in digital form so that it can be read aloud to him or her by a text-to-speech computer application.

- If a student is working on academic material at a lower level than that of most other students in the classroom, then he or she will need to have the general education materials modified to his or her reading and comprehension level but still aligned with the same general education content.

Learning General Education Academics and Skills for Participation in Inclusive School and Community

What is important for students with IDD to learn while they are in school? Teaching developmentally appropriate skills was considered best practice prior to and during the 1970s. For example, Jorgensen and Calculator (1994) described a classroom of this era that used developmentally based practices.

In the Rainbow Connection classroom, 12 students ages 3–21 with severe disabilities were enrolled. First thing in the morning, all students were "toileted," and they practiced combing their hair and brushing their teeth. Therapists worked on oral-motor skills and labeling of food items using sign language or picture boards. The PT worked with each student every day on neuro-motor developmental skills; the SLP had determined each student's "level" and worked with most on cause-and-effect and object permanence; and the teacher and the paraprofessionals used various pre-school toys to teach size, counting, colors, and other relationships. (p. 5)

No academics were taught because all the students were assumed to have significant intellectual disability and because the thinking at the time was that students needed to master a sequence of typical developmental milestones before they were ready for higher level skill instruction.

Brown, Nietupski, and Hamre-Nietupski (1976) introduced a functional, life skills model of educating students with IDD, which suggested that all students with IDD could learn functional, community-referenced skills, regardless of their developmental levels, if they were taught in natural environments outside the school building. This philosophy resulted in students with IDD leaving the school building for increasing portions of their school day as they got older to learn how to use public transportation, gain access to recreation facilities, make store purchases, and learn domestic skills at home. Although this model of education was an improvement over the developmental model because it showed that students with IDD could learn, they were still not taught academics, and they spent most of their school careers segregated from typical students.

With the increased advocacy for inclusion by families and their allies, advances in AT and AAC, research on effective instruction, and corresponding changes in special and general education laws, it is now apparent that students with IDD can learn academics in inclusive classrooms as well as functional skills in inclusive school and community environments alongside their typical classmates.

Students with IDD should be taught the same academic subjects that are taught to all students—language arts, math, social studies, science, health and physical education, computer literacy, the arts, a second language, and various elective subjects. Some students with IDD are expected to learn these subjects at the same level of rigor—the same depth, breadth, and complexity—as their typical classmates. Another very small group of students with IDD may be expected to master learning standards from these subject areas but at a reduced level of depth, breadth, and complexity. The learning standards that may be appropriate for these students are called *alternate achievement standards*. The most important aspect about these alternate achievement standards is that federal law requires that the standards be closely aligned with the same academic standards taught to students without disabilities. Table 1.1 shows the alignment between eighth-grade general education standards and the corresponding alternate assessment standards.

In addition to learning academics, myriad other skills are important for students to learn if they are to be fully included in school communities and have an enviable adult life. These skills fall into the domains of communication, social competence, self-determination, wellness and safety, and prosocial behavior. Students whose disabilities affect movement and the senses

Table 1.1.   Comparison of general and alternate assessment standards in Massachusetts eighth-grade English language arts cluster of key ideas and details

General education standards as written	Alternate assessment standards at the lowest entry point for students with significant cognitive disabilities
Cite the textual evidence that most strongly supports an analysis of what the text explicitly says as well as inferences drawn from the text.	Summarize key events in a literary text.
Determine a theme or central idea of a text and analyze its development over the course of the text, including its relationship to the characters, setting, and plot; provide an objective summary of the text.	Describe the main idea of a story, poem, or drama.
Analyze how particular lines of dialogue or incidents in a story or drama propel the action, reveal aspects of a character, or provoke a decision.	Describe how the setting affects one or more characters in the story. Identify the conflict in a story or poem. Describe the feelings between two characters in a literary text (e.g., friendly, loyal, afraid, suspicious).

(e.g., vision, hearing, self-regulation) may also need to learn strategies for making the most of the abilities that they have, utilizing AT and other supports to accommodate for the skills they lack, and gaining access to natural and specialized supports from peers, co-workers, and paid support providers. All the skills in this category are appropriate for annual goals and short-term objectives on students' IEPs.

Team Collaboration and Administrative Support

Team collaboration and administrative support form a base for all the other elements in Figure 1.1. Although situations exist in which a single committed teacher has successfully included a student with IDD without support from either his or her administrators or other members of the student's IEP team, it is a rare occurrence and rarely translates into a successful inclusive experience the following year. Team collaboration provides an avenue through which general and special educators and related services providers pool their knowledge to support students' learning and inclusion.

Team Collaboration   The following is an example of ineffective team collaboration.

Seth's team was scheduled to meet for 1 hour from 11 a.m. until noon. Invited team members included his grandmother, who was his legal guardian, his case manager, a fourth-grade general education teacher, a speech-language pathologist (SLP), an occupational therapist (OT), a one-to-one paraprofessional, and the assistant principal. Seth's grandmother and the OT chatted about his progress during his pull-out occupational therapy sessions for the first 15 minutes of the meeting. A couple of other team members wandered in around 11:15, and they joined in that conversation. His case manager arrived a few minutes later and attempted to call the meeting to order. There was no agenda, although most team members thought the purpose of the meeting was instructional planning for the upcoming week. Because the general education teacher never arrived (she had been delayed by a telephone call from a parent), the team was unsure about what lessons she had planned, so they were unable to discuss the supports Seth would need to successfully participate. The SLP finally arrived and took over the meeting by discussing the problems she was having with Seth's AAC device. She had little training in AAC for students with ASD and relied on quarterly visits from an AAC consultant who was responsible for programming and trouble-shooting the device. The OT left half way through the meeting, apologizing because she was scheduled to provide services to another student during this time.

People talked over one another's comments, side conversations between the grandmother and paraprofessional made it difficult to hear when others spoke, and some critical decisions were not made because the assistant principal did not arrive until the final few minutes of the meeting. No notes were taken, and people began to leave one by one as the end of the meeting approached. Therefore, another week went by without a solid plan in place for Seth's participation in his general education class. After a month of meetings just like this, the school planned to recommend an out-of-district placement for Seth because inclusion was not working.

Meetings that represent best practices in collaborative teaming for inclusion have the following characteristics.

- A regular meeting time is on everyone's schedule, and there are no conflicts with required services for other students.

- An agenda specifically focused on instructional planning (not on behavior, scheduling, field trips, or other extraneous topics) is displayed in the meeting room.

- Time allotments are given for each item on the agenda, and if the discussion is not finished at the end of the designated time, then the team defers making final decisions until the next meeting.

- Past to-do action items are reviewed to ensure that they have been completed by the responsible person.

- All members arrive on time and stay for the duration of the meeting. Late arriving members are expected to read the minutes and talk to a colleague if they need to clarify what was discussed in their absence.

- There are no interruptions during the meeting (except for real emergencies).

- The following roles are distributed among the meeting participants—facilitator, notetaker, and timekeeper.

- Team members use effective meeting behaviors such as avoiding interrupting, seeking to understand another's point of view before offering their own, staying on topic, and not having side conversations.

- Major decisions are made using a formal process of seeking agreement among all team members.

- A to-do list of action items is generated with people responsible and time lines for completion.

- The meeting ends with a short evaluation of what worked, what did not work, unexpected ideas, and what could be done more effectively the next time the team meets.

Administrative Support   Administrative support for a student's inclusive education program takes many forms. This support comes from general and special education administrators, with the school building principal assuming the primary responsibilities for creating an inclusive school culture and climate. The principal leverages this responsibility in his or her conversations with the school board; the PTA; the community at large; and building faculty, staff, and students.

The principal and special education administrator work together on staffing, budgeting, developing resources, and building a school schedule that prioritizes common planning times for general and special education staff. They ensure that staff have the time, space, technology, and curricular resources necessary to teach diverse groups of students in general education. The school schedule and staffing allocation decisions bring specialized resources into general education classrooms, eliminating the silos of expertise that often prevent effective collaboration among general and special education, Title I, and English language learners (ELLs) staff.

Effective administrators take an active role in mediating disagreements or personal conflicts among team members. They implement strategic plans for involving families and the general community in supporting the inclusive mission of the school.

Souhegan High School has a mission and philosophy statement that underscores its inclusive values.

> The Amherst and Souhegan school districts aspire to be a community of learners born of respect, trust, and courage. We consciously commit ourselves:
>
> - To support and engage an individual's unique gifts, passions, and intentions;
> - To develop and empower the mind, body, and heart;
> - To challenge and expand the comfortable limits of thought, tolerance, and performance; and
> - To inspire and honor the active stewardship of family, nation, and globe.
>
> To this end [we] have determined that the skills and resources of special education will be available to assist any student with exceptional needs. To the maximum extent possible, all of our students are educated within the regular class. We strive to be an inclusive system: inclusive of all students and all teachers. In this way, we will develop students who are independent learners, who understand their educational needs, and who can advocate for themselves within the academic environment. Our goal is to become a community of learners in the truest sense of those words. (Fisher et al., 1998, p. 35)

Three Souhegan administrators were exemplars of effective inclusive leadership that they demonstrated in interviews for the video *Class of '96: An Inclusive Community of Learners* (Jorgensen, Mroczka, & Williams, 1997). Superintendent Dr. Richard Lalley articulated his rationale for both equity and excellence.

How do you create an environment where all children can excel? All children. Not some children, or most of the children, but all of the children. Every child is so important, so unique that to do anything less is a travesty. It's a simple view, not complicated. It's nice that the research supports it. But I think even if the research didn't support it, I wouldn't care. Because essentially schools need to be places where every child is respected for what he or she can do and worked with to raise that child's level of performance as high as we possibly can before we let them out into the cruel world where they not going to have our support. Let's give them the skills to fend for themselves. And I think more importantly the belief in themselves that they can be successful. We do that, I go home happy.

Souhegan principal Dr. Robert Mackin expressed a similar level of commitment to inclusion and heterogeneous grouping:

The principal is really a role model. I have to be solidly behind inclusion and keep people coming back to the table to figure out solutions even when the going gets tough. This year some of the math teachers came to me and wanted to remove a group of kids from our math program because they were having difficulty passing Math 1. I asked them, "If we pull these kids out, will they acquire the skills to move on to Math II?" The teachers admitted that they probably wouldn't. While I understand that there will be some variability in the skills that our kids leave Souhegan with, I'm not willing to establish a totally different set of standards for students with disabilities. I think that we need to hold them to high standards and through the curriculum and the support we provide, push them to reach those standards.

Kathryn Skoglund was Souhegan's Director of Special Instructional Services and was instrumental in developing the school's inclusive philosophy. Her commitment reflected a view from the trenches about what it takes to keep inclusive education at the forefront of the school restructuring conversation:

It may seem easy to talk about what is necessary for effective inclusive education, however there still exist hurdles, even here. It is difficult to maintain the inclusive momentum unless the focus is constant and overt. It is imperative that those of us who are involved in successful inclusionary practices take the time to gather data, particularly from a longitudinal perspective, that show where the successes are and why they are occurring. We must talk and talk and talk—about kids, curricula, schedules, pedagogy, shortcomings, strengths, planning, problem solving, miscommunications, and disagreements.

CONCLUSIONS

This chapter describes the fundamental elements of inclusive education and presents many reasons why inclusion is the right thing to do for students with IDD. In Chapter 2, step-by-step guidelines describe how families and educators can establish a vision for a student's inclusive education to serve as a road map to future educational decisions and future life outcomes.

2

Imagine an Inclusive Vision for Education and Adult Life

"He is a biter." "She is a runner." "He is nonverbal." "She is off in her own world." "There is nothing really there." "He is difficult to be friends with because all he talks about is train schedules." These statements are often used to describe students who have ASD and other developmental disabilities. They represent a belief that disability is a disease or disorder that needs to be cured and ultimately eradicated; that people with disabilities are abnormal and the rest of society is normal. The difficulties or challenges people with disabilities experience are placed within them when they are viewed this way, and, thus, they are required to change to be eligible to participate in the full range of inclusive school and community activities and environments. How often is it said, "She could never be included in a general education class because of her sensory issues?" or "He cannot hold a real job because of his challenging behavior issues?"

RATIONALE FOR CHANGING
THE FUNDAMENTAL VIEW OF STUDENTS WITH DISABILITIES

What if the fundamental way that students with disabilities are viewed could change so that their disability was viewed as a natural part of human diversity instead of a problem? What if people intentionally looked for their strengths and viewed their challenges as problems with their environment instead of trying to make people with disabilities like the rest of society?

What if the unique talents of students with disabilities were appreciated and the contributions that they might make to schools and communities were recognized? How would the lives of children and adults with disabilities be different? How would schools need to change? How would the role of professionals in education be different?

Completing a person-centered plan, such as Making Action Plans (MAPS; O'Brien & Forest, 1989), can help parents and professionals articulate a new view of a student with complex support needs based on a vision of an inclusive life in the community and open the door to an inclusive education that draws on students' strengths rather than their perceived impairments.

Best Practices for Inclusion

Here is a strengths-based way of introducing Erin McKenzie, a student with Down syndrome, in the student profile section of the IEP.

- Erin will have a life in a community that values diversity and accentuates strengths, and she will share her gifts and talents with that community.

- Erin will have reciprocal relationships with friends. She will communicate and advocate for herself.

- Erin will have the same opportunities to learn and participate in typical classroom, extracurricular, and community activities when they would typically happen. Erin will graduate from high school in 2004 with her class and have continued postsecondary educational opportunities and a career that interests her.

Erin's mother, Barbara McKenzie, shared Erin's vision statements with parents and educators attending a workshop at the 2014 TASH conference. She told the audience that her vision had evolved over the years since Erin was a preschooler, and they were what kept her and Erin's educators focused on the kind of life that Erin and her parents wanted for Erin someday in the future. It was this future vision—of living and working in an inclusive adult community—that provided the rationale for what Erin's educational program needed to look like until she graduated.

Writing a vision statement that goes on a student's IEP and articulating that vision in team meetings can help ensure that the myriad of small decisions made on behalf of a student with IDD are leading to, not interfering with, the ultimate goals he or she and his or her family have for the future.

This chapter provides several examples of vision statements and describes in detail a person-centered planning process that can help students and their families define their vision and make it operational for each year's IEP team.

ELEMENTS OF A VISION STATEMENT

A vision statement should come from the heart but be specific enough so that an unfamiliar person knows exactly what is important to the student and his or her family. There is not a template for a vision statement but most contain a brief description of what the student's education and future life after high school will look like with respect to living arrangements, health and safety, postsecondary education, employment, relationships, and how he or she will spend his or her leisure time. Adult life may be far in the future in the case of a 3-year-old or next year in the case of a 20-year-old. The second element of a vision statement describes what the student's and family's hopes are for the current school year.

Selena and Anna

Selena, a 10th-grade student with Down syndrome who is one of this book's profiled students, had this vision statement on her IEP.

Selena wants to work in the tourism industry when she graduates from high school. She needs to be comfortable working in a fast-paced and inclusive environment, have a good command of spoken and written English, maintain her conversational French skills, understand the history of our country and continent, responsibly manage her money, and increase her understanding of other cultures to be successful in that career. Although travel is her most passionate interest, her best subject has always been computers, and we want to encourage her interest in that area too. Therefore, our vision for Selena's 10th-grade education is that she be fully included in English, French, history, biology, computer technology, and math; and that she joins the social justice and technology clubs.

Selena was involved in writing this vision statement and advocated for her enrollment in the computer class. She read the statement to the school staff at the beginning of her 10th-grade IEP meeting. When school personnel raised some concerns about Selena's ability to master the rigorous academic curriculum, her parents told them that they would be happy if Selena learned some of the most important concepts from her academic classes, and they were not concerned whether she passed the New York State Regents examination.

Anna's vision statement had many of the same elements as Selena's, although it contained a greater focus on social relationships.

The most important thing for us is for Anna to have friends, not special buddies. Anna loves her friends, and she thrives when she is with them outside of school. She communicates more, learns more, and feels a real sense of belonging. Yes, academics are very important, but Anna's school experience and her adult life will be filled with loneliness without friends. We want Anna to be involved in the same classes and extracurricular activities as other sixth-grade students.

THE PROCESS OF DEVELOPING A VISION STATEMENT

Parents and school teams sometimes develop a vision statement together after they talk about the student's interests, strengths, personality, challenges, and family values. Other parents and school team members benefit from using a person-centered planning process such as MAPS (O'Brien & Forest, 1989), which was first developed as the McGill Action Planning System.

Initial Preparation

The preparation involved in conducting a MAPS meeting includes identifying a facilitator and a chart-paper recorder; inviting the student's family, friends, and education team members; asking all participants to read a short description of what the process is and is not designed to accomplish; and finding a comfortable location and convenient time for everyone to attend. Schedule about 2 hours for the meeting and send a reminder a day or so ahead of time. Some students write and deliver their own invitations. In other situations, a parent, guardian, or the student's educational program case manager or inclusion facilitator can issue the invitation. A MAPS facilitator needs to be a strong advocate for the student and believe that he or she has gifts and talents that are more important than his or her disability and so-called impairments. The facilitator should understand the MAPS process, and if he or she has not been formally trained, then conduct a practice session with a small group of people who provide feedback on effective facilitation techniques.

Making Action Plans

Families and education teams use MAPS to help students plan for their futures and guide their education team in making decisions about the focus of the current school year. The process uses a person-centered approach in which future plans are built on the family's and student's dreams, fears, interests, and needs. It is directed and guided by the student and family and facilitated by someone skilled in using the MAPS process.

The MAPS process provides a structured format that helps gather information that supports decisions during the current school year, develop an IEP, or prepare for making the transition from grade to grade or school to adult life. It is a new way of thinking about assessment, providing a much broader view of the student's life than the traditional perspective of outlining impairments in specific skill areas. The MAPS process can help build trust, a common purpose, and positive relationships among team members.

Participants

The following people are usually invited to a MAPS meeting, although this can be customized to ensure that the people who are the most emotionally connected to the student attend as well as people who may have a role in helping the student achieve his or her dreams and goals.

- Student

- Parent(s) or guardians, siblings, extended family

- The student's friends

- IEP team members, the school principal, the special education administrator

- If appropriate, members of the community who may be involved in supporting the student's postsecondary education, living situation, employment, social relationships, and leisure activities.

- Other people as requested by family (advocates, faith or community leaders)

Making Action Plans Agenda

Six questions are asked by the meeting facilitator during the MAPS meeting.

1. What is the student's history?

2. What is the family's and student's dream?

3. What is the nightmare? What are the fears?

4. Who is this student? What are his or her interests, talents, strengths, and personality?

5. What does the student need in this school year to put him or her on the path to achieving the dream?

6. What steps need to be taken, and who will put the plan into action? What is the time frame for completing the action steps? How will the team know that the action plan has been successful?

Making Action Plans Norms and Processes

MAPS meetings have established norms that the facilitator describes at the beginning of the gathering.

- At each step, the facilitator asks the student to respond first. Then family members and other team members are free to respond in random order.

- All ideas will be recorded, using actual wording if possible. Information or ideas can be revised or deleted at any time.

- Team members have the right to pass.

- Ideas are expressed in a positive way. The facilitator will ask that any negative information be restated in a more positive way.

- Team members will wait until the final step of MAPS to begin to evaluate the merits of specific ideas. It is acceptable to record ideas that appear to conflict with one another. To have a lengthy discussion of the pros and cons of each idea when it is initially expressed will rob the MAPS of its forward momentum and student focus.

What Happens After the Making Action Plans Meeting?

The chart paper—usually a combination of words and graphics—is given to the student and his or her family and the notes on the chart paper are transcribed and distributed to all participants. Individuals assigned to complete action steps do so in the time frame indicated. The group reconvenes within approximately 3 months to assess progress on the plan and revise any action steps as needed.

Using the Making Action Plans Vision Statement

First, a vision statement should be included on the student's current IEP and at the beginning of the transition section of the IEP for a student who is 16 or older. The IEP form in some school districts has a placeholder titled Vision for the Student's Education, Parent and/or Student Concerns, or Parent's Input for the Student's Education. Even if such a placeholder does not appear on an IEP form, the vision statement can be added as an attachment or recorded in the student profile section. The team should read this statement aloud at the beginning of every IEP meeting, and the statement should be updated on a yearly basis or when important changes occur in the student or in the family's expectations regarding the future.

Sample Making Action Plans

The MAPS created for James, a second-grade student with multiple disabilities, is summarized in the following case study, and the action plan that resulted from the MAPS is depicted in Table 2.1. A checklist for developing an inclusive vision is depicted in Figure 2.1.

Table 2.1. Action plan for James's Making Action Plans (MAPS)

Needs	Action steps	Person(s) responsible	Time line
Give back to community	Support James every Sunday afternoon after church services to participate in the parish beautification program along with the other children from his Sunday school class.	Gramma	Beginning next Sunday
Play Minecraft on iPad	Purchase and install app.	Parents	Tonight
	Consult state ADAPT Center to learn how to set up switch access.	Occupational therapist (OT)	Within 2 weeks
Play soccer at recess	Build adaptation to James's wheelchair that will allow him to kick the ball during a soccer game or practice.	Physical therapist (PT), OT, and physical education teacher	Next Monday for meeting One month to build and fine tune adaptation
Improve reading skills	Assess James's current reading skills.	Reading specialist and speech-language pathologist (SLP)	A week from Thursday
	Fully include James in guided reading group.	Second-grade teacher	Starting tomorrow
	Create adapted Power-Point or BookCreator books that read aloud and enable James to turn pages with switch.	SLP and OT	One month to create five adapted books
	Order trial version of *MEville to WEville* literacy curriculum.	Special education teacher	Team, including parents, will review the curriculum in 1 month or as soon as the trial version arrives
Establish planning time for team	Review all providers' schedules and identify 45 minutes each week when all can meet to plan upcoming units.	Special education teacher and principal	Beginning in 3 weeks
Give James more control over his environment	Identify 10 times a day when James can make a choice or control his environment.	OT	OT will bring list to team meeting 3 weeks from today, and the team will select the top three to implement right away

(continued)

Table 2.1.   *(continued)*

Needs	Action steps	Person(s) responsible	Time line
Allow James more down time	Observe other students to identify two times per day when they have unscheduled or choice time and allow James to choose a leisure activity to do with a friend during these times.	Special educa- tion teacher and paraprofessional	By next week
Increase interactions with peers in class	Make sure that James is working with his table mates when they are doing a cooperative activity.	Paraprofessional Second-grade teacher	By next week
	Program key phrases on his AAC device related to coopera- tive group work.	SLP	
Ride bus with Sam	Meet to discuss assigning an acces- sible bus to James's neighborhood.	OT and PT Principal and special education director	Next administrative team meeting
	Do a trial run to plan who James will sit next to, who will strap down his wheelchair, emer- gency procedures, and who will get him off the bus at school.	District transportation director Parents Bus monitor Bus driver Paraprofessional	Two weeks before start of school in the fall
Assign some homework	Give James one modi- fied reading and one modified math homework assign- ment per week that will take no longer than 15 minutes to complete.	Second-grade teacher, special education teacher, parents	Next week

JAMES'S MAKING ACTION PLANS

1. What Is the Student's History?

Mom: We thought James was just perfect when he was born. You know, 10 fingers, 10 toes. About 5 minutes later we found out that his Apgar score was only 4, and they rushed him to the intensive care unit because his color did not pick up like they thought it should. Our pedi- atrician came to see us about an hour later and told us that he sus- pected that James might have suffered from a lack of oxygen, either sometime when I was carrying him or during the birth process. We were devastated, even though the doctor tried to reassure us. Over the

❑	Ask the student if he or she wants to participate in a Making Action Plans (MAPS; O'Brien & Forest, 1989) meeting.
❑	Ask the student's family if they want to participate in a MAPS meeting.
❑	Identify a facilitator and chart-paper recorder for the meeting and have an initial meeting with the student and family to discuss the process and identify participants.
❑	Schedule the meeting in a welcoming space.
❑	Be sure that the meeting space is accessible for all participants.
❑	Schedule at least 90 minutes for the meeting.
❑	Invite meeting participants.
❑	Provide snacks and drinks.
❑	Set up chairs around the focus student, with family and close friends in the front row and other participants behind.
❑	Post flip chart pages at the front of the room.
❑	Use markers with no scent.
❑	Conduct the meeting.
❑	Describe the student using person-first (e.g., student with Down syndrome) or identity-first (e.g., autistic student) language, depending on the student's and parent's wishes.
❑	Develop an action plan to implement the recommendations that arise from the meeting.
❑	Give the flip chart paper to the student and his or her family and a typed version to all participants
❑	Follow up on the action steps on a regular basis.
❑	Write a vision statement and include it in the IEP.

Figure 2.1.   Checklist for developing an inclusive vision.

next few months, during his well-baby visits, we learned that James had cerebral palsy. This started a whole round of visits to specialists at the children's hospital, and they found that James had some hearing and vision problems at well. He had to have a special enriched formula because he did not nurse well. Our worst fears were realized when he did not reach some of the important early milestones, such as holding his head up at 5 months or crawling at 9 months. His doctor referred us to the early intervention network, and our days were filled with visits from nurses, nutritionists, SLPs, and physical therapists (PTs).

Dad: All of these folks tried to be encouraging, but I lost a lot of sleep because every day my wife would have a new problem to talk to me about when I came home from work.

Mom: We had to admit to ourselves that our little boy was not just going to catch up if he had enough therapy, but our son would have a disability that would likely stay with him his whole life.

Gramma: I know that Gina and Don have gone through an awful lot since James was born, but I have always just looked at him as my precious grandson. He is cuddly, he smiles a lot, and he just seems to be a happy boy. I do not want to dismiss their concerns, but I have always thought that James's parents can handle just about anything that comes their way and that James can have a great life.

Early intervention OT: I have known James since he was about 6 months old, and, even though I do not provide services to him anymore, I do occasionally babysit him so that his mom and dad can have a night out. You know how some kids just tug at your heart strings? That is James. He has a lot of determination and has made some really good progress over the years with his AT, and I hope that people continue to see all of his strengths and not only the scores on his assessments.

2. What Is the Student's Dream?

James (using his AAC device): Pilot!

Dad: Yeah, my son wants to fly airplanes! You know when your kids are young and you do not want to discourage them from being whatever they want to be? I do not know if we should kind of tell him the reality of what he will be able to do and not do.

Mom: I want us to keep an open mind for as long as we can. We decorated James's room with posters of airplanes and spaceships. We have every DVD ever made about space, and he is actually able to play them by activating a switch that was hooked up to our DVD player. He plays them repeatedly. We made his wheelchair into a plane this Halloween, and he was the hit of the neighborhood party. It is hard to dream when you see all the challenges that lie ahead, but I guess we have the same dreams for James that other parents have for their kids. We want him to be happy, have a lot of friends, learn all he can in school, and do something he loves when he gets to be an adult. I cannot really think ahead to the specifics of his life when he leaves school, but right now my biggest dream is that he learns to talk or at least communicate with us so that we know what he is thinking. I just know that he knows more than he can tell us, but so far the technology is not that great.

Gramma: I want James to grow up to be a good person and give something back to his community and not always have to have people doing things for him. I guess independence and happiness are my biggest dreams for him.

3. What Is the Nightmare? What Are the Fears?

Gramma: I do not know if I can answer this without crying.

Dad: We have all had our worst case scenario thoughts over the years, and we try not to dwell on them. What good does that do? We just try to stay positive and let James know that we love him and will always be there for him.

Mom: Well, obviously, my biggest fear is about James's health. Thank God he has been healthy for the last few years except for the occasional cold. But when I listen to the PT, I worry about what will happen if he does not ever walk. Will his bones get brittle? I worry about him developing scoliosis. Other than the medical concerns, which are huge, I guess the fear that I hardly dare to say out loud is that James will be shut away in a segregated classroom and then shut away in a sheltered workshop when he gets older. My biggest fear is that he will be alone and be lonely, regardless of whether he ever learns to tie his shoes or wash his clothes. That would be the worst thing that could happen.

Gramma: Well, that will never happen if I have anything to say about it.

4. Who Is This Student? What Are His or Her Interests, Talents, Strengths, and Personality?

Dad: Like we said before, James loves airplanes, spaceships, anything that flies. I do not really know when it started, but it seems like he has been interested in those things since he was a little guy. Maybe he will design the next space shuttle—stranger things have happened!

Mom: I actually wrote some things down before this meeting so I would not forget anything. It is so easy to look at all the things your kid cannot do. James is really caring and tuned in to other people's emotions. If somebody in the house is sad or upset, then you can tell that he is concerned for them by his facial expressions and the sounds he makes. He is very curious. Even now, when we put him on the floor, he wants to roll toward his toys and play with them, even if they are out of reach and it is a struggle for him to get there. He loves using his switches to turn on the DVD player or when he was younger, we had some of those bears that clap or puppies that flip over that he could activate by just hitting a big button. I wish we had more things that he could control in his environment. Although he is usually happy, he can get frustrated, and I want to just make things easier for him.

Gramma: I know he loves books. I do not really know if he can read yet, but he calms right down when I read to him. I can see him looking out of the corner of his eyes to follow along with the pictures.

Third-grade teacher: I would like to jump in here, and do not quote me on this, but I am pretty sure that he has learned to read some words. When we have him read a book that has a predictable or repetitive storyline, I can see him trying to form the words even though he cannot say them. He clearly prefers informational text about planes and spaceships of course!

SLP: I second that. We have just started programming his AAC device with the ending words to familiar poems and repetitive storylines. He will reach out at the right time to hit those buttons when we set up the page for him and give him a little support at his elbow.

Sam (classmate):   James is funny. He makes these funny sounds, and we try to figure out what he wants.

Penelope (classmate):   James is my second best friend behind Hillary. He has some cool apps on his iPad, and we all like to play with him at recess or snack time. He lets us use the iPad too.

Theo (classmate):   I think if I were James I would want to fly right out of that wheelchair. One thing I know is that his favorite food is yogurt.

5. What Does the Student Need in This School Year to Put Him or Her on the Path to Achieving the Dream?

Mom: Communication is the number one priority.

Dad: I agree.

Gramma: Maybe a way for him to tell us when he is not feeling well. I would also like to see him do more reading at home.

Special education teacher: I think he needs more reading instruction. It seems like he is making some connections but not quickly enough for me and for the pace of the curriculum. I feel like we do not have enough hours in the day to give James everything he needs. We need some dedicated planning time every week to plan out how he will be more active in the classroom.

Theo: Can we figure out a way for him to play soccer with us on the playground?

Penelope: He needs Minecraft on his iPad.

Sam: Can James ride on my bus?

OT: More opportunities to control his environment.

SLP: I think we can do a better job helping James interact with his class-mates. It is hard when he is just learning how to use his AAC device, but maybe we can set up a communication circle for him and teach his classmates how to be better communication partners.

Mom: Wow, that sounds amazing!

Paraprofessional: Give James some time during the day when we are not all on him. All the other kids get to take minibreaks and we do not even notice, but if James is a little bit off task, then we all think that he must get right back to work. I hope this does not offend anyone.

Dad: I wonder if he should be getting more physical therapy. Should we start letting him control his wheelchair? I know one thing that he, or rather his mother and I, need is some idea of what we should be doing

What We Like and Admire About James	What Is Important to James
• Determined	• Being around friends all the time
• Curious	• Space, spaceships, space travel
• Attracts both girls and boys as friends	• Having apps and games on his iPad that other he and other kids like to play
• Persists until we understand what he is trying to communicate	• Getting out of his wheelchair several times a day
• Caring	• Giving him space to just sit back and observe several times a day
• Intuitive about others' feelings	
• Knows a lot about space science	

How We Can Best Support James

- Listen hard to what he is trying to communicate.
- Don't put words into his mouth but give him choices about what he wants to communicate.
- Tell him when we are going to move his body.
- Tell him that we know he has a lot to say and is smart and that we are trying our best to give him a way to communicate.
- Make sure that his friends are involved in updating his iPad with games and apps.
- Include his parents and grandmother in problem-solving.
- Make sure that information is sent home over the weekend so that family can preview upcoming books and lessons.
- Encourage his interest in space.

Figure 2.2. James's one-page profile.

with him at home related to his academics. I feel like we spend a lot of time with our older daughter on her homework, but James is just kind of sitting there.

6. What Steps Need to Be Taken, and Who Will Put the Plan Into Action? What Is the Time Frame for Completing the Action Steps? How Will the Education Team Know That the Action Plan Has Been Successful?

See Table 2.1 for the action plan that was created at the end of James's MAPS meeting.

CONCLUSIONS

James's parents crafted this vision statement as a result of participating in the MAPS meeting.

> James is a curious and loving boy. He has great strengths as well as some challenges. As parents, we have some practical tools and suggestions for successful inclusion for James, and we hope the team will be supportive of these suggestions. As parents, we hope that the whole team has the right attitude and is fearless, is creative, acknowledges his challenges, is not afraid to make mistakes, and celebrates his success. We would like to see James communicate effectively—to be able to express his novel thoughts and knowledge. We feel it is important for the team to foster social interactions with peers and for James to be in the general education class all day, every day in order for him to achieve the dreams we have for him.

They also created a one-page profile (see Figure 2.2) to share with James's team at every meeting, and as he grew, they updated it with his new interests, talents, and needs for support.

3

Construct Learning and Communicative Competence

Chapter 1 introduced the principle of presuming competence as the least dangerous assumption that can be made about a student's current and future capabilities. Although a presumption of competence is necessary as the foundation of a student's inclusive educational program, it is not sufficient. It is not enough to simply hold a belief. Everyone involved with the student needs to actively construct—to build—his or her competence through their words, instruction, and supports that they provide him or her.

When Jack, a student with ASD, was a rising third grader, his education team faced a dilemma—keep him in a general education classroom with a focus on academic instruction or shift his educational program to focus on life skills. They asked staff from the Beyond Access (BA) project at the Institute on Disability at the University of New Hampshire to observe Jack and give them an opinion (Sonnenmeier et al., 2005). The BA staff observed Jack and saw a student who was an "island in the mainstream" (Biklen, 1985, p. 18). He had a desk seated alongside a classmate, but most of his instruction occurred at the side of the room with a paraprofessional. He did not have a way to communicate about academic or social topics. His instruction was not linked to what was being taught by the general education teacher and included a series of discrete trials on color, number, and letter recognition. He had great difficulty making transitions and often expressed his frustration by hitting his head.

Recommendations included the following: 1) set aside the results of a recent psychoeducational assessment that reported Jack's developmental level at 24 months and instead presume his competence to learn and communicate, 2) introduce a new AAC device that gives Jack access to core vocabulary and content- and situation-specific messages, 3) hold a weekly instructional planning meeting with all team members to plan for the supports Jack will need in order to participate in the same instructional routines as his classmates, and 5) invite the BA staff to provide weekly on-site technical assistance and monthly team professional development workshops. The school agreed to implement these recommendations. One year later, Jack was showing emergent literacy skills, improving his ability to communicate about social and academic topics, and actively participating in general education lessons. The team did more than just presume his competence over the course of that year, they intentionally constructed his competence through the services and supports they provided to Jack in general education.

RATIONALE FOR CONSTRUCTING COMPETENCE

The idea that someone's competence is something that can be constructed originates with the theory that disability is not a fixed characteristic of a person but is mediated by societal attitudes, policies, the quality of the educational program, the supports that are given, and other characteristics of the environment in which the person lives (Barnes, 2003). Although this idea is not supported by everyone in the field of special education (Anastasiou & Kauffman, 2011), it is ultimately a more helpful way of thinking about students with IDD than a purely medical model. A belief in the medical model of disability can lead to efforts to change the student through therapy and remediation to the exclusion of efforts to look for the student's gifts and talents and search for ways to design instruction and the environment to facilitate that student's belonging, participation, and learning. The following sections describe what parents, teachers, therapists, and classmates can do to construct students' academic and communicative competence.

TALK TO STUDENTS AS IF THEY UNDERSTAND

Crossley said, "Not being able to speak is not the same as not having anything to say" (1990). This is particularly true for students who do not presently have a way to communicate their understanding. When it is assumed that students who do not speak have cognitive disabilities, they miss out on rich information about their world because educators may not expose them to a rich general education curriculum and age-appropriate conversation. It may seem awkward to talk to someone who cannot talk back, but this is one of the most important things that can be done to construct a student's competence. Imagine if a child with IDD was not instructed about his or her neighborhood and community, the nuances of social relationships, or current news events. He or she would experience significant barriers to engaging with his or her typical classmates and the increasingly demanding core curriculum. Talking to students as if they understand is the first step, and explaining what was said puts the least dangerous assumption of presuming competence into action. Many instances have occurred in which teachers and parents have reported that a student previously thought not to understand has talked about something that he or she heard weeks, months, or even years ago.

Best Practices for Inclusion

Parents and educators who always talk to students about age-appropriate topics show that they think students are competent. Using an age-appropriate tone of voice conveys the expectation that students have the capacity to understand. Sometimes typical students as young as 5 years old use a babying tone of voice when speaking to their classmates with disabilities. This happens because these little people are astute observers of how the adults in their lives talk to their classmates with IDD, and their default behavior is to copy those adults. If the student with IDD happens to be smaller than average, does not move around a lot, or is unable to communicate in conventional ways, then classmates often assume that the student is much younger than his or her actual age. It is up to adults to model an age-appropriate and respectful tone of voice and to speak to children about why it is important.

Open the conversation to the whole class by saying, "Friends, I have noticed that when you are playing with James you talk to him like he is a baby. James is 8 years old, just like you are, and probably feels embarrassed when you talk to him like he is 2 years old. Can you tell me what you are thinking about this James? Friends?"

Some people are wary of talking about issues such as these, thinking that inclusive education means trying to make every student the same. On the contrary, inclusive classrooms highlight, celebrate, and make student differences ordinary. The purpose of opening a conversation like this with a class is not to give students a lecture on disability etiquette but rather to open a dialogue about difference, demonstrate in a tangible way that all children are valued for their differences, and encourage them to think about ways that they can make their classroom welcoming to everyone.

GIVE STUDENTS A WAY TO COMMUNICATE ALL DAY, EVERY DAY

There is a crisis in American education because so many students with disabilities do not have the means or supports necessary to facilitate the development of their communicative competence. Kearns, Towles-Reeves, Kleinert, Kleinert, and Thomas (2011) investigated students participating in states' alternate assessments and found that only 50% of the total number of students who qualified as needing AAC received it. There are several reasons why this persists, despite the proliferation of knowledge about effective AAC. Developing students' communication abilities is the second strategy for constructing students' competence.

The Importance of Developing Communicative Competence

The following excerpt from Kleinert, Holman, McSheehan, and Kearns (2010) explains the importance of developing communicative competence through studies and considers Ben and Shelly, students who had not been properly identified and served by their educational system.

AAC includes all forms of communication (other than oral speech) used to express thoughts, needs, wants, and ideas. We all use AAC when we make facial expressions or gestures, use symbols or pictures, or use print. Special aids, such as picture and symbol communication boards and electronic devices, are made available to help people express themselves. Doing so increases social interaction, school performance, and a sense of self-worth.

All people communicate and can develop communicative competence. People with severe speech-language problems rely on AAC to supplement existing speech or replace speech that is not understandable and other methods of communication that are nonconventional. The ultimate goal of AAC for students in educational settings is to provide a vehicle for communication, social interaction, engagement in academics, and other school-related activities (e.g., extracurricular, work study). Beukelman and Mirenda (2005) discussed the "tendency to provide AAC students with communication systems that are solely designed to address wants/needs and social interaction functions rather than the information-sharing functions that are integral to classroom participation" (p. 420).

In the past, teachers and therapists believed that students had to demonstrate certain cognitive skills before they would benefit from communication services. Indeed, the interactions between the domains of cognition and language are certainly complex. In fact, sometimes teaching new communication skills can help a student develop other thinking skills. The appearance of a cognitive deficit should never be used to deny providing communication services and support (National Joint Committee for the Communication Needs of Persons with Severe Disabilities, 2003).

In a recent study of students labelled with significant cognitive disabilities participating in alternate assessments on alternate achievement standards across multiple states, Kearns, Towles-Reeves, Kleinert, Kleinert, & Thomas (2011) found that the majority of these students communicated using oral speech or symbol-based augmentative communication systems. A small percentage of students were identified by their teachers as using facial expressions, body movements, and cries to expressively communicate, and some were characterized as having inconsistent receptive responses across all grades up to and including high school. Of the students judged to need AAC, more than half did not have AAC systems. Furthermore, this study did not describe the extent to which the AAC included academic content but simply that the student used or did not use AAC.

Of all the groups of students identified with significant cognitive disabilities, we find that this group—those not yet using symbols for communication—presents the most unique challenges for schools. Vigilance is warranted, however, as some students in this group have simply not received the services and supports they need to develop communicative competence. This misidentification and subsequent failure of service are tragic but, sadly, not uncommon.

Consider Ben. Ben was a high school student with cerebral palsy who did not use oral speech, much like James, the student profiled in this book. His IEP team determined that he had an intellectual disability. He was dropped to consultation only from speech and language therapy as a related service due to failure to make progress in using oral speech. He received educational services in a segregated class for students with significant intellectual disabilities with limited access to the general curriculum. A new teacher recognized that Ben had not been appropriately identified or served, and requested the assistance of a speech and language expert external to the school and district. As a result, Ben received a speech-generating communication device and was able to answer questions about actual and predicted temperature as displayed on a mathematical graph within days of receiving his device.

It is clear that a series of unfortunate errors in the education system and low expectations from the IEP team across many years reduced Ben's ability to communicate and, thus, denied him access to the general education curriculum and a wide variety of social relationships. Sadly, Ben exited school without a high school diploma and without the communication device, which gravely limited the opportunities available to him after high school and placed him at serious risk for neglect and even abuse (Cox-Lindenbaum & Watson, 2002). Ben's story illustrates an unfortunate example of a systemic failure of education and of the IEP team.

Accountability within the education system for providing AAC services and supports remains absent. IEP teams are also limited by the knowledge they have available to them and the extent to which they have access to high-quality professional development and technical assistance. Given the American Speech-Language-Hearing Association (ASHA) ethical practice guidelines, SLPs should seek technical assistance for any student who needs to develop communicative competence if SLPs are unsure about how to provide services themselves (American Speech-Language-Hearing Association [ASHA], 2010a, b; National Joint Committee for the Communication Needs of Persons with Severe Disabilities, 2003).

Consider Shelly. Shelly, a high school student considered to have significant cognitive disabilities, communicates with cries, body movements, and facial expressions. After talking to her mother about activities that Shelly loved, she was provided with a switch requesting GO SOME MORE, indicating that she would like to be pushed rapidly in her chair (a favorite activity for her). In as few as eight trials, Shelly consistently responded by using the switch to request GO MORE. In Shelly's case, we aren't sure about tested cognitive abilities, but improving receptive responding is the first step in helping others see her communicative potential and, at a minimum, improving her skills in requesting assistance. The consistent use of a switch to request assistance will improve Shelly's overall communicative competence and lead to other opportunities to make choices in everyday activities.

Both stories represent the serious challenges that result when communicative competence is not identified as the highest priority in any student's educational program. Given that both students were likely identified as needing specialized supports and services from infancy; therefore, the continued lack of supports and services years later suggests a serious need for professional development and training for the wide range of professionals who work with these children and youth.

Communicative Competence Defined

Light (1997) described communicative competence as "being able to meet the changing demands and to fulfill one's communication goals across the lifespan" (p. 63) and accomplishes four main purposes, including expressing wants and needs, developing social closeness, exchanging information, and fulfilling social etiquette routines. For example, "Infants communicate primarily to express wants and needs and to develop social closeness," whereas "school-aged children need the means and skills to meet all four communication goals" (p. 62). Similarly, Beukelman and Mirenda (2005) recommended that chronologically age matched students without disabilities provide the communication target with which we do our discrepancy analysis. In other words, we are always continuing to develop AAC for students until they can communicate the same things (academically and socially) to the same extent as students without disabilities.

Research-based Interventions
to Improve Communicative Competence

Snell et al. (2010) reviewed twenty years of literature examining the development of communicative competence among students labelled with significant cognitive disabilities. These researchers found that 96% of the reviewed studies reported positive changes in some aspects of communication for most students. These findings unequivocally support providing communication intervention for people with complex support needs.

In terms of the length and intensity of time required to see results of a communication intervention, Rowland and Schweigert (2000) found that most students experienced success with as little as 15 minutes per day of instruction over an average of 6.5 months. These children experienced varying sensory and multiple disabilities and were also identified as having no functional symbolic communication skills. Indeed, twenty-eight of the participants learned novel symbols within the first three exposures. These authors concluded, "No single handicapping condition among our participants was exclusively associated with the outcome of intervention" (p. 74). That is to say that no student judged as severely cognitively disabled is unable to benefit from communication supports and services. The research clearly shows that students with the most significant cognitive and sensory disabilities can learn to use symbolic augmentative communication in six months or less.

The Importance of Augmentative Communication Combined With Literacy Instruction

In their review of the literature regarding AAC for students with significant disabilities, Romski and Sevcik (1997) cited many examples in which students with limited cognitive and language skills successfully learned to use AAC. Application of this knowledge in our schools is central to the educational success of students with significant disabilities. Indeed, the importance of AAC in supporting access to and progress in the general education curriculum, in particular literacy skills, cannot be underestimated.

Despite the evidence-based research indicating that even students with multiple and developmental disabilities can benefit from literacy instruction, including phonemic awareness, reading, and writing programs (Fallon, Light, McNaughton, Drager, & Hammer, 2004; Light, McNaughton, Weyer, & Karg, 2008; Millar, Light & McNaughton, 2004), Strum et al. (2006) reported that "most students who use AAC do not become conventionally literate and few of those who do achieve literacy skills beyond the second grade level" (p. 21). Similarly, Light and McNaughton (1993) suggested that without functional literacy skills, individuals who use AAC systems are "severely restricted in their access to educational and vocational opportunities" (p. 33). These disturbing realities require each and every member of a student's education team to make a commitment to begin developing a student's communicative competence as early in life as possible.

Early Communication Intervention   Romski and Sevcik described the many roles AAC may play in facilitating communicative competence in young children with complex communication needs.

> Using a developmental perspective, AAC interventions can be viewed as a tool that aids or fosters the development of early language skills and sets the stage for later vocabulary development and combinatorial language skills regardless of whether the child eventually talks or not. In fact, it is critical that AAC be introduced before communication failure occurs. AAC is not only for the older child who has failed at speech development but also for a young child during the period when he or she is just developing communication and language skills, to prevent failure in communication and language development. (2005b, pp. 178–179)

Romski and Sevcik (2005b) further cited many research studies documenting the efficacy of communication services and supports provided to infants, toddlers, and preschoolers with a variety of severe disabilities. Beukelman and Mirenda (2005) explained that many students with severe communication disorders unfortunately enter elementary school without communication systems that permit them to participate in typical curricular activities. Thus, "it is important to ensure that by the time children who use AAC reach first grade, they have the tools necessary for academic participation and instruction" (p. 392). In order for children with significant cognitive disabilities to access the academic standards in early primary (kindergarten through grade 2), system level supports must include the following.

- All professionals providing services to students with significant cognitive disabilities must consistently practice and respond across disciplines. This includes educators, speech language pathologists, and other related service personnel (Rainforth, York, & Macdonald, 1997).

- Early intervention supports for communication, as well as the transition to school services, must prioritize the development of communicative competence as a matter of first priority for the student and individual service plans (Light & Drager, 2007; Romski & Sevcik, 2005a).

- Students with significant cognitive disabilities must make the transition from preschool services to kindergarten by demonstrating communicative competence using AAC similar to their kindergarten peers if they are to maximize their right to a free appropriate public education (FAPE). This is important if students are to gain full access to the general curriculum (Beukelman & Mirenda, 2013).

- Student documentation (included with the IFSP and IEP) should also include videotaped records of the student's present level of communicative competence to ensure smooth transmission of accurate information on the student's communication and use of AAC.

Collaborative Planning: A Cornerstone for Success

A cornerstone to delivering the supports and services that foster communicative competence among students with significant cognitive disabilities is collaborative, transdisciplinary teaming (Rainforth et al., 1997). Hunt, Soto, Maier, Muller, and Goetz (2002) evaluated the effectiveness of a team collaboration process designed to increase the academic, communication, and social competence of three students with severe disabilities with AAC needs within an inclusive educational setting. They found that collaborative teaming supported by a unified planning process resulted in

- Increased levels of student initiated interactions

- Increased use of AAC

- Decreased levels of assistance provided by the instructional assistants

- Increased engagement in classroom activities

A particular strength of their planning process was its integration of supports in classroom activities. As a result, all three teams reported substantial gains in the students' academic performance. "The general education curriculum became the context for intervention, and academic and social participation became the ultimate goals" (Hunt et al., 2002, p. 34). A process for using this planning process is presented in Chapter 9.

Similarly, Calculator and Black (2009) followed the work of Jackson, Ryndak, and Billingsley (2000) in identifying 91 evidence-based practices around eight major themes for using AAC and including students with significant disabilities. The resulting themes included the following.

- Promoting inclusive values

- Collaboration between general and special educators

- Collaboration between educators and related services providers
- Family involvement
- Choosing and planning what to teach (which included the topic of challenging behaviors)
- Scheduling, coordinating, and delivering inclusive services
- Assessing and reporting student progress
- Instructional strategies (p. 330)

These authors emphasized the importance of academic and social interactions among peers and adults, frequent opportunities to practice, and use of AAC in academic content using evidence-based practices.

In teaching literacy skills to students labelled with significant cognitive disabilities, Fallon and Katz (2008) supported the importance of collaborative literacy teams, including teachers and SLPs, and emphasized

> in-service education activities for practicing professionals are also crucial in facilitating improved literacy services for students with complex communication needs. Repeatedly, the lack of professional training in AAC is cited as a factor related to ineffective literacy instruction for students who use AAC. (2008, p. 117)

These studies demonstrated the positive impact of a collaborative cross-disciplinary team in facilitating the academic and communicative competence for students with significant disabilities by incorporating many of the key evidence-based components described by Calculator and Black (2009).

Barriers to the Provision of AAC to Develop Communicative Competence

There are several key barriers related to the limited use of AAC with individuals and students in this population. The National Joint Committee for the Communication Needs of Persons with Severe Disabilities position statement delineated several of these factors under the overarching theme of eligibility concerns.

> Eligibility determinations based on a priori criteria violate recommended practice principles by precluding consideration of individual needs. These a priori criteria include, but are not limited to: (a) discrepancies between cognitive and communication functioning; (b) chronological age; (c) diagnosis; (d) absence of cognitive or other skills purported to be prerequisites; (e) failure to benefit from previous communication services and supports; (f) restrictive interpretations of educational, vocational, and/or medical necessity; (g) lack of appropriately trained personnel; and (h) lack of adequate funds or other resources. (2003, p. 2)

Without AAC, students such as Ben or Shelly may appear not to be making progress in communicative competence or developing cognitive or academic skills. The following outcomes will result only when communicative competence and AAC are considered.

- Students are able to display their actual level of cognitive and communication competence.
- Students have the opportunity to continuously learn and develop symbolic communication from early intervention throughout their educational career.

- With appropriate supports and instruction, students do continue to make progress in communicative competence and use of symbolic language into adulthood (National Joint Committee, 2003).
- Academic content is symbolic content—access to the general curriculum is only meaningful if one can understand and express that content.
- In order to maximize educational opportunities, students must come to kindergarten with AAC and use of symbolic language.
- There is no more fundamental support for and outcome of education than the right and the ability to communicate (National Joint Committee, 2003).

On the other hand, without the provision of communication intervention and the provision of AAC

- Lack of communication competence is highly predictive of poor post-school outcomes (Kleinert et al., 2002).
- If the use of AAC is not offered to these students, they are less likely to learn and evidence symbolic behaviors.
- Without use of AAC, students with significant disabilities cannot indicate their true abilities and do not have access to literacy, which is essential to participation in the school curriculum.

From Kleinert, J., Holman, A., McSheehan, M., & Kearns, J. (2010). *The Importance of Developing Communicative Competence. Synthesis Report #1.* Lexington, KY: University of Kentucky National Alternate Assessment Center.

ENSURE EVERYTHING IS AGE APPROPRIATE

Providing students with IDD clothing and other accoutrements, educational opportunities and materials, and leisure activities has been an essential best practice for more than 40 years.

Clothing and Other Possessions

When a typical 16-year-old girl has a *Hello Kitty* backpack, her friends might think she is quirky or cool. When a 16-year-old student with IDD has the same backpack, it can stigmatize her as her classmates may have preconceived notions that she is developmentally younger than her age. The problem here obviously does not lie with the student with IDD but with the attitudes of her classmates. Nevertheless, students with IDD should have exposure to and the right to choose age-appropriate clothing, backpacks, DVDs, songs, and so forth. Whenever people say, "But he likes *Sesame Street!*" one wonders if that student has had the opportunity to watch *Glee* or *High School Musical.* Parents are in the position of influencing many choices for their children. Instead of taking a 13-year-old to *Disney on Ice,* why not pick up a couple of classmates and take them to see *School of Rock?*

Classroom Membership

The principle of age appropriateness also applies to the classrooms in which students are enrolled. Instead of sending a fifth-grade student with emergent literacy skills down to the first-grade class for guided reading, why not set up reading buddies for all fifth and first graders? It may be tempting to place a small-statured 8-year-old in kindergarten but that denies the student the opportunity to learn age-appropriate academic content and develop same-age friends. Another unintended consequence of enrolling students with IDD in classrooms that are below their chronological age is what happens to that student when he or she reaches the age of 20 or 21 and he or she is a senior in high school. The student ages out of the entitlements of IDEA 2004 and may miss out on school district funded learning opportunities during the 18–21 years, such as pursuing postsecondary education, navigating the community, and sampling a variety of jobs.

Reading Material

What students are given to read is another aspect of age-appropriate educational choices. It may be easier to give a Dr. Seuss book to a 10th-grade student with emergent literacy skills, but it is more appropriate to find texts written at the student's current reading level that match 10th-grade literacy and informational text content. Chapter 5 describes a variety of sources for finding or making high-interest, low reading level texts.

Sexual Health Education

Selena

Selena's parents and teachers began to worry when she started taking a greater interest in her appearance in seventh grade and had crushes on boys. They realized that the old stereotype about people with disabilities being asexual was not valid, but they were fearful that she would not have the judgment to make safe choices and might be taken advantage of by a peer or sexual predator. They realized that not educating Selena about sexuality would deprive her of the very knowledge and skills she would need to prevent abuse. Furthermore, her parents fully anticipated that Selena would someday date and then get married, and they wanted her to enjoy sex as a natural part of life.

Educational teams often decide that they do not want their students with IDD to participate in the same sexuality education that typical students receive, but Selena's family wanted her to learn about these topics alongside her classmates. Selena's health teacher developed the course curriculum based on the *Guidelines for Comprehensive Sexuality Education: Kindergarten–12th Grade* (Sexual Information and Education Council of the United States [SIECUS], 2004). They supplemented the SIECUS curriculum with visuals and text from two sexual health curricula for students with IDD, including *The Facts of Life and More: Sexuality and Intimacy for People with Intellectual Disabilities* (Walker-Hirsch, 2007) and *Teaching Children with Down Syndrome About Their Bodies, Boundaries, and Sexuality* (Couwenhoven, 2007).

Social Activities

Anna

Anna's parents enrolled her in a local Brownie Girl Scout troop when she turned 7 years old. Although the troop leader expressed some initial concerns about her lack of experience working with children with ASD, Anna's parents assured her that their hope was that Anna would have fun and perhaps increase her communication skills by being around the other girls. Their hopes for an inclusive scouting experience aligned well with the Girl Scouts' mission of welcoming all girls into membership and that the diversity of the troop made it stronger. Anna's mom became an assistant troop leader and helped figure out the supports that Anna needed to have a productive experience. Anna's mom found that meeting with the girls on an occasional basis to get their ideas for Anna's participation allowed her to take a secondary role in supporting Anna. The suggestions that the girls came up with often proved to be simple yet effective, such as giving all the girls a movement break midway through their weekly meeting and offering a Make Your Own Badge activity that allowed Anna to pursue her interest in iPad technology alongside a friend who had a similar interest.

All three of the students profiled in this book participated in a variety of inclusive school- and community-based social activities rather than Special Olympics. Their parents knew that their children might not have access to the full range of social experiences if they relied on a special program that depended on specialized resources and funding rather than on the same activities that were available to any student in their communities.

Best Practices for Inclusion

When students with IDD are encouraged to join inclusive groups and make friends with children with and without disabilities, it communicates that they are more alike than different, a slogan coined by the National Down Syndrome Congress. It also communicates that when they become adults, they will be living and working in a world that is not always designed especially for their needs but can be made accessible through a little ingenuity and close connections with others.

Work Experiences

Including students with disabilities in age-appropriate and inclusive work and career learning experiences alongside their classmates without disabilities is another way to construct students' competence. Educators began taking students with IDD out into the community, depriving them of valuable academic instruction time, when the idea of a functional, community-based curriculum was developed in the late 1970s—a major improvement from the strict developmentally based programs of earlier years (Brown et al., 1976). What do typical students do to learn the dispositions and skills they will need for productive careers as adults? They assume chores at home when they are just entering school. They learn to set the table, load the dishwasher, make purchases at the grocery story, put their laundry in the hamper, and maybe feed the dog or cat. They may take on the responsibility of mowing lawns, having a paper route, babysitting, or volunteering during community clean-up days as they enter their teenage years. Many students get their first summer job when they turn 16 years old. Think of all the skills they acquire just through these natural opportunities that go along with moving from childhood into being teenagers—filling out a job application, dressing appropriately for the work environment, getting to work on time, working collaboratively with others, taking a city bus, managing their earnings, and so forth.

These same opportunities can be given to students with IDD if educators think creatively about the supports they will need. A student named Amro Diab was fully included at Souhegan High School in southern New Hampshire during the mid-1990s (Jorgensen et al., 1997). Rather than take him out of the mainstream of high school academic classes to teach him work skills, Amro worked one period a day in the school store, was assistant manager of the football team 4 years in a row, and held a summer job alongside a classmate who did not have a disability. Although the boys learned painting and carpentry skills one summer, they also honed their fast-food purchasing and "checking out girls" skills too!

One of the best times for students with IDD to learn work skills is between the ages of 18 and 21—after they have participated in senior year graduation exercises but before receiving a regular high school diploma or aging out of IDEA-mandated services. Students with IDD should have the opportunity to move on to postsecondary education and work.

INTERPRET STUDENTS' BEHAVIOR AS MEANINGFUL

Anna showed a fascination with books when she was a preschooler and had already been diagnosed with ASD—not only board books or picture books but also dictionaries, almanacs, and books that her older brother brought home from school. She would sit for an hour at a time holding them, flipping through the pages, smelling the pages, and putting her face close to the pages when she fanned them. Anna even liked to sleep with her favorite books under her covers. Anna's parents assumed that she was actually interested in what the words inside those books had to say instead of interpreting this behavior as stimming. They read to her every morning at breakfast and every night before she went to sleep. Anna's parents were not surprised when she was able to read in kindergarten because they constructed her competence by giving meaning to her behavior rather than just writing it off as some idiosyncratic behavior of a child with ASD. This idea of interpreting students' behavior as having meaning is another strategy for constructing students' competence. If Anna's parents had concluded that she was just stimming on the books, then they might have taken those books away and denied her the early experiences that are so important to students' future literacy development.

People looking at a behavior exhibited by a student with IDD may interpret it through their own biases about the characteristics of individuals with a particular disability. If Anna likes flipping through books, then a traditional interpretation of this behavior might be that she is getting sensory stimulation from the moving air. A constructing competence view interprets that behavior as Anna having an interest in reading. If James holds an iPad up close to his face, then a traditional interpretation might be that he is just looking at the bright colors on the iPad screen. A constructing competence view interprets that behavior as James searching for the app that he wants to open. If Selena frequently clutches at her lower abdomen, then a traditional interpretation might be that she is masturbating. A constructing competence view interprets that behavior as meaning that she might have a gastrointestinal problem or menstrual cramps.

Although interpretations of students' behavior are important, overt reactions to students who exhibit those behaviors are even more so. All three of the students' parents and members of their education teams responded to the students' behavior in a manner that constructed their competence. Anna's SLP shaped Anna's page-flipping behavior into a request on her AAC device—WANT TO READ. James's vision consultant taught his team how to make the icons on the iPad screen larger so he could see them more clearly. Selena's OT made a "How I am feeling" picture communication board for Selena so she could tell her parents or the school nurse when she had a stomachache or if some other part of her body was hurting.

Even behaviors that are perceived as negative can be interpreted through a constructing competence lens. When James repeatedly pointed to the "I need a break" symbol on his communication device, his team members might have interpreted that to mean that the information being presented in his class was too difficult for him to understand and he was trying to escape. Instead, James's inclusion facilitator spent some time observing James in class and identified times when James seemed most disengaged and prone to requesting a break. James's team determined that he needed more visual supports and manipulative objects during math to understand the steps of working through a math problem. Anna sometimes ran over to a table and swept all the items off or pulled all the computer plugs out of the electrical sockets. Her team realized that they needed to develop more active ways for Anna to be engaged in teacher-led instruction because she had a short attention span and was not going to be able to sit quietly while the classroom teacher lectured for 20 minutes. They used the Clicker Connect app to create note-taking forms for Anna so she could be as actively involved as her classmates when the teacher was delivering information. Selena sometimes did not answer questions during classroom instruction. She would look away or put her head down and just sit quietly. Rather than interpret that behavior as stubbornness or not knowing the answer, her team hypothesized that Selena needed additional visual supports to translate the thoughts in her head to verbal speech. They created an aided language board depicting the main character, places, and events in the book that was being discussed in her English class. She now had a visual symbol right in front of her to support answering questions about character traits, rising and falling action in the story, and the story setting.

ENSURE STUDENTS HAVE ACCESS TO EVERY PART OF THE GENERAL EDUCATION CURRICULUM

The following statements reflect several beliefs that can lead to harmful consequences to students' acquisition of knowledge and skills: "Oh, she does not really need to take math. How will she use algebra in her adult life anyway?" "Let's schedule her pull-out speech services during history. Students do not get tested on it, and, besides, she is not really going to be able to learn the seventh-grade material anyway."

First, there is the belief that students with IDD are not capable of learning general education academic content. Browder and Spooner (2014) debunked that myth through their description of a variety of evidence-based practices that promote student learning of English language arts, math, and science.

Another belief is that if students with IDD are not capable of learning all the material covered in a general education class and pass the state test, then there is no benefit to them being in that class and learning some of the material. IDEA 2004 regulations states that "a child with a disability is not removed from education in age-appropriate regular classrooms solely because of needed modifications in the general education curriculum" (U.S. Department of Education, 2006, p. 46765). That applies to students participating in alternate assessments too. Taking the alternate assessment is not a reason why a student should not be in a general education class. The Dynamic Learning Maps (2015) *Alternate Assessment System Consortium* illustrated the alignment between the general standards in English language arts and math and the alternate achievement standards. This makes it easy for a team to imagine how students with and without disabilities working on similar learning goals can learn alongside one another in a general education classroom.

A third belief is that the choice between a student being in a general education class and getting his or her individual needs met is an either/or

❑ Apply the least dangerous assumption of presuming competence, even if there is uncertainty about the student's abilities.

❑ If the student does not have a way to communicate in ways that are commensurate with his or her peers without disabilities, then interpret assessment results with caution.

❑ If the student does not have a way to communicate in ways that are commensurate with his or her peers without disabilities, then conduct an augmentative and alternative communication (AAC) evaluation, regardless of his or her diagnosis or perceived cognitive ability.

❑ Provide the student with a way to communicate about all the same academic and social topics as students without disabilities.

❑ Think about disability as another kind of natural difference rather than an impairment or deficiency.

❑ Do not judge a student's competence solely by the way he or she looks, moves, or communicates.

❑ Talk to the student about age-appropriate topics and events.

❑ Talk to the student in the same way as a peer without a disability.

❑ Educate classmates to speak to the student in an age-appropriate tone of voice.

❑ Bring in an outside expert to support the team and the student if the speech-language pathologist does not have AAC competence.

❑ Follow the guidelines of the American Speech-Language-Hearing Association regarding eligibility for speech-language services.

❑ Provide the student with a way to communicate about wants and needs, feelings, academic topics, and social topics as well as establishing social closeness.

❑ Teach language, communication, and literacy skills through an integrated approach.

❑ Teach all the elements of a balanced literacy approach, including phonemic awareness, phonics, vocabulary, comprehension, fluency, and writing.

❑ Ensure that the student leaves preschool with a fully functioning AAC system and supports that enable participation in academic instruction and establishment of reciprocal social relationships.

❑ Provide communication supports across activities, environments, and service providers.

❑ Utilize a collaborative teaming approach to plan for the supports the student needs to participate in and communicate about all academic and social topics.

❑ Support the student to wear age-appropriate clothing and use age-appropriate materials.

❑ Enroll the student in age-appropriate general education classes.

❑ Provide age- and grade-appropriate instructional materials.

❑ Teach the student about age-appropriate sexual health topics.

❑ Engage the student in age-appropriate and inclusive extracurricular and social activities.

❑ Provide an older student with work experiences at the same time and in the same places as their classmates without disabilities.

❑ Interpret all behavior as having meaning.

Figure 3.1. Constructing learning and communicative competence checklist.

situation. Students who are provided related services and supplementary aids and services primarily within a general education class are in a both/and situation. Having the SLP work with a guided reading group can help the student with IDD learn language, literacy, and communication. The SLP can also benefit other students in the group. Using the OT's expertise during art or computer class can help promote access for a student who has difficulty with fine motor control. Bringing a PT into a physical education class or extracurricular activity might open up possibilities for the use of adapted equipment to support a student's participation.

Students with IDD must have accessible instructional materials specified in the IEP in their annual goals and short-term objectives and in the section that addresses supplementary aids and services for them to participate and make progress in the general education curriculum. Their service providers must understand how individualized instruction and supports for participation can be provided within the context of general education instruction.

CONCLUSIONS

Each of the strategies for constructing competence that are presented in this chapter makes sense if a student is presumed capable of learning and communicating when given the right supports (see Figure 3.1). If that idea seems far-fetched and concrete evidence of a student's capabilities is needed before he or she is given supports to gain access to the instructional and social world, then recall the principle of the least dangerous assumption. Is the potential for harm to a student greater if it is presumed that he or she can learn, can communicate, and take steps to give him or her a means to do so? Is the potential for harm greater if his or her behaviors are dismissed as meaningless? The lessons of history clearly show that society has underestimated the abilities of people with disabilities, and people are destined to continue making this mistake unless they change their underlying assumptions and actions.

4

Write an Inclusive, Standards-Based Individualized Education Program

Anna's IEP notes that she has severe autism and frequent tantrums, bites and kicks when frustrated, does not have a conventional means of communication, and makes eye contact with familiar adults for 5 seconds without running away. How would most teachers feel about including Anna in a general education class if they read this on her IEP?

How would teachers feel about including James in a general education class if they read his IEP and learned that he functions at a 6-month developmental level, and has a severe seizure disorder?

Do these student profiles give a picture of why and how they will engage in instruction in a general education classroom? Do they present ideas for how Anna and James will establish social relationships with their classmates? How will they communicate about history or science? Will either student be able to read the informational text that is part of a state's large-scale assessment?

RATIONALE FOR FOCUSING ON STUDENT STRENGTHS

If Anna's and James's IEPs described their strengths in addition to their challenges, if their annual goals were aligned with the general education standards being taught to all students, and if supplementary aids and services supported their full participation in general education instruction, then their teachers and other team members would have a road map for including them in general education and helping them prepare for postsecondary education, employment, and community living.

IEP teams are encouraged to write standards-based IEPs because of increasing accountability for improving the academic achievement of all students with disabilities. This recommendation stems in part from IDEA 2004, which ensures that students with disabilities participate and make progress in the general education curriculum. Writing an IEP with a presumptive placement in a general education class is consistent with IDEA 2004 and some landmark education court cases (Huefner, 1994; *Oberti v. Board of Education*, 1993). In addition, ESSA (the reauthorization of NCLB) requires that students participate and make progress in the general education curriculum—the same curriculum as the one taught to students without disabilities. State accountability under ESSA includes assessing students with disabilities on the general education standards of the grade in which the student is enrolled. Alternate assessments for students with severe cognitive disabilities must be aligned with grade-level general education standards.

This chapter describes how to write an inclusive, standards-based IEP. This kind of IEP, however, does not supersede the requirement that students' IEPs are individualized based on their unique needs. Excerpts from this book's profiled students' IEPs will provide specific examples of student profiles and present levels of performance, annual goals, short-term objectives, supplementary aids and services, and special education service options. The characteristics of an inclusive, standards-based IEP are depicted in Figure 4.1.

Marked differences exist between inclusive, standards-based IEPs and traditional IEPs. Some of these differences are evident in the student profile section of the profiled students. The left column of Table 4.1 presents descriptors taken from the IEPs prior to the profiled students' full inclusion in general education, and the right column reflects the student profile sections after the students' teams received professional development and coaching on inclusive education.

UNDERSTAND IEP CONTENTS

Many variations of the IEP format are used by local school districts, but IDEA 2004 requires that every IEP contain the following items.

- A statement of the student's present levels of academic achievement and functional performance, including how the student's disability affects his or her involvement and progress in the general education curriculum

- A statement of measurable annual goals, including academic and functional goals

- Short-term objectives or benchmarks that will enable students participating in alternate assessments to make progress toward the annual goals

- A description of how the student's progress toward meeting the annual goals will be measured and when periodic progress reports will be provided

- ❑ Portrays the student's strengths as well as needs

- ❑ Describes the student's present levels of performance relative to general education curriculum standards as well as reports his or her performance in functional domains

- ❑ Describes the results of assessments in the context of the student's prior opportunities to learn, whether he or she has been taught using evidence-based instructional practices, and the limits of his or her current communication abilities and supports

- ❑ Presumes the student's competence to communicate

- ❑ Anticipates that the student can acquire literacy and mathematics skills

- ❑ Bases the IEP on the long-term goal of postsecondary education, integrated employment and community living, and satisfying social relationships

- ❑ Uses grade-level academic achievement standards as a guide for determining annual goals

- ❑ Annual goals and short-term objectives or benchmarks are measureable

- ❑ Identifies supports necessary for the student to achieve IEP goals

- ❑ Contains goals that can be implemented and achieved in a general education classroom

- ❑ Specifies that special education and related services are delivered primarily in the general education classroom

- ❑ Specifies that a student is in an inclusive learning environment nearly 100% of the day

- ❑ May also address communication, prosocial behavior, sensory regulation, technology skills, social relationships and skills, participation in extracurricular activities, work and community living skills, executive function, and health and fitness

- ❑ Describes the supports that the team needs on behalf of the student, such as common planning time, time to adapt materials, and professional development

- ❑ Checks the box that indicates the student's need for accessible instructional materials

- ❑ Indicates that the student will ride the regular school bus (with supports, if necessary)

- ❑ Describes inclusive extended year services (if the student needs them)

- ❑ Matches the accommodations available on large-scale assessments to the accommodations the student receives during instruction

- ❑ Clearly recognizes the differences between accommodations and modifications

- ❑ By the student's 16th birthday (or younger if the team decides it is necessary), describes postsecondary goals, IEP goals and objectives related to those goals, transition services related to meeting the goals, and the student's projected course of study for the remainder of high school

Figure 4.1.   Inclusive, standards-based IEP indicators checklist.

Table 4.1. Comparison of student profiles in traditional versus inclusive standards-based individualized education programs (IEPs)

Traditional IEP	Inclusive standards-based IEP
James is nonverbal. He is wheelchair bound. James is unable to read.	James requires one-to-one assistance to support his participation in the classroom, maintain personal safety, and meet his complex medical needs.
James requires one-to-one assistance throughout his day.	James's primary means of communication is through an augmentative and alternative communication device. He and his communication partners require training and coaching to use it with consistency. James is an emergent reader and has demonstrated early print awareness. James actively engages in listening to books read aloud by activating a switch to turn the pages and play an animation.
Anna has severe autism and is very low functioning.	Anna has improved communication skills.
Anna experiences significant behavioral challenges. She often scratches, pinches, screams, and falls to the ground kicking and flailing.	Anna loves music, computers, art, and listening to stories being read.
Anna has a 5-second attention span.	Anna is showing an increase in reciprocal interactions with classmates and adults.
Anna is not toilet trained.	Anna needs to use sensory tools and have frequent movement breaks to maximize her attention.
Anna frequently runs away from instructional tasks and on the playground.	Anna is highly energetic and needs support and supervision in order to be safe. Anna participates in the general education curriculum with modifications and some accommodations. Anna needs one-to-one adult support to meet her personal hygiene needs.
Selena has low muscle tone.	Selena enjoys swimming and is eager to improve her personal best time in freestyle.
She functions within the mild to moderate range of intellectual disability.	Selena's diagnosis of intellectual disability does not fully capture her strengths and abilities.
Selena's spoken language has 50% intelligibility.	Selena's speech intelligibility is rated at 90% within familiar contexts with familiar people.
Selena misses subtle social cues.	Selena needs to have picture supports with unfamiliar conversational partners or when communicating novel information to effectively express her ideas. Selena is eager to be part of a social group and benefits from peer support to understand subtle social cues.

- A statement of the special education and related services and supplementary aids and services to be provided to the student or on behalf of the student

- A statement of the program modifications or supports for school personnel that will be provided

- o To enable the student to advance appropriately toward attaining the annual goals

- o To be involved in and make progress in the general education curriculum and to participate in extracurricular and other nonacademic activities

- o To be educated alongside and participate with other students with and without disabilities

- An explanation of the extent, if any, to which the student will not participate with students without disabilities in the regular class and in extracurricular and nonacademic activities

- A statement of any individual accommodations that are necessary to measure the academic achievement and functional performance of the student on state and districtwide assessments

- o If the IEP team determines that the student must take an alternate assessment instead of a regular state or districtwide assessment of student achievement, then the IEP must include a statement of why the student cannot participate in the regular assessment and why the particular alternate assessment selected is appropriate for the student

- The projected date for the beginning of the services and modifications and the anticipated frequency, location, and duration of those services and modifications

- The IEP must include the following, beginning no later than the first IEP when the student turns 16, or younger if determined appropriate by the IEP team.

- o Measurable postsecondary goals based on age-appropriate transition assessments related to training, education, employment, and, where appropriate, independent living skills

- o The transition services (including the course of study) needed to assist the student in reaching those goals.

Also, beginning no later than 1 year before the student reaches the age of majority under state law, the IEP must include a statement that the student has been informed of his or her rights under Part B of IDEA 2004 (if any) that will transfer to the student on reaching the age of majority.

STEPS TO WRITING AN INCLUSIVE, STANDARDS-BASED IEP

Figure 4.2 depicts the 15 steps involved in writing an inclusive, standards-based IEP.

These steps are described next; examples from this book's profiled students are provided to demonstrate each step.

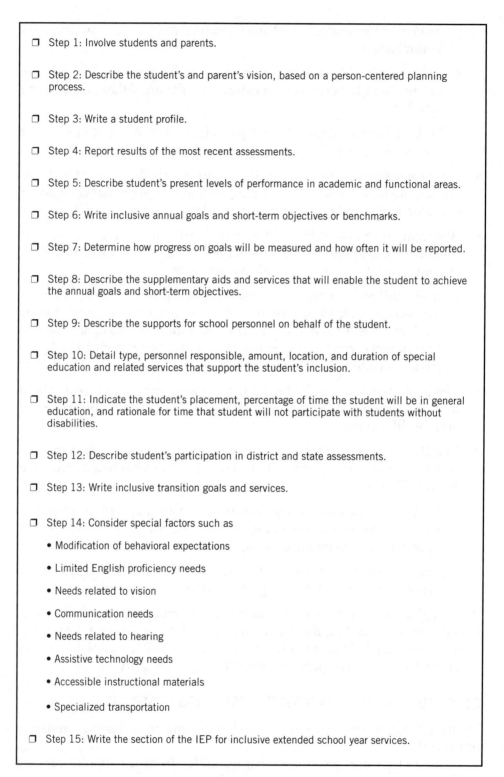

❒ Step 1: Involve students and parents.

❒ Step 2: Describe the student's and parent's vision, based on a person-centered planning process.

❒ Step 3: Write a student profile.

❒ Step 4: Report results of the most recent assessments.

❒ Step 5: Describe student's present levels of performance in academic and functional areas.

❒ Step 6: Write inclusive annual goals and short-term objectives or benchmarks.

❒ Step 7: Determine how progress on goals will be measured and how often it will be reported.

❒ Step 8: Describe the supplementary aids and services that will enable the student to achieve the annual goals and short-term objectives.

❒ Step 9: Describe the supports for school personnel on behalf of the student.

❒ Step 10: Detail type, personnel responsible, amount, location, and duration of special education and related services that support the student's inclusion.

❒ Step 11: Indicate the student's placement, percentage of time the student will be in general education, and rationale for time that student will not participate with students without disabilities.

❒ Step 12: Describe student's participation in district and state assessments.

❒ Step 13: Write inclusive transition goals and services.

❒ Step 14: Consider special factors such as

• Modification of behavioral expectations

• Limited English proficiency needs

• Needs related to vision

• Communication needs

• Needs related to hearing

• Assistive technology needs

• Accessible instructional materials

• Specialized transportation

❒ Step 15: Write the section of the IEP for inclusive extended school year services.

Figure 4.2.   Checklist for writing an inclusive standards-based IEP.

Step 1: Involve Students and Parents

Avoid presenting students' parents with a completed IEP document without first getting their input. Completing the document without their input communicates to parents that their ideas and contributions are an afterthought. There are several ways that parents and students can be invited to offer input on the IEP.

- Send parents a copy of the grade-level academic standards or a curriculum guide and ask them to prioritize learning goals for the upcoming year.

- Use the *Choosing Outcomes and Accommodations for Children* (COACH; Giangreco, Cloninger, & Iverson, 2011) educational planning process to help parents prioritize their child's needs.

- Meet with the student, the student's parents, and classmates before the IEP meeting to ask about

  o His or her interests and achievements outside of school

  o Academic subjects and topics that are of interest to him or her

  o His or her likes and dislikes

  o His or her learning style

  o What he or she is good at doing

  o What he or she has trouble with

  o His or her favorite subjects

  o Things he or she would like to learn

  o The kind of instruction he or she likes best (e.g., one to one, from a peer, in a cooperative group)

  o How he or she likes to be provided with support (e.g., by whom, where, how)

  o Extracurricular activities he or she would like to join

  o Whether he or she wants to go to college

  o What he or she wants to be when he or she grows up

All students should have a role during the actual IEP meeting, regardless of their age. An elementary student such as James can talk about his favorite sports team, iPad app, or book. Anna, a sixth-grade student, might describe her favorite singer, things that help her concentrate, and extracurricular activities she would like to join. Selena might do a short PowerPoint presentation about her goals after high school. Students can attend 5 minutes of the meeting or be present and participate the entire time. Obviously, students' preferences and those of their parents should be respected.

Step 2: Describe the Student's and
Parent's Vision, Based on a Person-Centered Planning Process

Depending on a district's IEP template, the student, parent, or team vision statement is part of the student profile and is included in a specific section labeled "Vision" or is part of a section labeled "Parent Concerns." See Chapter 2 for sample vision statements.

Step 3: Write a Student Profile

The student profile section of the IEP should describe the student's interests, strengths, achievements in and outside of school; academic and functional areas of need; supports that maximize the student's performance; and personality. It should describe the impact of the student's disability on his or her ability to gain access to the general education curriculum and should reflect the perspectives of the student him- or herself, his or her friends (particularly if he or she is unable to effectively communicate), his or her parents, and other members of the education team. Selena's profile is presented in Figure 4.3.

Be specific when describing the impact of the student's disability on his or her ability to make progress in the general education curriculum. Do not write "Selena's intellectual disability affects her ability to gain access to 10th-grade learning standards and curriculum." Do write "Selena's difficulty with short-term memory and slow processing skills affect her receptive understanding and expressive demonstration of 10th-grade learning standards."

Step 4: Report Results of the Most Recent Assessments

This section presents the results of a variety of assessments, including standardized and classroom tests of academic knowledge and functional performance; speech-language, occupational therapy, and physical therapy evaluations; teacher observations; analysis of work samples; scores on large-scale assessments; and achievement of prior IEP goals.

It is prudent to provide some context for interpretation of an assessment of intellectual functioning for students who are diagnosed with or suspected of having an intellectual disability.

- James's performance on standardized assessments must be interpreted cautiously because he does not yet have a reliable means of communication.

- Anna's relatively low scores on measures of adaptive behavior do not reflect an intellectual disability but are a function of her sensory processing and movement difficulties.

- Selena's identification as someone who has an intellectual disability does not present a comprehensive picture of her as a learner. Selena can demonstrate learning of prioritized general education standards when she is consistently provided with effective supports.

Individualized Education Program

Student's name: <u>Selena</u>
Projected date IEP is to be implemented: <u>May 2018</u>
Projected date of annual review: <u>May 2019</u>

Student Strengths, Preferences, and Interests

Selena is a confident and outgoing young woman. She loves school and is happy about being fully included in the high school social scene. She is kind to others and quick to offer a comforting or encouraging word. She is generally very laid back and not flustered by unforeseen events, with the exception of fire drills. She is very close to her two sisters and older brother and enjoys the support of both parents. Selena has many of the same interests as her classmates without disabilities, such as pop music, celebrities, and the high school sports teams. She has been on the swim team since middle school, and she works hard at practice several times a week. Participation in extracurricular activities, service learning opportunities, and sports are essential for Selena to develop age-appropriate and functional skills such as following the unwritten rules of social interaction, solving problems, dedicating herself to lifelong fitness, navigating around the community, and developing career and independent living skills.

Selena's social, pragmatic, and interpersonal skills are strengths that serve her well during academic tasks and promote her connections with classmates at school. She is motivated to learn, demonstrates effort when working on assignments, conforms to expected classroom behavior, and willingly engages in group work and presentations. Selena is very sociable and has a network of peers that she interacts with at lunch and during transition times. Her positive attitude and desire to learn and to do well assist her both in and out of the classroom. Selena's magnetic personality, upbeat attitude, and confidence contribute to her success in the school environment. Selena's strengths must be considered in the context of her family system. Selena's family is very involved in her education and works with school staff in a respectful and collaborative manner.

Academic, Developmental, and Functional Needs of the Student

Selena's long-term memory is optimized by ensuring that all text and other instructional materials are presented during instruction and assessment at her reading and comprehension level and supplemented with pictures, graphic representations, and semantic maps or schema. Selena's recall difficulties may be due to language retrieval problems rather than the absence of knowledge or conceptual understanding. She benefits from supports such as using word banks, giving her a choice of several answers, restating questions with familiar vocabulary, making connections to her background knowledge, and using analogies to help her understand figurative language. If Selena is distracted by noise, movement, or changes to routine, then the least intrusive prompts should be used. Structures that support her to follow classroom routines include using task cards, encouraging her to follow what her classmates are doing, using her iPad reminder app, and chunking academic tasks into smaller steps.

Selena uses a variety of technology for both academic and functional purposes that are described in the Accommodations and Modification section.

Selena easily navigates the building and can meet her self-care needs independently.

Selena demonstrates anxiety during fire drills. She requires support and supervision from an adult during these events.

Figure 4.3. Selena's Individualized Education Program.

Step 5: Describe Student's Present Levels of Performance in Academic and Functional Areas

Because formal assessment results may be up to 3 years old, this section of the IEP describes the student's present levels of performance in academic and functional areas as last measured during the current academic year. Selena's present levels of performance are depicted in Figure 4.4.

Present Levels of Performance and Individual Needs

Selena enjoys reading popular magazines and mystery series books written at the third-grade level that feature girls or young women as the main character. She listens to books read aloud on her iPad, such as *The Hunger Games* series. Selena decodes at approximately the fifth-grade level, but her silent reading comprehension is at approximately the third-grade reading level. She recalls details better when unfamiliar vocabulary is previewed before reading and when she is asked to summarize what she has read after every page. She can give answers to "who," "what," and "when" questions but needs guided support to answer "why" questions and make inferences.

Selena participates in many sports but fatigues easily due to poor core strength. Using adaptive seating is being explored because Selena's posture deteriorates toward the end of the school day.

Selena is generally a happy young woman, but she is sensitive to being left out of social activities. This year she has expressed to her parents a wish to be part of more extracurricular activities and go on outings with friends on a more regular basis.

Selena writes notes and letters to friends using a pencil or pen but does all of her academic writing using word prediction software on her laptop or iPad. She makes frequent spelling errors and does not accurately use punctuation. She sends text messages on her smartphone. She writes most expansively when she has created an outline or graphic organizer prior to writing. She is beginning to use Inspiration software to develop an outline and the word prediction and other features of Read&Write.

Selena can state big ideas and recall up to five vocabulary words from recent science and social studies units. Long-term recall is difficult for her without prior review.

Selena has mastered addition and subtraction facts up to 12 in math and is able to complete multidigit multiplication and division problems when using a calculator. She needs to have word problems displayed as computation problems to successfully solve them. She uses a calculator to determine how much a group of items costs and uses the "next higher amount" strategy to determine how much to give the cashier. She can use an ATM to withdraw money and a debit card to make purchases at the store. Selena generally scores 80% or better on math tests modified to about the third-grade level.

Selena's receptive and expressive communication skills are a strength. Her abilities in social conversation are on par with her closest same-age peers without disabilities with whom she shares activities and social experiences. She initiates conversation with unfamiliar peers but has difficulty sustaining them. Her articulation of multisyllabic words is sometimes unclear, although familiar people are generally able to understand her meaning. Her intelligibility improves when she is asked to slow down or repeat what she has said.

Selena wears glasses to correct her vision to 20/20, and her vision does not present a barrier to safely navigating the school or familiar community environments. Her perceptual motor difficulties sometimes present a barrier to looking at the board and copying notes, so she should have copies of all notes provided after a lecture.

Selena has difficulty comprehending novel academic information, and her understanding is compromised by difficulties with long-term memory, particularly of decontextualized information. Selena does best learning new concepts when they are presented verbally, in writing, within a graphic organizer, through video, with concrete objects (when possible), and when she has had the opportunity to talk about these ideas with her classmates as well as at home. Selena's concentration is best when her daily schedule is varied (i.e., one period of academics, a period of music, a short academic support period, another academic class, lunch, physical activity, another academic class). Her attention will fade and she will not do her best work on those days when she has several academic classes in a row.

Selena received grades of 85 in English, 78 in math, 89 in biology, 74 in history, and 92 in culinary arts during the previous academic semester with modified general education content. She received a nonmodified grade of 90 in physical education.

Selena has had two volunteer jobs. The first job was at the local parks and recreation department after ninth grade where she assisted the campers with arts and crafts. Her second job was with a law office where she did filing, mailing, and photocopying. She recently spent a day at the computer company of a family friend and has expressed an interest in an internship or job there in the future.

Figure 4.4.   Selena's present levels of academic and functional performance.

Step 6: Write Inclusive Annual Goals and Short-Term Objectives or Benchmarks

Annual goals represent knowledge and skills that the IEP team projects the student can reasonably achieve within 1 year, or the term of the IEP. Write annual goals and short-term objectives or benchmarks that can best be implemented in an inclusive classroom and other inclusive contexts. These goals do not represent everything that the team hopes the student will achieve in a year, but rather the highest priority goals that will help the student make progress toward achieving grade-level standards and other functional skills or developmental milestones. IEPs that contain 50 goals are invariably not implementable. Short-term objectives and benchmarks reflect intermediate steps between the student's present levels of academic achievement and functional performance and the attainment of the annual goal.

Annual Goals

Measurable annual goals contain the following elements describing what the student will do.

1. Will do what (demonstrated skill/behavior)

2. To what level or degree (criterion—percent, number of opportunities, number of points)

3. Under what conditions (conditions)

4. In what length of time (time frame)

5. As measured by (performance measure)

Goals that reflect what staff will do (e.g., "Staff will provide James with opportunities to play with friends during recess") should be reframed as supplementary aids and services (e.g., "James will use adapted playground equipment with support of an adult to engage with peers during recess"). Four types of annual goals are consistent with an inclusive, standards-based IEP (Jorgensen et al., 2007).

Annual Goal Type 1 Type 1 annual goals relate directly to grade-level general education or alternate assessment standards.

Math Goal for James Given plane figures outlined in red on a black background (the condition), James will use eye gaze as measured by observation of the SLP (performance measure) to match congruent figures (demonstrated skill), one of which has been rotated once, 75% of the time (level or degree of mastery) during the fall grading period (time frame).

Reading Goal for Anna Anna will use her AAC system during spring semester English language arts class (condition and time frame) to describe the author's purpose (demonstrated skill) in three pieces of connected literary text (condition), scoring 3 out of 4 on an evaluation rubric (performance measure and degree of mastery).

Science Goal for Selena   When provided with text written at her reading and comprehension level, graphic organizers, pictures and symbols, schema, and Read&Write supports on a computer or iPad (the conditions), Selena will master one enduring understanding/big idea, five vocabulary words/terms, and three facts/concepts/skills within each unit of the physical science curriculum (demonstrated skill), scoring 75% (level or degree of mastery) on teacher-made end-of-unit tests (performance measure and time frame).

Reading Goal for Selena   When provided with text written at her reading level, graphic organizers, pictures and symbols, schema, and Read&Write supports on a computer or iPad (condition), Selena will improve her reading skills (demonstrated skill) within connected literary and informational texts to the criterion required to meet modified English 10 course competencies (level or degree of mastery) as measured by classroom assignments and teacher-made tests (performance measure) during the spring semester (time frame).

Annual Goal Type 2   Type 2 annual goals relate directly to content area foundational skills (in some cases, lower than grade level) that can be addressed while learning the grade-level standards. The following example is for a student who is an emerging communicator and not yet demonstrating knowledge of the grade-level standards.

Math Goal for Marcus   Given a rectangle or triangle and two plausible distractors (condition), Marcus will identify a rectangle or triangle (demonstrated skill) by making a selection on his AAC device (performance measure) 100% of the time (level or degree of mastery) when given on four consecutive trials throughout the week's math lessons (time frame).

Annual Goal Type 3   Type 3 annual goals address communication, social, behavioral, executive function, or movement skills that facilitate participation in general education instruction based on the general education curriculum and other inclusive activities and environments. Teaching these types of goals during content area instruction more effectively utilizes instructional time by reducing the need to pull a student from class to work on what might traditionally be viewed as a functional skill that people often think cannot be addressed in a general education classroom.

Reading Comprehension Goal for Suri   Suri will use facial expressions as observed by the SLP (performance measure) during guided reading (condition) to select answers to questions about the story (demonstrated skill) when provided with four word-picture choices with a latency range of 1–15 seconds (condition), 90% of the time (level or degree of mastery), in 3 out of 4 opportunities every day during the fall term (time frame).

Communication Goal for Jacob   Jacob will participate in turn-taking during buddy reading (condition) by pressing a switch that plays a prerecorded portion of the text (demonstrated skill) 90% of the time out of 10 trials (level or degree of mastery), as measured by data forms (performance measure), during each week of the spring semester (time frame).

Notice the targeted skill is communication rather than reading in Jacob's buddy reading goal. When students such as Jacob do not have an accurate and reliable way to communicate, assessments of their current or potential abilities are not valid or reliable, and the team's job is to work toward finding a communication system and related supports that will enable them to engage in instruction and social interactions.

Annual Goal Type 4   Type 4 annual goals address knowledge and skills within other inclusive school and community settings, including self-determination and transition.

Technology or Transition Goal for Selena   When provided with instruction and modeling (conditions), Selena will use a variety of technology hardware and software applications for organizing her schedule and communicating with her summer job supervisor (demonstrated skill), meeting the computer technology graduation requirements through an extended learning opportunity contract, and obtaining a 3 out of 4 (level or degree of mastery) on a rubric (performance measure) during a summer extended school year (ESY) program (time frame).

Transition Goal for Selena   After visiting two college campuses and meeting with staff from admissions and disability services office (conditions), Selena will demonstrate knowledge of two postsecondary educational opportunities (demonstrated skill) by doing a PowerPoint presentation in her advisory class (performance measure) at the end of the fall semester (time frame), providing five facts with 100% accuracy (level or degree of mastery).

Short-Term Objectives or Benchmarks

With few exceptions (check each state's special education regulations), short-term objectives or benchmarks are only required for students participating in a state's alternate assessment. A *short-term objective* breaks the annual goal into discrete components that are measurable intermediate steps. For example, "James will demonstrate knowledge of letter sounds and letter patterns by reading regularly spelled one-syllable words with 80% accuracy," and "James will demonstrate knowledge of letter sounds and letter patterns by reading irregularly spelled one- and two-syllable words with 80% accuracy." Sample short-term objectives (without their performance criteria) include the following.

- Identify regularly spelled multisyllabic words by using knowledge of sounds, syllable types, or word patterns.

- Use strategies to unlock meaning.

- Locate and record information to show understanding.

- Use a range of self-monitoring and self-correction approaches (e.g., predicting upcoming text, monitoring, adjusting and confirming).

- Use strategies while reading or listening to literary and informational text (e.g., using prior knowledge); predicting and making text-based inferences; determining importance; generating literal and clarifying questions; constructing sensory images (e.g., making pictures in one's mind); making connections (e.g., text to self, text to text, text to world); and locating and using text features (e.g., headings, parts of the book).

- Distinguish fact from opinion.

- Describe characters, setting, problem, solution, and major events.

- Sequence key events.

- Compare stories or texts with personal experience, with prior knowledge, or to other texts.

- Identify the author's basic message.

Appropriate skills that can be reflected in short-term objectives can often be found in a state's general or alternate assessment standards.

A *benchmark* breaks the annual goal into milestones that the student is expected to reach within a specified period of time. For example, "Chelsea will utilize eye gaze to correctly answer questions with 60% accuracy by the end of the first quarter; with 70% accuracy by the end of second quarter; with 75% accuracy by the end of the third quarter; and with 80% accuracy by the end of the year."

Benchmarks can change over time as indicated by an increase in the level of mastery (e.g., increasing difficulty of the reading material); an increase in the complexity of the learning environment (e.g., in natural settings with classmates as opposed to a one-to-one session with a therapist); or an increase in independence as reflected in less intense supports (e.g., fading prompts from full physical to partial physical to verbal to gestural). Sample benchmarks include the following.

- By the end of the first marking term, James will identify main characters (in response to questions) from a primer level literal text that he has listened to with 90% accuracy as measured by the Qualitative Reading Inventory-6 (2017).

- By the end of the second term, James will identify main characters (in response to questions) from a primer level literal text that he has read with 90% accuracy as measured by the Qualitative Reading Inventory.

- By the end of third marking term, James will identify main characters and setting (in response to questions) from a first-grade literal text that he has listened to with 90% accuracy as measured by the Qualitative Reading Inventory.

Step 7: Determine How Progress on Goals Will Be Measured and How Often It Will Be Reported

Deciding how and how often progress on goals will be reported to parents is an essential step in writing an inclusive, standards-based IEP. Acceptable ways to measure student performance include the following.

- Letter, number, or percent grades

- Inventories

- Rubrics

- Checklists

- Observations

- Audio analyses of verbal responses

- Video analyses of hands-on performance

- Portfolios

- Quizzes and tests

- Homework completion

- Ratings of drawings, illustrations, and models

- Reports from internships and vocational experiences

- Self-evaluation scales

The methods used should communicate to the student, parents, and other readers (e.g., college admissions committees, future employers) what students know and are able to accomplish. Perhaps the most common measures used to quantify student achievement of their short-term objectives is 3 out of 5 trials. Does it make sense to write a goal that states, "Darren will cross the street safely 5 out of 7 times?" Of course not, and that is a ridiculous way to assess that particular skill. This type of performance measure may not be appropriate for reporting student performance on complex, multicomponent skills such as reading, writing, or communicating, unless a students' educational program is based on strict applied behavior analysis teaching. Consider the student who has comprehension goals on his or her IEP. Is it best to measure his or her achievement of those goals within a tightly controlled assessment situation with an unfamiliar text, or would doing periodic assessments over the course of several weeks' reading assignments in the regular class be a better measure?

Progress is usually reported every 6 weeks, although there is nothing in IDEA 2004 that requires that or any other reporting interval other than it must be at least as often as progress is reported for students without disabilities. Because report cards are issued approximately every 12 weeks, perhaps doing twice as many assessments makes sense for students whose progress depends on the quality of their instruction. Schools that use response to intervention or multi-tiered systems of support to organize instruction and progress monitoring may dictate that progress reports for the neediest students are issued on a much more regular basis, often every week.

Step 8: Describe the Supplementary Aids and Services That Will Enable the Student to Achieve Annual Goals and Short-Term Objectives

Step 8 involves describing the supplementary aids and services that will be provided to the student to enable him or her to achieve the annual goals and short-terms objectives or benchmarks within an inclusive classroom and other inclusive contexts. This step is addressed in Chapter 5 because of the amount of information involved and the depth with which it will be covered.

Step 9: Describe the Supports for School Personnel on Behalf of the Student

Many people are unaware that part of supplementary aids and services is a section within the IEP usually titled "Supports to the Team on Behalf of the Student." This issue is also covered in Chapter 5 and includes resources for professional development, other kinds of training or coaching, consultation from experts outside of the school, school–home communication books, and common planning time.

Step 10: Detail Type, Personnel Responsible, Amount, Location, and Duration of Special Education and Related Services

Specifically listing the type, personnel responsible, amount, location, and duration of special education and related services that support the student's inclusion is another essential step in writing an inclusive, standards-based IEP. The service grid of a student who is included in a general education class looks very different from a student who is in a substantially separate classroom. James—who is now a full-time member of a general education classroom—receives services during the regular school year (September to June) according to the schedule depicted in Figure 4.5.

Step 11: Indicate the Student's Placement, Percentage of Time Student Will Be in General Education, and Rationale for Time That Student Will Not Participate With Students Without Disabilities

This step entails listing the student's placement, the percentage of time the student will be in general education (required by many states), and the

Service provider	Type and location of service	Length of service	Frequency of service
Inclusion facilitator	Instructional planning meeting/conference room	60 minutes	Weekly
Inclusion facilitator	Direct/general education classroom	40 minutes	5 days per week
Inclusion facilitator	Indirect/preparation of adapted materials	60 minutes	5 days per week
Paraeducator	Direct/general education classroom and other school environments	6.5 hours	5 days per week
All team members	Instructional planning/conference room	60 minutes	1 time per week
Speech-language pathologist (SLP)	Direct/general education classroom	60 minutes	3 times per week
SLP	Consultation with occupational therapist (OT)/conference room or general education classroom	40 minutes	1 time per week
SLP	Indirect/programming augmentative and alternative communication device	60 minutes	1 time per week
OT	Direct support in the classroom	60 minutes	1 time per week
OT	Consultation with SLP/conference room or general education classroom	40 minutes	1 time per week
Physical therapist	Direct support in physical education	40 minutes	1 time per week
Reading specialist	Direct instruction in reading lab	30 minutes	3 times per week

Figure 4.5. James's services schedule.

rationale for time that the student will not participate with students without disabilities. Of course, the goal of this book is for all students to be fully included in general education instruction in a general education class taught by a general education teacher. Therefore, this part of the IEP should indicate that the student is spending the maximum amount of time available as a choice on the district's IEP form.

The following phrases are examples of the IEP team justifying time spent outside of a general education: "Jeremy will not participate in general education instruction in the general education class because he needs individualized instruction in a quiet environment due to his distractibility." "Marissa is working on an alternate curriculum that cannot be addressed in the general education environment." Using these reasons to justify time outside of the general education classroom is discouraged. Teams should identify strategies for engaging Jeremy's attention during individual seat work, small-group instruction, or whole-class instruction in the inclusive classroom. Even students who are participating in alternate assessments based on alternate achievement standards can be successfully included in a general education class if the team aligns the alternate achievement standards with the general achievement standards. They do not necessarily need an alternate curriculum. And remember that the final regulations issued for the implementation of IDEA 2004 state that the amount of curriculum modification needed cannot be the sole reason for removing a student from a general education classroom (U.S. Department of Education, 2006, p. 46765).

Step 12: Describe Student's Participation in District and State Assessments

Step 12 involves describing the student's participation in district and state assessments, including accommodations to the general assessment or rationale for why the student will participate in the alternate assessment based on alternate achievement standards. When students do not have a way to communicate in ways that are commensurate with their same-age peers without disabilities or when their measured IQ results in a diagnosis of intellectual disability, people often assume that they are not capable of learning the general education academic content, rather than assuming the problem is a lack of quality instruction, supports, or not having a way to demonstrate what they know. These students are usually considered among the 1% who should participate in a state's alternate assessment based on alternate achievement standards. The debate about what students are expected to learn and therefore what assessments best measure that learning is not over, however. McGrew and Evans (2004) synthesized that debate concisely:

> Considerable controversy surrounds the issue of what can and should be expected for these students. Some people argue that the vast majority of students with disabilities, when given appropriate access to high quality curriculum and instruction, can meet or exceed the levels of proficiency currently specified. Many special education advocates believe that subscribing to the same high expectations and accountability for student progress will ultimately lead to improved instruction and learning for all students. Others argue that a student's disability will ultimately prevent the student from attaining grade level achievement standards, even when provided appropriate instruction and accommodations. This latter group believes that it is unjust to punish schools when these students fail to perform at the proficient level. (p. 2)

McGrew and Evans (2004) concluded the following based on their analysis of the tenuous relationship between measured IQ scores and the achievement of students with disabilities that often surpasses expectations.

> Stereotyping students with disabilities (often on the basis of disability label or test scores) as a group that should be excluded from general education standards and assessments is not supported by the best evidence from current science in the field of psychological and educational measurement. The potential soft bigotry of setting a priori I.Q. or disability label-based low academic expectations (for students with disabilities) needs to be recognized, understood, and minimized, if all children are not to be left behind. (p. 10)

Where does that leave educators and parents? Parents are rightfully concerned that agreeing to have their child participate in an alternate assessment will decrease the team's expectations for their child and lead to a non-inclusive educational placement (although there is no legal reason to link the two). They may think that subjecting their child to assessments on which they will do poorly is neither fair nor humane. Many parents also strongly believe, however, that schools need to be accountable for all students' learning. Parents who use this line of reasoning want their children to be assessed and their scores counted when evaluating a school's effectiveness.

Educators are concerned that requiring participation in the general assessment for students they perceive to have significantly lower than average intellectual functioning is not fair and even cruel to those students. Furthermore, teachers and administrators worry that these students' poor performance on a general assessment will negatively affect their school's ability to meet performance standards required by ESSA. IEP teams must account for all points of view, maintain high expectations, and keep the student and his or her learning at the center of their decision-making process because they determine the large-scale assessment a student will complete.

Step 13: Write Inclusive Transition Goals and Services

Writing inclusive transition goals and services is an IEP step for students who are 16 years old and older. This step is also completed for younger children if the IEP team determines it is necessary. Chapter 10 describes the transition-related requirements of the IEP and presents examples of goals and services.

Step 14: Consider Special Factors

Teams must consider the following special factors when writing a student's IEP: behavior; limited English proficiency; blindness or visual impairment; communication needs, especially, but not only, deafness; and AT.

Teams must check a box on some IEP forms to indicate they have considered the impact of these factors on the student's educational program, which may lead them to think that this section of the IEP does not carry as much weight as others. Nothing could be further from the truth because checking the box obligates the team to determine what steps they will take to make their considerations tangible in other sections of the IEP (including annual goals and short-term objectives, supplementary aids and services, special education and related services, participation in assessments, placement, transition goals and services, and the need for specialized transportation). This is why it is important to have all the professionals who represent the student's areas of need affected by his or her disability attend the IEP meeting.

Students who demonstrate challenging behavior can benefit from having a functional behavioral assessment (FBA) and a positive behavior support plan. If a student's challenging behavior is attributable to his or her disability, then special rules protect the student from the consequences that might be faced by a student without a disability, such as suspension or expulsion. If there is any uncertainty regarding this issue, then it may be wise to check this box to protect the student's rights.

Students who have limited English proficiency may require specialized instructional materials, staff with special qualifications, and large-scale assessments specifically for them. The Center for Parent Information and Resources (2010) published a document titled *A Checklist for IEP Teams: Considering Limited English Proficiency* that helps teams consider the needs of this group of students who also have a disability.

Students who have vision or hearing differences are eligible for specific services and supports, so teams should check these boxes if the student's disability includes these areas of functioning. Although it is not included in the same category as those previously listed, the student's need for accessible instructional materials must be considered by the IEP team. The very definition of IDD includes challenges in gaining access to, processing, and demonstrating learning that can be ameliorated by the provision of accessible instructional materials. Again, this section on the IEP is usually addressed in a single sentence requiring a checkmark by the team. The team might discuss the following questions to determine if a student needs accessible instructional materials.

- Does the student have difficulty seeing the material?

- Does the student have difficulty physically manipulating the material?

- Does the student have the physical stamina necessary?

- Does the student have difficulty decoding words?

- Does the student have difficulty with fluency?

- Does the student lose his or her place while reading or tracking?

- Does the student have difficulty with comprehension skills?

Some people think that accessible instructional materials considerations only relate to students who have visual or movement difficulties, when, in fact, many other disability-related conditions require accessible instructional materials. Checking the accessible instructional materials box prompts teams to review their list of supplementary aids and services to determine if the needed materials and technologies provide full access to information, the means to fully participate in general education instruction, and a way to demonstrate learning. Chapter 5 describes accessible instructional materials that may be part of a student's supplementary aids and services.

Step 15: Write the Section of the IEP for Inclusive Extended School Year Services

The topic of extended school year (ESY) services may be one of the most common areas in which parents and school personnel have misunderstandings that lead to disagreements. This section represents information from three primary sources—the South Dakota Department of Education (2012), the U.S. Department of Education (n.d.), and Wright's Law (2011). It is always wise to consult each state's regulations about ESY as they vary across the United States. Six reasons are generally recognized as providing the rationale for ESY services.

1. Regression and recoupment (i.e., Is the student likely to lose critical skills or fail to recover these skills within in a reasonable time after a vacation or other absence?)

2. Degree of progress toward IEP goals and objectives

3. Emerging skills present a breakthrough opportunity (e.g., a lengthy school break causes significant problems for a student who is learning a key skill)

4. Interfering behavior (i.e., Does the student's behavior interfere with his or her ability to benefit from special education?)

5. The nature or severity of the student's disability

6. Special circumstances that interfere with the student's ability to benefit from special education

Some of these reasons for ESY services are open to interpretation, requiring parents and educators to use guidance from their state department of education and sources that describe the results of case law on the subject. Here are some fast facts about ESY services.

- A new IEP is not written for ESY services.

- Services do not have to include a focus on all of the student's annual goals and short-term objectives, just those that are related to the six factors previously cited.

- For some students, skills that support continued placement in the LRE can be maintained only by ESY services. For example, an ESY program may be justified if a student has challenging behavior and the continuation of a learning program in the summer will give the student the opportunity to maintain his or her skills in dealing with anxiety, frustration, or transitions in a general education class the following school year.

- ESY decisions must be made every year; having had ESY services in the past does not automatically qualify a student for them in the future.

- ESY decisions should be based on objective criteria, such as data showing that a student has or has not lost skills during a holiday break.

- If objective data are not available, then team members' best professional judgment can be used as a rationale to support or deny ESY services.

- One or more related services may be appropriate for an ESY program; instruction from a special education teacher is not required.

- ESY services do not have to be limited to the summer break. Although this is generally the longest break from the normal school year, ESY services may be needed during shorter breaks of 1–2 weeks in length (e.g., winter and spring breaks). ESY services can even be an extension of the student's normal school day, such as a special tutoring program after school.

- Parents are sometimes offered a 4-week program in July or services 3 days a week for 6 weeks, but schools may not "unilaterally limit the type, amount, or duration of those services" (U.S. Department of Education, 2006, p. 46763). A student's ESY services must be based on his or her individual needs, not the convenience of staff or scheduling.

- ESY services are not designed to maximize a student's benefit from his or her educational program.

- ESY services generally are not provided to enable to the student to learn more than the annual goals and short-term objectives on his or her IEP unless special circumstances provide an opportunity for a student to take advantage of a developmental window for learning new skills.

- Acceptable ESY programs include

  - The same summer school provided to students without disabilities but with special education or related services provided to focus the student's learning on his or her IEP goals and objectives.

  - Attendance at a summer camp with special education or related services provided to focus the student's learning on his or her IEP goals and objectives. Although an argument can be made that the school should pay the camp fee, some parents and schools agree that parents will pay the camp fee and the school will provide support personnel.

  - A home- or school-based tutoring program a few hours a day, a few days a week.

  - A summer job either on a volunteer or paid basis with support from special education personnel.

ESY services must be individualized to meet each student's unique needs.

CONCLUSIONS

Writing a high-quality inclusive IEP is equal parts science and art. The purpose of an IEP is to identify the student's highest priority learning goals and identify the supports and services he or she will need to attain those goals. The IEP is not the student's entire educational program but rather a road map containing the most important stops along the way to the final destination of learning and inclusion.

5

Identify Supplementary Aids and Services as Part of an Inclusive Standards-Based IEP

This chapter describes and provides examples of supplementary aids and services that enable students to fully participate and learn within general education instruction in a general education classroom and enable their team members to implement students' educational programs well.

✱CATEGORIES AND EXAMPLES OF SUPPLEMENTARY AIDS AND SERVICES

Supplementary aids and services or student supports fall into nine general categories: 1) physical and environmental; 2) emotional and behavior; 3) sensory; 4) vision and hearing; 5) accessible instructional materials; 6) communication; 7) executive function; 8) personalized instruction; and 9) technology, equipment, and tools. Teams should be mindful of the differences between two major types of supplementary aids and services—those that qualify as accommodations and those that qualify as modifications because these differences have implications for a student's receipt of a regular high school diploma. Some supplementary aids and services are considered *accommodations* that change the format of presenting information and demonstrating learning, the amount of time, and the location of instruction and assessment. Accommodations do not change the rigor or difficulty of the standard being taught. Accommodations through the lens of universal design for learning (UDL) means the varied ways that teachers present information to students, the diverse ways that students interact with information, and the multiple ways that students show what they know—all with respect to the general education learning standards and curriculum (Meyer, Rose, & Gordon, 2014).

Other supplementary aids and services are *modifications* that do change the rigor or difficulty of the standard being taught. Some students can gain access to the general education curriculum only with accommodations, others need a combination of accommodations and modifications, and some students need modifications to be successful. In the past, students whose learning objectives were highly modified and who participated in alternate assessment were often not allowed to pursue a regular high school diploma. This is no longer the case after the passage of the ESSA, and any student who meets a district's or state's graduation requirements may receive a regular high school diploma, subject to certain requirements. As legislation and regulations are revised, teams should check the special education rules applicable to their situation.

Supplementary aids and services also include the supports that the team needs on behalf of the student. These supports might be professional development, coaching, common time for planning, visits to inclusive schools, creation of a professional learning community to support team learning, and methods of communication between school and home. Teams are encouraged to consult Causton and Tracy-Bronson (2015) for a comprehensive list of supplementary aids and services, and a supplementary aids and services team decision-making toolkit from the Pennsylvania Training and Technical Assistance Network (2008).

Physical and Environmental Supports

Physical and environmental supports enable a student with movement, endurance, and positional challenges to sustain attention, manipulate objects in the environment, and maintain postural integrity. The supports are provided to the student or adaptations are made to equipment, such as wheelchairs, classroom chairs, desks, computers and keyboards, or laboratory tables, including the following.

- Push a student's wheelchair.
- Provide support to a student's arm as he or she types or activates an AAC device.
- Use adjustable mounts to position an iPad or dedicated AAC device for easier access.
- Take notes for a student.
- Give a student a keyboard such as BigKeys that supports typing and spelling.
- Provide adaptive seating.
- Seat the student close to the teacher or SMART Board.

Emotional and Behavioral Supports

Some students with IDD also have emotional and behavioral support needs. A formal system of rewards and punishments is too often implemented before taking a close look at the student's communication and other needs that lead to challenging behavior. Judith Snow, a renowned disability advocate, once led a workshop for a group of high school students who were involved in supporting their friend who had significantly challenging behavior. She guided the students to draw that student's circle of friends (see Chapter 8) and asked them to reflect on how the student probably feels because he is surrounded by adults all day long and does not have one classmate in his closest relationship circles. The students generated words such as *sad, left out, hopeless, worthless,* and *frustrated.* Judith then asked the students to reflect on how a person might act if he or she had those feelings. The students said he or she might hit someone, hurt themselves, run away, refuse to do his or her work, abuse drugs, and so forth. Make sure that the student's basic human needs are being met before doing an FBA, and make a conscious effort to provide the following supports.

- Presume the student's competence, have high expectations, and provide the supports that actively construct the student's competence (see Chapters 1 and 3).

- Provide the student with a means of communication so that he or she can interact in both academic and social contexts in a way that is commensurate with his or her classmates without disabilities (see Chapter 3).

- Express confidence in a student's capabilities.

- Acknowledge a student's feelings.

- Teach stress or anxiety management strategies.

- Include the student in more general education classes.

- Facilitate social relationships (see Chapter 8).

If these supports do not work, then conduct an FBA and develop a positive behavior support plan that reflects the values of humanistic behavioral support pioneered by Lovett (1996) and others (Causton, Tracy-Bronson, & MacLeod, 2015; Pitonyak, 2005).

Sensory Supports

Sensory supports should be given to students with sensory needs that influence their ability to stay calm, be organized, pay attention, and regulate their responses to sensations in their environment. Students with sensory regulation needs are sensitive to touch, visual stimuli, sound, taste, smell, movement, or joint position. Students who are unable to regulate and balance these sensitivities may go through their school day feeling confused, anxious, or frightened about what will happen next and even physically uncomfortable or in pain. Dunn (1997) organized students with sensory difficulties into four categories.

Category 1: Low Registration These students need a greater amount or intensity of sensory input to recognize or register information and do not seek out sensory information from the environment. They may

- Not feel where their body is until they are leaning or crashing into another person or object

- Not register or recognize pain when falling

- Not respond to being called until their name is said multiple times

- Appear inattentive or confused

Category 2: Sensory Seeking These students need a greater intensity of sensory input to register or process information, and they may seek out this input to alert or wake up their system. They may

- Seek out movement and deep pressure input by running, fidgeting, crashing, and being generally physically active

- Hum, sing, tap their hands or feet, flap their hands, or flutter their fingers against a lighted background to get sensory input

Category 3: Sensory Sensitivity These students can be sensitive to sensory information and are sometimes passive in their response to their environment. They may

- Be very observant of their environment and those around them

- Complain or be hesitant to participate in or try new activities

- Like to watch before trying

Category 4: Sensory Avoiding These students can be sensitive to sensory information and act to avoid uncomfortable situations that involve undesirable sensory situations. They may

- Avoid situations or settings in which they could encounter uncomfortable sensory information

- Cover their eyes or ears to block out sight or sound

- Bite their hands or hit their heads

- Be anxious or develop anxieties related to uncomfortable sensory experiences

- Be rigid and rule bound

Some disagreements exist in the fields of special education and physical and occupational therapy about what constitutes evidence-based interventions for students with these challenges. Reviews of classical sensory integration therapy and other strategies, such as using a sensory diet, have found weak evidence of efficacy (Jordan, n.d.). Yet, many parents and educators have found that using these techniques yields positive outcomes for some students. Teams are advised to establish strong baseline data, implement supports or interventions with fidelity (i.e., accurately and consistently), and carefully evaluate the impact of those supports or interventions, whether or not there is a strong research evidence base. Teams should be flexible enough to abandon strategies that are not working, particularly with a sensory diet (a schedule of sensory activities provided throughout a student's day), and try new ones when the novelty of a new object or activity has worn off. A sample sensory diet is depicted in Table 5.1.

Stimmel (2010) described a variety of sensory supports that represent environmental adaptations or tools and techniques used by students themselves to address their sensory processing differences.

Therapy Ball

A therapy ball can provide students with the movement they seek while also keeping them within a designated area. The ball enables students to move while staying at their desk. A therapy ball can also be used to provide deep pressure. Think of how a big hug or heavy down comforter can make someone feel relaxed.

Fidget Tools

These are toys or tools that can be manipulated in the hands or mouth, providing different textures or resistances, and include spinners, porcupine balls, putty, and chewy necklaces and bracelets. OTs have access to a variety of vendors that sell these tools inexpensively. Increasing textures to the hands or resistance to the hand joints can be alerting to a student with low registration. Simply occupying the hands can be focusing and calming to many students. Some people seem to concentrate better when they are simultaneously doing something with their hands, such as tapping their pencil or twirling their hair.

Proprioceptive Activities

Lifting heavy objects (never more than 30% of student's body weight), using TheraBands, pulling or pushing weighted objects, or wearing a weighted vest or lap pad may be organizing or calming for some students. Putting one's body weight through joint or limb movement might give students the proprioceptive input they need. Students might engage in animal walks,

Table 5.1. Sample sensory diet

Level 1	Lethargic Head down	Stretch arms/trunk Stretch for objects out of reach Bounce on a gym ball (do not get overstimulated) Chew on something/snack

Level 2	Distracted
	Stares at the wall
	Slow to respond
		Stretch arms/trunk
		Go for a walk
		Walk quickly for 20 steps and stop. Continue
		  the length of a hallway. Incorporate abrupt
		  changes in direction.
		Bounce on a gym ball or minitrampoline for
		  3–5 minutes (do not get overstimulated)
		Brain gym
		Chewing/snack

Level 3	Optimal learning level
	On task
	Attends to verbal and visual
	  directions
	Follows established daily
	  routine
	Makes transitions easily
	Responds when called by name
	Looks at the speaker
		Build heavy work activities into the school
		  routine on an hourly basis
		Brushing routine
		Brain gym
		Stretch/change position
		Snack, suck on a water bottle, blow through a
		  straw, chew on an object

Level 4	Difficulty following routine/
	  directions
	Low frustration level
	Performing school tasks
	  inefficiently
	Anxious
		Decrease verbal directions. Rely on picture
		  cues/gestures
		Talk in a low, quiet, and calm voice when verbal
		  input is needed
		Prepare for changes in routine
		Talk through expectations
		Provide fiddle objects
		Provide deep compression materials (bean bag
		  chair, cover with a heavy mat or blanket)
		Slow, steady paced walk
		Heavy work activity
		Incorporate movement into class tasks

Level 5	Tantrum Loud Does not respond to verbal cues Face flushed Fetal position Swear	Provide only visual cues Dim the lights Lower the noise level Go to a quiet area Provide sensory items to calm

crawl through tunnels, do wheelbarrow walks, or do push-ups on the floor or against a wall, depending on their ages and available space in the classroom or other school locations. Seated arm push-ups, a quick in-place exercise, are done when a student simply pushes his or her body up with stiff arms from the surface of their chair.

Movement Activities

Movement activities are increasingly used by teachers at every grade level to give all students in a classroom a break from cognitive tasks. These can take the form of dancing, doing yoga or exercises along with a DVD, using scooter boards, taking a walk around the classroom or hallway, or using the playground equipment during recess.

Tactile Activities

Tactile activities give students a chance to touch objects that have different textures, such as

- Sand or bean box

- Textures from nature (e.g., brick, sand, tree bark, grass)

- A piece of scratchy Velcro stuck under a desk

- A smooth rock or rough sandpaper kept in a pocket

- Feathers or a clean paintbrush

Sound

Some students may benefit from being able to block out certain sounds and others may find that adding sounds helps them balance other irritating sensory input. Strategies include

- Using music in the classroom to set a calm tone or provide white noise to block out other sounds and noises

- Wearing headphones or ear buds to block out ambient noise or listen to music or sound recordings

- Doing rhythmic drumming or tapping on one's thigh

- Humming or singing softly to block out other sounds

Smell and Taste

Consider the smell of classroom materials and settings (e.g., paints, dry erase markers, the lunch room, air fresheners, perfume). Some students and staff who have sensitivity to smell may ask for particular classrooms or even whole schools to be free of perfume. In other cases, students who are sensitive to scents might find certain fragrances calming or alerting. Students who have food sensitivities—either to textures, taste, or ingredients—may bring their own snacks and lunch so that they are not exposed to foods that irritate them or even cause illness.

Anna, the sixth-grade student with autism, needed a host of sensory supports to be happy, well regulated, and productive at school. Figure 5.1 depicts a daily schedule of her sensory supports.

Vision and Hearing Supports

Students with vision and hearing differences need access to specialized technologies that enable them to navigate school, home, and community

Time	Activity	Sensory supports
8:30	Arrival	Anna's parents send a short note to school letting her team know whether she got a good night's sleep and how the morning routines were tolerated. Peers accompany Anna from the bus into the building, often holding hands.
8:45	Enter classroom	The paraeducator helps Anna put on her weighted vest after she takes her coat off.
9:00	"Do Now" seat work	The classroom teacher stands behind Anna and gives her shoulder presses. Anna chooses to listen to music through her headphones while she is doing her seat work.
9:15	English language arts	Anna sits on a therapy ball during the teacher's lecture. The occupational therapist (OT) provides Anna with hand-under-hand support while she types her story into her iPad using BigKeys.
10:30	Snack	Anna walks around the classroom during break and hums quietly while she looks out the window.
10:45	Physical education	Anna uses a small trampoline for the entire warm-up time.
11:30	Lunch	Anna brings her lunch from home and it does not contain any of the foods that cause her tactile distress.
12:00	Recess	Anna and three girls play clapping games.
12:30	Math	Anna uses a Whisper Tilt 'n Spin prior to the beginning of math class to provide her with vestibular input.
1:30	Science	Anna uses a computer simulation to dissect a frog instead of a real amphibian.
2:30	Art	Anna uses nonsmelling paints sourced by her OT.
3:15	Dismissal	No sensory supports are necessary. A note about Anna's day is sent home so her parents can anticipate her sensory needs to help make the transition from school to home.

Figure 5.1. Daily sensory supports schedule for Anna.

environments and interact with instructional materials, tools, technologies, and other people. Most are well beyond the scope of this book, and readers are encouraged to seek assistance from teachers of the visually impaired, teachers of the deaf, and orientation and mobility specialists as well as resources from organizations such as the American Printing House for the Blind, Perkins School for the Blind, Texas School for the Blind and Visually Impaired, and the National Technical Institute for the Deaf. Two supports used by the profiled students in this book are described next.

Supports for Auditory Engagement   Some students who are hard of hearing and others who have difficulty paying attention to the teacher during whole class instruction or to classmates during small-group interactions may benefit from the use of personal "FM" technology. This system functions like a miniature public address system and consists of several portable parts, including a small, teacher- or classmate-worn microphone/transmitter and a receiver worn by the student or contained in a small desktop unit (Updike, 2006). Anna's teacher and classmates used an FM system during whole class instruction and small-group work.

Supports for Students With Cortical Visual Impairment   Because one of the students profiled in this book has cortical visual impairment (CVI), this section provides information to teams that will help them ask the right question about their students with CVI and participate as informed team members with a teacher of the visually impaired or others knowledgeable about CVI. Morse (1999) noted that to know one student with CVI is to only know about that one student.

> We should be cautious not to assume that all children with CVI exhibit the same behaviors. The diagnosis means different things for different children; the effects depend on factors such as how extensive and severe were the insults to the brain, the developmental period during which the insult occurred, the child's previous experience, the presence or absence of additional disabilities, medications being taken, and the child's motivation. Some individuals with CVI have no observable visual responses; others have occasional responses to stimuli, whereas still others have a significant amount of usable vision. (p. 22)

CVI is a term used to describe visual impairments that occur due to brain injury (Blind Babies Foundation, 2010). CVI is sometimes referred to by other terms, including *cerebral visual impairment, neurological visual impairment, brain damage* and *related visual impairment*. These terms refer to visual dysfunction resulting from injury to the visual centers of the brain, not to abnormalities in the eyes. CVI differs from other types of visual impairments that are due to physical problems with the eyes. CVI interferes with communication between the brain and the eyes. The eyes can see, but the brain does not interpret what is being seen. Asphyxia, perinatal hypoxic-ischemic encephalopathy, intraventricular hemorrhage, periventricular leukomalacia, cerebral vascular accident, central nervous system infection, structural abnormalities, and trauma are the most common conditions associated with a diagnosis of CVI. The typical characteristics of CVI include

- Preference for a specific color

- Need or preference for movement in order to see an object

- Delayed response when looking at objects (visual latency)

- Difficulty with visual complexity, particularly when trying to process unfamiliar images

- Light-gazing and non-purposeful gazing

- Visual field preferences

- Impaired distance vision

- Impaired or absent visual blink reflex

- Preference for familiar objects versus novel ones

- Impaired visually guided reach manifested in looking away from an object the student wants to touch or grasp

CVI is the only visual impairment that can get better over time with intervention. Roman-Lantzy (2007) developed an assessment and found that most children start in Phase I (of three) of CVI, which means that most of the CVI characteristics are present. Many of these characteristics begin to resolve as a child progresses through the three phases. This process can take several years and requires specific interventions. Children in Phase III approach near normal vision to varying degrees.

James, a second-grade student with cerebral palsy and CVI, was evaluated by a teacher of the visually impaired using the Roman-Lantzy (2007) assessment and was found to be in late Phase II. His team developed a guide that described the CVI accommodations he needed to visually process his environment, interact with others, and gain access to instructional materials (see Figure 5.2).

Accessible Instructional Materials

IDEA 2004 requires that students with disabilities have accessible instructional materials provided to them at approximately the same time as instructional materials are made available to students without disabilities. Nevertheless, when students with IDD cannot read books, web sites, or other image or text-based materials, educators too often just read the text or verbally describe the image for them. This results in students missing the opportunity to build their literacy skills and be more independent in gaining access to information now and in the future. Text and other visual displays can be made accessible by

Cortical visual impairment consideration	Accommodation
Color	Use neon color to highlight up to three salient features of visual information.
Movement	Use movement of the teacher's hand or pointing wand to get visual attention.
Latency	Allow wait time between presentation of materials and expected attention and response.
Visual fields	Present material no more than 45 degrees from midline on a plane from his eyes to his chin but not higher or lower.
Complexity	Ensure that the instructional space is free from clutter and objects not needed for the activity. Reduce the complexity of the object, the background, and the sensory environment.
Light	Use light (e.g., backlit materials, a lighted wand) to focus attention.
Distance	Distance viewing is closely related to the characteristic of complexity. The farther an object is from James, the more background clutter can be seen. Visual targets should be presented within arm's reach of James.
Visual novelty	Objects that are familiar to James are more easily processed. Novel objects have to be explicitly taught (through salient features and comparative language).
Visual motor	Provide hand-under-hand support when James is reaching for an object within his visual field.
Visual reflexes	James does have a blink reflex, so this is not an area that needs accommodation.

Figure 5.2. James's cortical visual impairment considerations plan.

- Changing the visual characteristics of the text or image (e.g., changing the size, color, or spacing; reducing the complexity of an image; adding outlining to identify the salient features of a letter, word, number, or graphic image)

- Supplementing classroom materials (e.g., adding pictures, symbols, audiovisual media, models, graphic organizers, manipulatives)

- Substituting different materials (e.g., creating a synopsis of a book or other text at the student's current reading level)

- Adding something to help the student make sense of the material (e.g., adding an aided language board to a reading lesson to help a student keep track of the characters; providing schema to help the student understand the steps in a process; using a graphic organizer to help a student understand a text; using technology to translate the text into speech)

Teams have two choices for providing accessible instructional materials—finding materials that have already been created by someone else or creating their own. It will clearly save a lot of time and effort if the needed materials can be found rather than created.

Commercially Available Adapted Texts   Table 5.2 lists sources for commercially available adapted texts that enhance accessibility. Sometimes these texts are accessible to students just as they were written and other times teams must further customize them for a student's unique needs.

Creating Accessible Books or Other Text   If an already created adapted book cannot be found, then create one using Microsoft Word, a book creator app such as Pictello, or an online tool such as Book Builder. Instructions for creating switch access to adapted books for students with significant movement difficulties are available from Musselwhite (2016) or Burkhart (2016). The instructions that follow can be used to create an adapted version of a literary text (e.g., *Romeo and Juliet, The Outsiders, Stone Fox*) or an informational text (e.g., butterflies, the solar system, the Civil War).

Create a Book Using Microsoft Word *Step 1:* Search Google Images or use a symbol set such as Boardmaker Picture Communication Symbols that

Table 5.2.   Accessible text resources

Resource	Source
Adapted literary (fiction, poetry, fantasy, science fiction) and informational (science, social studies, technology, the arts) texts *Free*	Tar Heel Reader CAST Book Builder Paul V. Sherlock Center on Disabilities Pinterest Dade County Florida Public Schools New York City Department of Education Baltimore City Schools Newsela
Adapted books with original and side-by-side text, chapter summaries, photographs and other images to enhance multiple-choice study guides and quizzes, cartoon versions of books and plays, flashcards and quizzes, character summaries *Free*	Schmoop
Online summaries, character analysis, and quotations from literature, math, and science *Free*	Spark Notes
Classic literature for children and youth written at a lower reading and comprehension level *Cost*	Don Johnston Start-to-Finish Literacy Starters
Collection of adapted books and lessons *Free*	The Autism Helper
Communication boards to go with adapted books *Free*	Baltimore City Schools
Digital versions of books and periodicals *Free* for students with documented print disabilities	Bookshare
Digitally recorded textbooks and literature *Free*	LearningAlly
Informational texts for adolescents written at a lower reading level *Cost*	Don Johnston Core Content

relate to the topic of the text. Copy and paste the images into a Word document. Do this prior to every unit of study or book that will be the subject of lessons for an extended period of time (e.g., solar system, water cycle, Civil War, *Romeo and Juliet*) because the images will be used to make the book and create visual supports such as aided language/topic boards, vocabulary activities, and adapted writing templates. Save the Word images document in a file named for the unit of study or book.

Step 2: Rewrite the story in Word or another word processing program, keeping most or all of the essential story elements such as characters, settings, and major events. See the text box titled "Considerations and Tips for Simplifying Text" for guidelines for rewriting text so that it is true to the intent of the original and accessible for students with decoding or comprehension challenges. Additional considerations for simplifying text include using

- High-frequency words
- Concrete versus abstract words
- Mostly one- and two-syllable words
- Sentences with only one independent clause
- Sentences written in active voice
- Fewer sentences in a paragraph
- Similar syntactic structures
- Repeated content words

Minimize or avoid using

- Negation words
- Passive voice
- Words that have multiple meanings and other forms of figurative language
- The number of conditional sentences (i.e., those that use *and, but,* and *not*) (Schuster & Erickson, 2014)

Because rewriting from scratch—going through every page of every chapter and writing summaries—takes a great deal of time, two free online tools make the task more efficient. Find a chapter summary on the Spark Notes or Schmoop web site and cut and paste it into a new Word document. If the chapter summary looks like it will work for your student, then go on to Step 3. Use a free online text summarizer, such as Auto Summarize, if you need to reduce the amount of text further. Use another free online text simplifier, such as Rewordify, if you need to reduce the reading level of the text.

Considerations and Tips for Simplifying Text

Having language challenges significantly affects students' literacy skills (Sturm & Clendon, 2004). Some of these language challenges are related to vocabulary, sounds, tenses, complex sentences, figurative language, metaphors, inferences, and perspective. These skills are integral to literacy learning and directly affect students' abilities to read a complete text with comprehension. Thus, easing the language demands in a text may make it more accessible to students.

It is important to have enough content when creating accessible texts so key themes, details, plot, dialogue, or voice of the author are not lost. Not enough simplification could result in too many language demands that might keep students from getting at the deeper meanings in the text. Six strategies for creating accessible text using the book *On My Honor* (Bauer, 1986) are found in the accompanying examples adapted from Hanser (G. Hanser, personal communication, October 15, 2014).

1. Break down compound and complex sentences by substituting easier vocabulary, removing connecting words, and making them into two separate sentences.

Original: A shiver convulsed Joel, though the sun was still bright and hot, and he began to move woodenly toward the spot where he had left his clothes.

Simplified: Joel shivered even though it was hot. He walked to the place where he left his clothes.

2. Be careful with the use of pronouns.

Try not to have too many pronouns because the referent (e.g., who, what) may be confusing. Make sure that the referent of the pronoun is right before it or in the preceding sentence. Do not use too many pronouns with character names or dialogue. Using the actual name might make it easier to follow the conversation.

Original: Maybe Tony could still be saved if he got help.

Simplified: Maybe Tony could be saved if Joel got help.

3. Simplify vocabulary words.

Keep some rich vocabulary words to explain and teach, but keep it in balance to allow time for teaching all the other text concepts and connections.

Original: Joel fell over and vomited again.

Simplified: Joel fell over. He threw up again.

4. Consider the students' background knowledge.

Clarify concepts and terms that students may not have the background knowledge to understand. For example, a student who has never ridden a bicycle before may not know the name Schwinn.

Original: Tony said, "I get dibs on the Schwinn!"

Simplified: Tony said, "I want the Schwinn bike!"

5. Clarify figurative language.

Original: Joel gave Tony a high five, taking in his friend's face as he did.

Simplified: Joel gave Tony a high five. Joel looked closely at Tony's face.

6. Delete information that is not necessary to understanding the main theme.

There is so much involved with teaching comprehension; there are a lot of balls to juggle for any student. It may be helpful to choose a few to juggle for beginning readers to help make them more successful. It is important to provide instruction at a level just a bit beyond students' current abilities. Try to do this while maintaining the integrity of the story.

Original: It took only about 10 minutes to reach the edge of town. On their way past the school, Tony stuck out his tongue in the direction of the sixth-grade classroom where they had spent last year. Joel, deciding he might as well get into the spirit of the day, followed suit, though he liked school well enough.

Simplified: It took 10 minutes to reach the edge of town. The boys rode past their school. Tony stuck out his tongue at the school. Joel did the same, even though he liked school.

From Hanser, G. (2016). *Tips for Simplifying Text*. New York: Hanser.

Table 5.3 compares the original text of Lincoln's *Gettysburg Address* with a Rewordified version. The Snap&Read Universal app allows for dynamic text leveling and reduces the difficulty of the text even further than Rewordify.

Step 3: Adapt the visual look of the adapted text by creating more white space between letters, words, or lines; customizing the font; or manipulating the color of the font and background. Create extra line spaces in the document to insert pictures above the words the student does not know. The purpose of this adapted version is to promote participation in buddy reading, read-alouds, and comprehension, not to teach decoding of individual

Table 5.3. Comparison of original and adapted text

Original text	Rewordified text
Four score and seven years ago our fathers brought forth on this continent, a new nation, conceived in Liberty, and dedicated to the proposition that all men are created equal.	Eighty-seven years ago our fathers created on this continent, a new nation, created in Freedom, and dedicated to the possible plan of action that all men are created equal.
Now we are engaged in a great civil war, testing whether that nation, or any nation so conceived and dedicated, can long endure.	Now we are involved in a great war between groups that all live in one country, testing whether that nation, or any nation so created and dedicated, can long last.

Figure 5.3. Sample topic board for *Sarah, Plain and Tall*.

words. Research shows that picture supports should not be used when teaching individual word decoding (Pufpaff, Blischak, & Lloyd, 2000).

Step 4: Copy and paste the images above the words that need to be enhanced with visual support. Change the spacing of the words in the text to accommodate the pictures, if necessary.

Step 5: Print the book in color, slip the pages into clear transparencies, and insert them into a three-ring binder. Make a cover for the book and insert it into the clear pocket on the front of the binder. Alternatively, leave the book in digital form and activate a text-to-speech reader to support the student's listening comprehension.

Step 6: Create laminated topic boards for the book to support receptive understanding during classroom read-alouds and discussion. This strategy is a variation of aided language stimulation for AAC (Goosens', 1989). Even if a student does not use AAC, it may be an effective strategy to promote learning vocabulary and comprehension. Figure 5.3 depicts a sample topic board for *Sarah, Plain and Tall* (McLaughlin, 1985).

Make another laminated copy of the topic board and cut out individual squares that can be used for vocabulary teaching and review and for light-tech fill-in-the-blank writing activities.

Communication Supports

Presuming that students can develop communicative competence is central to developing effective communication supports and providing a way to communicate about feelings, wants and needs, academics, social topics, and the world around them. If a student cannot communicate in ways that are commensurate with their classmates without disabilities, then they are candidates for AAC. The importance of developing communicative competence among AAC users is thoroughly described in Chapter 3.

Definition of AAC   AAC includes all forms of communication (other than oral speech) that are used to express thoughts, needs, wants, and ideas. People use AAC when they make facial expressions or gestures, use symbols or pictures, or write. People with severe speech-language problems rely on AAC to supplement existing speech or replace speech that is not functional. Special augmentative aids, such as picture and symbol communication boards and electronic devices, are available to help people express themselves. This may increase social interaction, school performance, and feelings of self-worth. AAC users should not stop using speech if they are able to do so. The AAC aids and devices are used to enhance their communication.

AAC takes two primary forms—unaided methods using only one's body, such as gestures, body language, or sign language—and aided communication systems that range from light-tech methods, such as paper communication boards and books, to high-tech devices with speech output (i.e., speech generating). Some devices are used solely for communication, such as a Prentke-Romich Accent or a Tobii-Dynavox T-10. Other devices, such as an iPad, can be used for academic work and communication when an AAC app or piece of software is installed (e.g., Proloquo-2-Go, TouchChat).

Myths About AAC   Some parents and educators subscribe to several myths about AAC (Cress & Marvin, 2003; Romski & Sevcik, 2005b).

- AAC will interfere with speech development.

- Cognitive prerequisites are needed to successfully use AAC.

- Students must understand concepts or vocabulary before that vocabulary can be used for communication.

- Abstract words (e.g., *have, is, are*) are more difficult to teach (learn) than concrete words (e.g., *drink, bathroom, book*).

- There is a representational hierarchy of symbols from objects to written words (traditional orthography), and students with supposedly low IQ cannot learn more complicated symbols.

- Students who are not motivated to communicate are not candidates for AAC systems.

- Teaching AAC symbols and navigation must first be done in a controlled environment before the student can be taught to use the device in natural communicative interactions.

None of these myths is true, and breathing is the only prerequisite for using AAC! It cannot be stated more strongly; if a student cannot meet his or her communication needs in ways that are similar to his or her classmates who do not have disabilities, then he or she needs an AAC assessment immediately. It is not justifiable to say, "Well, she communicates pretty well for a student with Down syndrome," or "He needs to learn the Picture Exchange Communication System before we even consider an AAC device."

AAC Assessment and Recommendations Conducting a comprehensive assessment is the first step in providing a student with an AAC device and related supports. Beukelman and Mirenda (2013) and ASHA (2016c) are comprehensive resources for AAC assessment, procurement, and use. If the SLP on a student's team does not have AAC expertise, then it is incumbent on him or her to seek outside consultation, per ASHA's (2016b) Code of Ethics.

Teaching Students to Use AAC Through Aided Language Stimulation Once a student has an AAC device or light-tech communication supports, an evidence-based technique for teaching AAC use is called *aided language stimulation*. Aided language stimulation involves a communication partner—a parent, a teacher, or a peer—teaching symbol meaning and modeling language by combining his or her own verbal input with selection of vocabulary on the device or paper communication aid (Goosens', 1989). This does not mean pointing to a light-tech communication board, book, or speech-generating device (SGD) and saying, "Show me *want*," or "Point to *drink*," but rather using the board or device to supplement spoken words while interacting with the student (Zangari, 2012a). Zangari (2012b) provided several tips for supporting all members of a student's education team, including parents, siblings, and classmates, to use aided language stimulation.

- Take the pressure off of teaching the AAC user for now. Focus the team on getting used to the new tool themselves so that they can be good interventionists in the weeks to come.

- Set a specific goal and time frame. "For the next 2 weeks, we're each going to use the XYZ device/app when we talk to Johnny. Let's each shoot for using it at least once in each activity."

- Lead by example. Use the AAC tool when talking to the student so that others on the team see its importance. The more they see aided language input being used, the more likely they will be to try it themselves.

- Be authentic. Educators should use aided language input to their best ability and not worry if they struggle at first. Other team members might feel more relaxed about their own less-than-perfect attempts once they have seen others make mistakes. The message is that everyone is in this together, learning and striving each day/session to be a little bit better at supporting people who use AAC.

- Recognize effort. Be generous with compliments and stingy with criticism. Although it seems like the focus is on this one strategy, the real prize is building a team that constantly moves forward in building their intervention skills.

- Hold people accountable. Doing this in a respectful and positive way can help create a culture of learning and mutual support. For example, "Hey, did you have a chance to use Johnny's communication board when you were talking to him at recess? No, oh okay. Maybe you can try it tomorrow. I will stop by and see how it went."

Another significant benefit to using aided language stimulation is that team members quickly discover shortcomings in the student's device or light-tech aids and can make revisions. If an adult cannot find a way to use the device to effectively communicate, then surely the student will not be able to either.

Executive Function Supports

Executive function is a term used to describe a set of mental processes that helps people connect past experience with present action. Executive function is used when activities such as planning, organizing, strategizing, and paying attention to and remembering details are performed. People with executive function problems have difficulty planning, organizing, and managing time and space. They also show weakness with working memory (or seeing in the mind's eye), which is an important tool in guiding one's actions (National Center for Learning Disabilities, 2008).

Examples of support strategies for students with executive function difficulties include using within-activity checklists, providing visual and procedural schema for solving problems, and using one of the increasing number of task and schedule management apps such as the Functional Planning System that provides a visual approach to daily planning. It is like a cross between a video playlist and a calendar through which activities can be scheduled, alarms can be set, and step-by-step videos prompt the user through the completion of the activity.

Personalized Instruction

Once students have qualified for special education services, their IEPs must contain a description of the special education—specially designed instruction and related services—that will help close the gap between their present levels of performance and their achievement of grade-level academic standards and age-appropriate functional performance. According to the final regulations for IDEA 2004 (U.S. Department of Education, 2006), special education means specially designed instruction including

> adapting, as appropriate to the needs of an eligible child under this part, the content, methodology, or delivery of instruction to address the unique needs of the child that result from the child's disability; and to ensure access of the child to the general curriculum, so that the child can meet the educational standards within the jurisdiction of the public agency that apply to all children. (p. 46762)

Creating schema or graphic representations to support a student to move through the steps in a problem is a third support for executive functioning.

Figure 5.4 shows an example of a schema that was created for Tobias, a fourth-grade student with Down syndrome, to use in a math lesson about rounding numbers. Create an Explain Everything presentation on a tablet computer that animates every step in the process to teach this task in an engaging and visual way.

Specially designed instruction does not dictate pull-out instruction but includes instruction in a general education classroom provided by a special educator or related services provider (including a paraprofessional) in collaboration with a general education teacher. Using systematic instruction is the cornerstone of all the research on learning for students with complex support needs. This means that instructional targets are carefully chosen, a clear teaching plan is implemented with fidelity, and data on student performance are used to guide ongoing instructional decision making. Table 5.4 draws primarily from comprehensive literature reviews by Browder, Wood, Thompson, and Ribuffo (2014) and the National Professional Development

---

Best Practices for Inclusion

Paper-based checklists are easy to create and easy to use. For example, the following checklist was created and laminated to help Selena manage the steps to get ready for gym class. The team decided that adding pictures to each step would not be necessary because Selena is an accomplished reader. Selena used a dry erase maker to check off each step as she completed it when she was first learning the routine. After a few weeks, she only needed to look at each step as a reminder of what to do next, and soon thereafter, she did not need to refer to the checklist at all.

❐ Walk to locker with Bethany

❐ Unlock locker

❐ Take off shoes

❐ Take off pants

❐ Take off shirt

❐ Put clothes and shoes in locker

❐ Put on T-shirt

❐ Put on gym shorts

❐ Put on trainers

❐ Lock locker

❐ Walk to gym with Bethany

For Anna, a sixth-grade student with autism, the team took photographs of her going through each step and added those to the checklist.

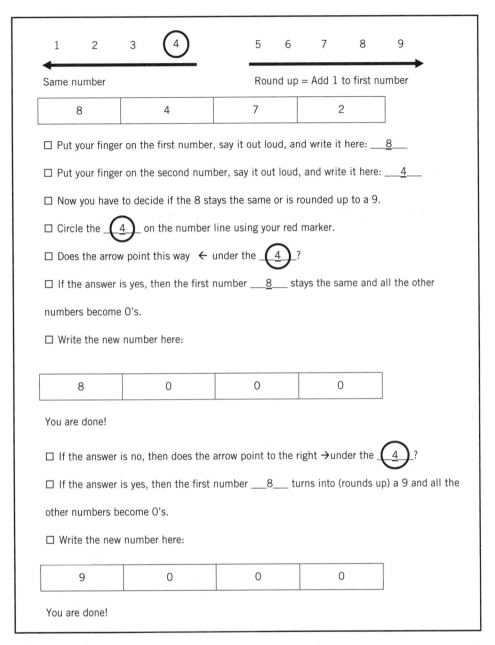

Figure 5.4. Schema for rounding numbers.

Center on Autism Spectrum Disorders (2016) and lists several instructional strategies that have a strong research base with examples of how they might be used in the context of general education instruction.

Technology, Equipment, and Tools

Few examples of AT, other than wheelchairs and the first AAC devices, were used in the mid-1980s when students with IDD were first included in

Table 5.4. Opportunities to use systematic instructional strategies in an inclusive classroom

Strategy	Description	Example
Naturalistic interventions	Use within the typical settings, activities, and routines in which the learner participates. Establish the student's interest in a learning event, provide necessary support for the learner to engage in the targeted behavior, elaborate on the behavior when it occurs, or arrange natural consequences for the targeted behavior or skills.	The principles of this intervention are frequently used by James's, Anna's, and Selena's teams. For example, James's classroom teacher says the following when she speaks to him during a small guided reading group: "James, we are going to be reading this paragraph for the purpose of identifying the main idea and three supporting details. When you hear a friend name a main idea, let us know by saying THAT ONE on your device." At the same time she speaks out loud, she uses his augmentative and alternative communication (AAC) device and selects the following words/phrases: READ, IDEA, DETAIL, HEAR, FRIEND THAT ONE. Each time he selects THAT ONE while listening to a peer read, the teacher says to the group, "James thinks that is a main idea. Who agrees? That is right, you got it!"
Modeling	A teacher or peer demonstrates a behavior or skill, and the student is taught to copy what they did. To use video modeling, a video of a target behavior or skill is shown to the student. The model can be done by a same-age student who is proficient at the skill or by the student him- or herself when he or she is correctly performing the skill.	Anna's speech-language pathologist (SLP) made a short video of one of Anna's classmates going through the lunch line and paying with her school debit card.
Computer aided instruction	Computer aided instruction includes using computers to teach academic skills and promote communication and language development and skills. It includes computer modeling and computer tutors.	Selena uses Kahn Academy math tutorials to improve her algebra knowledge and skills.
Scripting	Scripting involves providing verbal or written descriptions of a specific skill or situation that serves as a model for the learner. Scripts are usually repeatedly practiced before the skill is used in the actual situation.	James's SLP uses the TapSpeak Sequence app and records a six-question script for him to use to interview classmates during a math graphing activity. James presses the large TapSpeak Sequence buttons on his iPad sequentially, and his paraeducators enter each student's response into a tally sheet.
Time delay	In a setting or activity in which a student should engage in a behavior or skill, a brief delay occurs between the initial question or demand) and the opportunity to use the skill, without giving any additional prompts. The purpose of the time delay is to allow the student to respond without having to receive another prompt; which might lead to more dependence on prompts rather than learning to do a task more independently.	This strategy is used by James's, Anna's, and Selena's teams because all three students need extra time to think about what they want to say and then say it using their AAC devices (James and Anna) or natural speech. Selena has become very prompt dependent, so using time delay helps to discipline the team to give Selena a chance to respond before they provide an extra prompt.

Strategy	Description	Example
Least to most intrusive prompts	Determine the skill that the student needs to perform. Do a task analysis of the individual components of the skill. Develop a teaching, prompting, and reinforcement schedule that begins with the least intrusive prompt, add up to two more prompts if necessary to elicit the desired behavior, and build in a schedule of prompt fading.	Anna's team frequently uses this strategy because they want to keep her from becoming dependent on adult prompting to successfully move through her day. Her special education teacher developed a teaching routine for personal hygiene and diligently fades prompts so that she preserves Anna's privacy in the bathroom as quickly as possible.
Backward and forward chaining	Develop a task analysis of the multiple components of a behavior to be taught. The instructor using forward chaining teaches the first step to the student and then performs the other steps him- or herself. The instructor then teaches the first and second step together, and so forth, once the student has mastered the first step. The instructor using backward chaining does all the steps in the task except the last ore, which is taught to the student. The next to last and last step are taught together, and so forth, once the student masters the last task.	Forward chaining is used to teach James the rounding numbers procedure according to the schema depicted in Figure 5.4.
Self-Determined Learning Model of Instruction (SDLMI) (Shogren, Wehmeyer, Burke, & Palmer, 2017)	The SDLMI teaches self-directed learning to students in three units: 1) setting a goal, 2) taking action, and 3) adjusting the total or plan. Students are taught to solve problems using four steps: 1) identify the problem, 2) identify possible solutions, 3) identify possible barriers, and 4) identify consequences of each solution.	Selena's special education teacher uses this model with Selena to help her decide what summer job she wants, prepare a résumé, determine potential employers, fill out applications, and write a thank-you note after each interview. He helps Selena decide what to do if she receives a rejection.
Peer tutoring	A peer tutor is typically a same-age or older student who delivers instruction to a student with disabilities. Peer tutors are trained to incorporate active student responding, opportunities to respond, feedback, and reinforcement in instructional sessions.	Selena receives peer tutoring in algebra from a senior who excels in math and provides peer tutoring to preschoolers attending an early childhood program at her high school.
Directed inquiry	Students use directed inquiry, such as a KWHL chart, to answer questions about science and social studies topics.	James's teacher uses the Know-What-How-Learn (KWHL) method with all students when they begin a science unit. James's SLP programmed several phrases onto his AAC device so that he can fully participate by saying I KNOW..., I WANT LEARN..., I WILL..., and I LEARNED....

general education classrooms. The options for students have increased as AT laws have strengthened and software applications for personal computers have evolved to mobile applications on tablets and smartphones. IDEA 2004 dictates that teams consider students' AT needs.

> Each public agency must ensure that assistive technology devices or assistive technology services, or both are made available to a child with a disability if required as a part of the child's special education, related services, or supplementary aids and services. On a case-by-case basis, the use of school-purchased assistive technology devices in a child's home or in other settings is required if the child's IEP Team determines that the child needs access to those devices in order to receive FAPE. (IDEA, 2006, 46753)

See the text box for IDEA 2004 definitions of AT devices and services.

AT is one area of intervention that is underused and sometimes misused because teams not only lack the technical knowledge and skills related to using AT, but also, perhaps even more important, the understanding of how to identify whether a particular piece of AT is appropriate for a particular student.

IDEA 2004 Definitions of AT Devices and Services

The term *AT device* means any item, piece of equipment, or product system, whether acquired commercially off the shelf, modified, or customized, that is used to increase, maintain, or improve functional capabilities of a student with a disability. The term, however, does not include a medical device that is surgically implanted or the replacement of such device.

The term *AT service* means any service that directly assists a student with a disability in the selection, acquisition, or use of an AT device. The term includes

- Evaluating the needs of a student with a disability, including a functional evaluation of the student in his or her customary environment

- Purchasing, leasing, or otherwise providing for the acquisition of AT devices by students with disabilities

- Selecting, designing, fitting, customizing, adapting, applying, maintaining, repairing, or replacing AT devices

- Coordinating and using other therapies, interventions, or services with AT devices, such as those associated with existing education and rehabilitation plans and programs

- Training or technical assistance for a student with a disability or, if appropriate, his or her family

- Training or technical assistance for professionals (including individuals providing education or rehabilitation services), employers, or other individuals who provide services to, employ, or are otherwise substantially involved in the major life functions of that student

The Wisconsin Assistive Technology Project created a tool for assessing students' needs for AT based the SETT framework—student, environment, tasks, tools—pioneered by Zabala (2005), and this tool should be used prior to the IEP meeting. There are too many important AT considerations to do the topic justice within the IEP meeting itself. Several categories of AT that can be applied in a general education class are described in Table 5.5.

SUPPORTS FOR THE TEAM ON BEHALF OF THE STUDENT

IDEA 2004 describes supports for the team on behalf of the student, as part of supplementary aids and services, that will enable them to successfully implement the student's educational program.

- Professional development related to the student's unique needs in the areas of AAC and other communication supports, positive behavior supports, AT, facilitating social relationships, using person-centered planning, and so forth

- Professional development on inclusive education and collaborative teaming, including processes for writing inclusive, standards-based IEPs, planning a student's full participation in general education instruction, and choosing inclusive roles for IEP team members

- Outside consultation to the team by AAC, AT, or other experts to supplement the team's current knowledge and skills

- In-class coaching that supports the implementation of the student's inclusive educational program with fidelity

- Visits to inclusive schools to talk with members of a similar student's team

- Parent training

- Common planning time

- Using a daily communication notebook to share information between school and home

Following are some examples of statements detailing such supports for the education team on behalf of the student. "James's team—including his classroom teacher, paraeducators, special education teacher, SLP, and OT—will meet for 1 hour each week to develop participation plans for the following week's instruction." "Six hours of professional development, 6 hours of in-class coaching, and 6 hours of consultation at home will be provided for Anna's team on the topic of positive behavior supports." "A skilled and experienced facilitator will work with Selena's team to update her personal futures plan yearly until she reaches the age of 21."

Table 5.5. Examples of assistive technology that supports learning and inclusion

Function	Technology	Classroom use
Alternate keyboard access for writing support	BigKeys https://www.bigkeys.com/	James uses a switch to select letters from his keyboard to create writing assignments on his computer.
Customized worksheets	GoWorksheet Maker http://www.attainmentcompany.com/goworksheet-maker	Pictures of worksheets are taken with Selena's iPad, her occupational therapist customizes them for Selena's reading level, and Selena types her answers into the blanks.
Differentiated reading, writing, and math instruction for students with complex support needs	Classroom Suite https://www.ablenetinc.com/emails/New_Product_Anncmnt/ClassroomSuite-v5-May2015.html	Science study guides are created for Anna using Classroom Suite so that she answers comprehension questions about a concept before going on to the next topic.
Student presentations and reports	Explain Everything http://explaineverything.com/	Anna uses Explain Everything in history to create class presentations that are enhanced with video and photographs from Google Images.
Study tools	Bitsboard https://itunes.apple.com/us/app/bitsboard-education-games/id516422102?mt=8	Anna uses a variety of flashcards made with Bitsboard to study sight words and math facts with her advisory classmates.
Symbol enhanced English language arts and math lessons	Boardmaker Instructional Solutions https://www.boardmakeronline.com/	The classroom teacher's math lessons are adapted for Anna using Boardmaker Instructional Solutions because the numbers and operations signs can be customized for level of understanding.
Text to speech	Kurzweil https://www.kurzweiledu.com/default.html Read&Write https://www.texthelp.com/en-us/products/read-write/ Microsoft add-on to Quick Access toolbar https://support.office.com/en-us/article/Using-the-Speak-text-to-speech-feature-459e7704-a76d-4fe2-ab48-189d6b83333c iPad apps http://appadvice.com/appguides/show/text-to-speech-apps-for-ipad	James listens to books on his iPad while riding in the car to build his background knowledge and listening comprehension. James activates a switch to read his book aloud during buddy reading.
Visual organizers	Kidspiration and Inspiration http://www.inspiration.com/Kidspiration	Selena uses Inspiration to create a visual map of a lab experiment and then switches to outline mode to add details for her lab report.
Writing	Clicker Connect http://www.cricksoft.com/us/products/clicker-apps/clicker-connect.aspx First Author http://donjohnston.com/firstauthorsoftware/	Selena completes writing assignments in history using a combination of words and words with pictures that have been preprogrammed into Clicker Connect on her iPad.
Text simplification	Snap & Read Universal http://donjohnston.com/snap-read/	Selena uses Snap & Read Universal to level the text to her listening comprehension level on websites related to current events in history.

❏ Clarify the meaning of accommodations and modifications with all team members.

❏ Determine which supplementary aids and services the student needs in the following areas:

- Communication supports

- Physical or environmental supports

- Emotional supports

- Humanistic and positive behavior supports

- Sensory supports

- Vision supports

- Cortical visual impairment accommodations

- Hearing supports

- Attention supports

- Executive function supports

- Accessible instructional materials

- Personalized instruction

- Assistive technology

- Adapted tools or equipment

❏ Determine what supports the team needs on behalf of the student.

Figure 5.5.   Supplementary aids and services checklist.

CONCLUSIONS

Supplementary aids and services provide the means through which students master their annual goals and objectives and participate and make progress in the general education curriculum in a general education classroom. IEP teams must consider the full range of supplementary aids and services before considering a placement other than a general education classroom. Figure 5.5 contains a checklist for teams to follow when developing the student's supplementary aids and services for the IEP. A process for incorporating a student's supplementary aids and services into daily general education lessons is described in Chapter 9.

6

Describe Inclusive Team Member Roles and Establish Collaborative Teaming Processes

S tudents with the most complex support needs were being effectively included in general education classrooms in the mid-1980s, when inclusive education was in its infancy. These students had no reliable means of communication, no AT, required support to move every part of their bodies, and had extensive medical needs. The beliefs and commitment of their team members and their collaboration skills are what made it work. Success comes down to the same thing today—team members who believe in inclusion and work together to make it successful. This chapter describes inclusive roles and responsibilities of students' IEP team members and the collaborative processes that support their planning and implementation of individualized student supports.

INCLUSIVE TEAM MEMBER ROLES AND RESPONSIBILITIES

Figure 6.1 depicts the roles and responsibilities of IEP team members and school administrators in creating a culture of inclusion and teaching a diverse group of learners in the general education classroom and within other inclusive school and community environments. The roles of special education teachers and related services providers dramatically change when students with complex support needs are included in general education.

This figure describes some of the key roles and responsibilities of IEP team members. It is not meant to be a comprehensive job description, reflect staff members' legal obligations, or describe every relevant professional practice. It highlights how all members of the team and administrators can work together to make inclusive education successful for all students.

Definition of Terms

Lead: take the initiative in an action, serving as an example for others to follow

Facilitate: encourage full participation, promote mutual understanding, cultivate shared responsibility, find inclusive solutions, and build sustainable agreements

Coordinate: bring order and organization to a task or enterprise

Collaborate: work together on a shared goal

All Staff

❑ Communicate respectfully, effectively, and regularly with students, families, and school staff and administrators

❑ Use research-based education practices

❑ Develop positive relationships with students' families/guardians

❑ Contribute to a school climate that celebrates diversity, inclusion, and cooperation

❑ Utilize the principles of universal design for learning (UDL) during instruction and assessment

❑ Implement schoolwide positive behavior interventions and supports (PBIS)

❑ Engage in continuous professional development to improve skills in teaching diverse students in inclusive settings

Student

❑ Understands his or her learning style

❑ Expresses his or her preferences for how support is provided

❑ Uses self-determination skills to participate in IEP meetings

❑ Approaches learning enthusiastically

❑ Provides service to classmates and the larger school community

Parents/Guardians

❑ Presume positive intentions by the IEP team

❑ Understand special education laws

❑ Establish an inclusive educational and postschool vision for their child

❑ Communicate priorities to the team prior to the IEP

❑ Support their child's completion of homework

❑ Contribute to the classroom and school community

General Education Teacher

❑ Welcomes all students as members of heterogeneous general education classrooms

❑ Leads curriculum and instructional planning teams comprised of special educators, Title I teachers, and others to create accessible curriculum, instruction, and assessments for a broad range of student diversity based on the principles of UDL and Common Core State Standards (CCSS)

❑ Teaches the whole class, small groups, and individual students using UDL principles, including

Figure 6.1. Sample inclusive team member roles and responsibilities.

- Providing multiple means of representing knowledge

- Providing multiple means of student engagement

- Providing multiple means of action and expression

❏ Coordinates the activities of other staff when they are providing instruction or support in the general education classroom

❏ Uses formative assessments and progress monitoring to improve instruction

❏ Collaborates with Title I, special education, and other staff to identify students who need additional supports and interventions to supplement core instruction or who may qualify for special education services

❏ Facilitates the development of students' social competence and social relationships

❏ Collaborates with special educators to assign grades to students with disabilities

Special Education Teacher

❏ Supports membership, participation, and learning for students with and without disabilities in inclusive classrooms:

- Participates on planning teams comprised of general educators, Title I teachers, and others to create accessible curriculum, instruction, and assessments for a broad range of student diversity based on the principles of UDL and CCSS

- Teaches the whole class, small groups, and individual students using UDL principles, including

  o Providing multiple means of representing knowledge

  o Providing multiple means of student engagement

  o Providing multiple means of action and expression

- Uses formative assessments and progress monitoring to improve instruction

- Facilitates the development of students' social competence and social relationships

❏ Collaborates with general educators, Title I, and other staff to identify students who may qualify for special education services:

- Uses a variety of assessments to evaluate students for special education services and inform the development of their IEPs

- Leads teams of general educators, Title I staff, related services providers, and other staff to develop, implement, and evaluate students' IEPs

- Conducts functional behavioral assessments and develops positive behavior support plans

❏ Facilitates instructional planning meetings to design individualized supports for students' full participation in general education instruction, learning CCSS, and meeting their IEP goals

- Identifies, locates, or develops adapted materials and other supports (e.g., assistive technology) that promote students' participation in general education instruction in the general education classroom and meeting their IEP goals

- Provides supplemental instruction to students who are not making progress within universally designed general education instruction

❏ Supervises, coaches, and models for special education paraprofessionals

❏ Collaborates with general educators to assign grades to students with disabilities

❏ Leads teams of general educators, related services providers, and others to develop students' postschool plans using the principles of person-centered planning

(continued)

Figure 6.1.   *(continued)*

- Collaborates with students, their families, other school staff, and community resources to facilitate students' transition from school to postsecondary education, career, and an inclusive life in the community

Speech-Language Pathologist

☐ Collaborates with other team members to write IEP goals and objectives that prioritize skills needed for students to fully participate in general education instruction, learn CCSS, acquire and maintain satisfying social relationships, and achieve their IEP goals

☐ Collaborates with other team members to implement communication supports and services (e.g., occupational therapist, paraprofessionals)

☐ Integrates services and supports within general education instruction and other school activities

☐ Provides services outside the context of general education instruction or other typical activities only if they result in students' generalization of communication skills to natural settings

☐ Utilizes Beukleman and Mirenda's (2005) Participation Model and recommendations from the National Joint Committee for the Communication Needs of Persons with Severe Disabilities (Brady et al., 2016) to design supports and services for students who do not use natural speech to communicate in ways that are commensurate with their same-age peers without disabilities

  - Obtains outside evaluation or consultation if the speech-language pathologist (SLP) does not have appropriate training and skills in the area of augmentative and alternative communication (ASHA, 2016c)

☐ Creates materials to use in general education instruction that support students' acquisition of IEP goals and learning of CCSS

Occupational and Physical Therapists

☐ Collaborate with other team members to write IEP goals and objectives that prioritize skills needed for students to fully participate in general education instruction, learn CCSS, acquire and maintain satisfying social relationships, and achieve their IEP goals

☐ Collaborate with other team members to implement supports and services (e.g., SLP, paraprofessionals)

☐ Integrate services and supports within general education instruction and other school activities

☐ Provide services outside the context of general education instruction or other typical activities only if they result in students' generalization of skills to natural settings

☐ Create materials to use in general education instruction that support students' acquisition of IEP goals and learning of CCSS

Reading Specialist

☐ Collaborates with general educators, special educators, Title I staff, related services providers, and others to design and implement accessible curriculum, instruction, and assessments in the area of literacy across the curriculum for all students based on the principles of UDL and CCSS:

  - Providing multiple means of representing knowledge

  - Providing multiple means of student engagement

  - Providing multiple means of action and expression

❏ Provides guidance, coaching, and professional development on literacy instruction to general and special educators

❏ Collaborates with general educators, special educators, related services providers, and others to develop, implement, and evaluate students' IEPs

❏ Provides intensive literacy intervention for students not making progress within universally designed instruction

❏ Creates individualized literacy materials (including those that are accelerated) to be used in core academic instruction or intensive interventions

Guidance Counselor

❏ Provides guidance to large groups, small groups, and individual students within and outside of the general education classroom

❏ Participates as a member of students' IEP teams

❏ Implements positive behavior supports for individual students

❏ Facilitates the development of students' social competence and relationships

❏ Leads response to intervention student study meetings

Special Education Paraprofessional, With Supervision From a Professional

❏ Provides large-group, small-group, and individualized instruction within the general education classroom and other school and community environments

❏ Creates instructional materials

❏ Gathers data on student performance

❏ Provides other supports as specified on students' IEPs, including ppositive behavior supports

Librarian/Media Specialist

❏ Acquires literary and informational reading materials, hardware, and software that provide multiple representations of knowledge based on state standards

❏ Includes all students in library lessons

❏ Provides professional development and coaching to staff on the use of accessible information resources

Building and District-Level Administrators

❏ Model and clearly communicate the district's inclusive education vision to all students, staff, and the community

❏ Provide professional development related to inclusive best practices both within and outside of the school day

❏ Secure resources related to UDL (e.g., accessible text, computer hardware, software licenses, adaptations to the physical plant)

❏ Evaluate staff using a variety of tools, including inclusive education quality indicators

❏ Provide common instructional planning time for grade-level and student-specific teams

❏ Create a school schedule that accommodates multiple priorities, such as common planning time, extended instructional blocks, time for tiered interventions, individual teacher planning, and so forth

❏ Are available to answer staff questions and assist with implementation

Special Educators Evolving to Inclusion Facilitators

The role of a special educator in an inclusive school shifts from being someone who teaches in a special education classroom to an inclusion facilitator. The inclusion facilitator supports teams to implement the best educational practices for students with complex support needs related to their membership, relationships, participation, and learning of the general education curriculum in inclusive classrooms in neighborhood schools (Jorgensen, Schuh, & Nisbet, 2006). They work alongside general educators and related services providers in general education classrooms and other inclusive school and community environments to support students to achieve the goals of their IEPs, develop and sustain typical social relationships and participate in social activities, learn and maintain appropriate behavior, make smooth transitions from year to year, and graduate to typical adult roles in the community. This role is typically assigned to the teacher who leads teams of students with diagnoses of developmental delay, intellectual disability, ASD, multiple disabilities, deaf-blindness, and, in some situations, students diagnosed with other health impairments or traumatic brain injury. These students need complex supports to be successfully included, defined by the uniqueness of the students' needs in a variety of learning and functional areas, including mobility, vision, hearing, communication, sensory, and behavior; their participation in large-scale assessments; and their need for instructional adaptations beyond those commonly considered as accommodations to the presentation of information and demonstration of learning.

Inclusion Facilitator Attitudes, Knowledge, and Skills A number of beliefs and dispositions are required for effective inclusion facilitators. Of course, they must value and respect the gifts and talents of all students, including those with the most complex support needs. Their commitment to inclusion is unwavering. They encourage and support family and school partnerships and have broad knowledge about the educational needs of students with complex support needs. Although they do not typically have the depth of knowledge of SLPs, OTs, and PTs, they understand students' movement, sensory, and communication needs and are fluent in using a variety of ATs in collaboration with those specialists. They have subject matter expertise that aligns with the general education curriculum of the grades in which their students are enrolled. They are effective leaders of other members of the IEP team and promote inclusion throughout the school community through their advocacy efforts. Inclusion facilitators have skills that support effective team collaboration, including facilitating, presenting, coaching, consulting, modeling, and mediating.

Inclusion Facilitator Responsibilities The inclusion facilitator's responsibilities include

- Reviewing records and evaluations
- Observing students and classroom instruction to identify participation opportunities

- Observing other team members working with students

- Interviewing parents, team members, and classmates

- Conducting formal and informal assessments

- Preparing reports and presenting to team members

- Developing students' learning and participation plans

- Developing team support plans

- Coordinating writing of the IEP

- Planning for ESY programming

- Planning for students' return to district from out-of-district placement

- Facilitating students' transition from self-contained to general education classrooms

- Developing instructional materials

- Conducting FBAs and working with others to develop positive behavior support plans

- Coordinating services

- Collecting, summarizing, and interpreting data

- Modeling appropriate instruction and supports

- Coaching team members

- Providing professional development to IEP team members and other school staff

- Identifying instructional and other resources

- Coordinating alternate assessment portfolios

- Facilitating social relationships and students' participation in extracurricular activities

- Facilitating team meetings

- Serving in leadership capacity within the school

Inclusion Facilitator Caseload and Schedule   A special education teacher in a self-contained classroom might be responsible for six to 12 students with complex support needs. He or she might supervise several paraprofessionals and work in collaboration with related services providers. An inclusion facilitator should have a caseload of five to eight students who have complex support needs who are included in various general education classrooms throughout a building. Rather than teaching in one classroom all day, the inclusion facilitator's schedule reflects his or her role with many general educators as well as other service providers. Figure 6.2 shows how

Elementary Self-Contained Special Education Teacher

8:15	Assist students off special education buses
8:30	Lead circle and calendar time
9:00	Facilitate language activity among students
9:30	Supervise toileting
10:00	Observe occupational therapist (OT) working with students during art activity
10:45	Observe physical therapist (PT) working with students on balance and strength
11:30	Teach students to make lunch
12:00	Eat lunch with students and paraeducators in classroom
12:30	Supervise teeth brushing and toileting
1:00	Teach math—time and money skills
1:30	Teach science—plant tomatoes
2:00	Supervise free play time
2:30	Get students ready for dismissal
3:00	Escort students to special education buses

Middle or High School Life Skills Special Education Teacher

7:30	Assist students off special education bus
8:00	Supervise students delivering the mail and doing recycling
8:45	Facilitate language activity among students
9:30	Supervise toileting
10:00	Observe OT working with students during art activity
10:45	Observe PT working with students on balance and strength
11:30	Teach students to make lunch
12:00	Eat lunch with students and paraeducators in classroom
12:30	Supervise teeth brushing and toileting
1:00	Teach students to learn to ride a city bus
1:30	Supervise students during a job shadowing experience
2:30	Return to school and escort students to special education buses

Elementary Inclusion Facilitator

7:30	Facilitate instructional planning meeting for a fourth-grade student's IEP team
8:45	Support a kindergarten student's participation in calendar time
9:30	Teach a reading group in a first-grade classroom
10:15	Meet with first-grade teachers to present a variety of ways to conduct read-alouds in their diverse classrooms
11:00	Prepare adapted instructional materials for math
12:00	Meet with librarian to discuss acquisition of digital books
12:30	Observe during lunch to assess students' access to the cafeteria line and their social interactions
1:00	Support a third grader's participation in science class
1:45	Support a second grader's participation in English language arts
2:30	Analyze data for upcoming IEP meeting
3:00	Supervise dismissal and chat with parents who are picking up their children

Middle School Inclusion Facilitator

7:30	Meet with paraeducators to preview the day
8:45	Support a sixth-grade student's participation in science
9:30	Teach a literature group in eighth grade

Figure 6.2.   Self-contained special education teacher schedules compared with inclusion facilitator schedules.

10:15	Meet with seventh-grade team to plan "Early Civilizations of the Americas" unit
11:00	Prepare instructional materials for social studies
12:00	Meet with librarian to discuss acquisition of digital books
12:30	Observe during lunch to assess students' access to the cafeteria line and social interactions
1:00	Meet with fifth-grade team to discuss math instruction
1:45	Meet with two paraprofessionals to teach them how to use Clicker Connect app
2:00	Observe dismissal and chat with parents
2:30	Attend computer club meeting to support the advisor's inclusion of a student who uses a switch to activate the computer

High School Inclusion Facilitator

- The inclusion facilitator meets one to one weekly for 15–20 minutes with all his or her students' general education teachers to find out about upcoming lessons, units, materials, and assessments

- The inclusion facilitator meets with each student's IEP team members (e.g., paraprofessional, SLP, OT) once a week to develop student participation plans for the following week or unit based on the information gathered from meetings with the general education teachers.

the daily schedule of a self-contained special education teacher contrasts with an inclusion facilitator's daily schedule.

Related Services Providers

Related services designed to assist a student with a disability to benefit from special education include

- Audiology

- Counseling services

- Early identification of students with disabilities

- Interpreting services

- Medical services

- Occupational therapy

- Orientation and mobility

- Parent counseling and training

- Physical therapy

- Some paraprofessional services

- Psychological services

- Recreation

- Rehabilitation counseling

- School health and school nurse services

- Social work services

- Speech-language pathology
- Transportation

The roles of SLPs, OTs, PTs, and AT specialists may have significant overlap. How individual providers' responsibilities are identified may be dictated by state law, state accreditation standards, and common practice. A variety of terms are used by local school districts to describe how related services are delivered, including *direct, indirect, consultative inclusive, integrated, embedded, push-in,* and *pull-out.* It is no wonder parents and educators are confused! A majority of related services for a student who is included in general education should be delivered within the context of inclusive, general education lessons and other inclusive activities and environments, based on research suggesting that such integrated services have a number of benefits to students and staff alike (Calculator & Jorgensen, 1991; Giangreco, 1986; Rainforth et al., 1997; Szabo, 2000), including the following.

- Students learn the skills they need in the places they will use them rather than having to transfer skills learned in isolated environments to natural ones.

- Students have increased practice opportunities throughout the day and in many environments.

- Students' social relationships are not disrupted by being out of the classroom.

- Students do not miss out on classroom instruction or activities.

- Students do not have to manage multiple transitions during the day.

- Teachers can see what strategies therapists use and carry them over when the therapist is not present.

- Therapists can see whether strategies are feasible and effective in natural environments.

- Teachers and therapists are more likely to prioritize skills that are needed in general education contexts that will be immediately useful for students.

- Students do not get the message that they need to be fixed before they can belong (Kunc, 1995).

- Assessment of progress can be done across a variety of routines.

In general, inclusive roles of SLPs, OTs, and PTs necessitate changes in several aspects of their IEP team responsibilities, including

- Writing goals and objectives that relate to learning general education curriculum in the general education classroom and participating in other inclusive school activities and environments

- Observing lessons and outside-of-classroom activities to identify communication, movement, sensory, and environmental demands

- Developing supports for participating and learning in general education contexts

- Providing supports within natural environments

- Empowering other team members to provide communication, sensory, and movement supports through transdisciplinary role release (York, Rainforth, & Giangreco, 1990).

A shift in thinking needs to occur from remediation to participation; shifting one's view of disability as deficiency to natural diversity; and shifting from thinking of oneself as the only expert to thinking about how all team members can support students' communication, sensory, and movement challenges.

Speech-Language Pathologists   IDEA 2004 defined speech-language services as 1) identification of students with speech-language impairments; 2) diagnosis and appraisal of specific speech-language impairments; 3) referral for medical or other professional attention necessary for the habilitation of speech-language impairments; provision of speech-language services for habilitation or prevention of communication impairments; and 4) counseling and guidance of parents, students, and teachers regarding speech-language impairments.

ASHA (2012) suggested that SLPs use a variety of service delivery models to meet student needs with an emphasis on delivering their services in the LRE.

> Federal law requires a full continuum of services in the LRE for all students, including those with speech and language impairment. For many students, services in the classroom constitute the LRE. By suggesting in-class services for some students, the SLP is beginning a gradual shift to a more diversified schedule reflecting a variety of service delivery models that more appropriately address individual needs. Providing services within the classroom may allow for more generalization and carryover of skills in a functional setting, as well as help the classroom teacher observe ways she can cue and support the student throughout the week. (p. 10)

ASHA (2012) also identified that SLPs have important roles in teaching students to acquire standards-based knowledge and skills. SLPs may collaborate with other members of students' education teams to work on appropriate academic and functional goals.

Causton and Tracy-Bronson (2014b) described numerous ways that SLPs can work within inclusive contexts, including preschool stations, circle and calendar, reading lessons, snack time, recess, advisory, extracurricular club meetings, and any time that language and communication are required. SLPs who embed their services within these contexts may teach a whole class, teach a small group, or sit next to a student with a disability and directly facilitate his or her participation in instruction or social conversation.

Sample IEP Goals Written by a Speech-Language Pathologist   The following examples show how SLP-written IEP goals can address the language and communication skills students need to fully participate in instruction and social interactions.

- When several passages have been prerecorded under buttons labeled 1, 2, 3, and 4 by a male classmate, William will use his Dynavox to participate in buddy reading by 1) choosing a partner, 2) selecting from among four of his favorite books on trains, 3) pressing the numbers sequentially to say the text aloud, and 4) commenting about his favorite part of his classmate's book.

- When provided with a digital note-taking form in GoWorksheet consisting of previously determined priority concepts and vocabulary, Cheyenne will fill in a guided note-taking form in science by choosing from among four possible word/picture icons with 80% accuracy in 8 of 10 lessons.

- With partial support at the elbow and when provided with color-coded, picture-enhanced symbols, Ethan will create a model of the element nitrogen by placing 80% of the electrons, protons, and neutrons in their correct position.

These goals represent the many skills that students must use within authentic learning activities in the general education classroom.

Occupational Therapists   Occupational therapy services are defined in IDEA 2004 as 1) improving, developing, or restoring functions impaired or lost through illness, injury, or deprivation; 2) improving ability to perform tasks for independent functioning if functions are impaired or lost; and 3) preventing initial or further loss of function through early intervention.

The American Occupational Therapy Association (AOTA; 2006) said "pull-out services built around a clinical model of predictable, routine 'appointments' have little support in the educational literature and do not necessarily promote the generalization of skills to the classroom or other appropriate skills" (p. 1). School-based OTs also support student progress in the state standard course of study (AOTA, 2013). Causton and Tracy-Bronson (2014a) gave numerous examples of how OTs can work in inclusive classrooms, including supporting a preschooler to manipulate fasteners on clothing in the dress-up area, making adaptations to science equipment for a student with fine motor difficulties, developing a schedule of sensory supports and breaks for a middle school student, and helping a student use an adapted keyboard during a writing activity.

Sample IEP Goals for Integrated Occupational Therapy Services   IEP goals that represent integrated occupational therapy services include the following.

- When prompted to recognize the need for a break using a visual sensory thermometer during the class just before lunch, Marcus will choose and do a 5-minute activity from among 10 provided in a sensory toolbox during 80% of 20 trials.

- When provided with a switch-activated computer-aided design (CAD) drawing program, Brandon will create plans for a picnic table with 80% accuracy in the table's dimensions over five class periods.

- Using one hand to open a folder and the other to grasp a paper, Nikhil will maintain an organized workspace 4 out of 5 days by using a color-coded folder system for storing his completed work, homework, and work in progress, with an end-of-the-day verbal prompt from his teacher.

It is difficult to determine whether these are movement goals, sensory goals, or academic goals because they are integrated goals that represent the many skills that students must use within authentic learning activities in the general education classroom.

Physical Therapists School-based physical therapy services generally address a student's posture, muscle strength, mobility, and organization of movement in educational environments. Physical therapy may be provided to prevent the onset or progression of impairment, functional limitation, disability, or changes in physical function or health resulting from injury, disease, or other causes. According to the American Physical Therapy Association (n.d.),

> The school-based physical therapist promotes motor development and the student's participation in everyday routines and activities that are part of the educational program. The physical therapist performs therapeutic interventions, including compensation, remediation and prevention strategies and adaptations, focusing on functional mobility and safe, efficient access and participation in activities and routines in natural learning environments.

The contributions of the PT to the student's outcomes directly facilitate functional skills that promote access and participation. Many opportunities exist for PTs to support students within inclusive classrooms and school environments, including

- Moving from the classroom to another room on the same floor using an assistive device or wheelchair

- Walking up and down stairs and ramps or gaining access to an elevator to move to other floors of the building

- Getting in and out of desks

- Taking a seat on a designated spot on the floor and getting up from the floor when making the transition between circle time and desk work

- Carrying materials from one area of the classroom to another

- Maintaining adequate seated posture for attention to instruction and completion of desktop activities

- Using lab, culinary arts, horticulture, and computer equipment
- Ascending or descending steps to use a bus or public transportation
- Negotiating curbs and ramps
- Moving to and from a seat on the bus or along the aisles
- Participating in driver's education
- Maneuvering through a crowded cafeteria while carrying food on a tray
- Getting in and out of a lunch table
- Sitting with appropriate posture to eat with peers within the time allotted
- Moving to and from the toilet and maintaining sitting on the toilet
- Gaining access to a sink, soap, and paper towels
- Safely gaining access to and using playground equipment
- Safely participating in age-appropriate gross motor games with peers during recess or physical education periods in conjunction with adapted physical educators if necessary

Sample Physical Therapy IEP Goals   Sample IEP goals in the area of physical therapy that focus on full participation include the following.

- When provided with a racing wheelchair and lane dividers enhanced with reflective paint, Charles will complete one lap around the track within 10 minutes during five successive practice sessions.
- When seated next to classmates, George will maintain his posture for 10 minutes during calendar activities to enhance his attention.
- During weight training class, Meredith will increase her time on the treadmill by 5% each week, achieving 20 minutes by the end of the year.

Assistive Technology Services   AT services are defined in IDEA 2004 as any service that directly assists a student with a disability in the selection, acquisition, or use of an AT device. The term also includes

- Evaluating the student in his or her customary environment
- Purchasing, leasing, or otherwise providing for the acquisition of AT devices
- Selecting, designing, fitting, customizing, adapting, applying, maintaining, repairing, or replacing AT devices
- Coordinating and using other therapies, interventions, or services with AT devices, such as those associated with existing education plans and programs

- Training other team members or providing technical assistance for a student with a disability or, if appropriate, that student's family

- Training or technical assistance for professionals (including individuals providing education or rehabilitation services), employers, or other individuals who provide services to, employ, or are otherwise substantially involved in the major life functions of the student.

There are six areas in the IEP where it is most appropriate to include AT.

1. Present level of academic achievement and functional performance

2. Transition

3. Annual goals and objectives

4. Assessment of the student's progress toward achieving goals and objectives in large-scale assessments

5. AT consideration within supplementary aids and services

6. Special education and related services

Although there is no reference in IDEA 2004 to a specific provider of AT services, these may be assigned to a special educator, SLP, OT, or an AT specialist certified by the Rehabilitation Engineering and Assistive Technology Society of North America on staff at the school or hired in a contractual capacity. Specifying AT devices without reflecting the need for AT services, including training in the use of devices, provided directly to the student, his or her classmates, family members, and other members of the team is perhaps the most common error made by IEP teams.

Sample IEP Goals for Assistive Technology   Sample IEP goals in the area of AT include the following.

- Jerome will use a single switch mounted on a switch-mounting arm positioned to the right side of his head and scan software to listen to reading assignments.

- Nate will compose a paragraph with three or more sentences with less than two spelling errors using Read&Write or another assistive writing app.

- Brianne will use an adapted keyboard with custom overlays and a computer with talking word processor to complete written assignments.

The question always arises about whether to name a specific AT device or software on the IEP. If the team has done a comprehensive AT assessment and identified a specific device or piece of software as a good match for the student's needs, then it should be listed on the IEP. If a family moves from its current school district to another, then the new team will save valuable instructional time and money if they know which AT supports have been prescribed for and successfully used with the student in the past. If a team has not yet conducted an AT assessment at the time the IEP is written, then they can use a generic statement such as, "Pending the results of a comprehensive AT assessment, Daniela will use a tablet computer and adapted keyboard for all written work" and then amend the IEP after the assessment to include the recommended device or software.

TEAM COLLABORATION

Once team members have defined their roles in supporting students' membership, participation, social relationships, and learning within an inclusive classroom, they need to determine how they will work together in planning and implementing students' educational programs.

Weekly Instructional Planning Meetings

Team members meet to develop IEPs, review progress, discuss case management issues such as scheduling services or reviewing the results of evaluations, problem-solve, and plan for the student's participation in upcoming lessons.

Figure 6.3 depicts a typical agenda that organizes team member discussion and decision making during instructional planning meetings. It is critically important that an agenda be followed at each meeting and team members avoid discussing issues that are unrelated to instructional planning. Keeping a "parking lot" list for issues that are not related to instructional planning but need to be discussed later is an effective strategy for recognizing a team member's concern but not addressing it during the time set aside for instructional planning.

Some teams hold weekly instructional planning meetings and then schedule an additional meeting once a month to address case management or other issues. More details about instructional planning meetings are provided in Chapter 9, including using a form to identify student learning objectives and assessment procedures during upcoming lessons and units and the supports the student needs to fully participate in commonly occurring instructional routines.

Collaboration Within Inclusive Activities and Environments

The second way that team members work together is within the context of general education lessons and other inclusive school and community activities. Figure 6.4 depicts how James's team members support James during a variety of activities in a typical school day. These providers obviously would not be in every class every day of the week, but this schedule shows how the SLP, PT, OT, and AT specialists are all involved in supporting his access to academic instruction in the classroom and other learning and social opportunities throughout his day. On days when two of his providers overlap with one another during a class period, they can take advantage of cotreatment opportunities (i.e., when two professionals from different disciplines work together to maximize goals and progress). For example, an inclusion facilitator comes into an English language arts class to teach a small group

Date:

In attendance:

Team member roles:

Facilitator:

Notetaker:

Timekeeper:

Crowd control:

1. Set agenda and times for each agenda item (2 minutes)

2. Announcements (5 minutes)

3. What did the student learn this week? Social highlights? (5 minutes)

4. Fidelity check of supports and student learning during the previous week (10 minutes)

   • How did the student do last week? Look at work samples, homework, tests, and projects.

   • How well did our support plans work? Did we deliver supports accurately and consistently? Where do we need to improve our fidelity of supports?

5. Weekly learning and participation plan: (30 minutes)

6. To do's: (3 minutes)

What	Who	When

7. Evaluate the meeting (how well the team collaborated during the meeting): (3 minutes) What worked? What didn't? Ah-ha's?

8. Prepare for next meeting: (2 minutes)

Date/time:

Facilitator:

Notetaker:

Timekeeper:

Crowd control:

Agenda items:

9. Parking lot

Figure 6.3. Sample instructional planning meeting agenda.

Time	Activity	Who is present	What they do
7:30	Arrival	Physical therapist (PT)	Support James to open door and then wheel through.
8:00	Unpack	Occupational therapist (OT)	Teach James how to unzip coat and hang it up
8:15	"Do Now" seat work	OT and inclusion facilitator	Support James to use GoWorksheet to fill in worksheet
8:30	Read-aloud	Inclusion facilitator	Support James to use his finger to track under each line in his adapted book
9:00	Guided reading	Speech-language pathologist (SLP)	Support James to ask questions, identify main character and three supporting details, and describe favorite part of the book
9:45	Writing	OT	Support James to use graphic organizer software to plan his writing project
10:30	Recess	PT	Support James to use wheelchair-adapted swing
11:00	Science	Assistive technology specialist	Support James to use adapted equipment to plant and water seeds
11:30	Lunch	OT	Support James to use adapted utensils to eat
12:00	Recess	PT and SLP	Support James and friends to play an adapted soccer game
12:30	Music	OT	Support James to play adapted keyboard
1:00	Social studies	Inclusion facilitator and OT	Support James to construct a map of 13 original United States colonies using iPad app
1:45	Math	Inclusion facilitator	Support James to use interactive math app to solve addition and subtraction problems
2:30	Dismissal	OT	Support James to put on his coat, hat, and mittens

Figure 6.4. Sample daily schedule for James's providers.

(that includes a student with complex support needs) and the SLP sits next to the student facilitating his or her use of his or her AAC device to answer comprehension questions. Another example is when an SLP supports a student to ask questions using his or her AAC device while the OT evaluates the most effective positioning of the student and the device.

Finding or Creating Time to Collaborate

Time is always a barrier to effective inclusion and, in particular, common planning time for all IEP team members. Administrative leadership and support is the primary means through which common planning time is given to teams. Administrators and other school leaders first set the expectation that common planning time will be utilized by all staff. Then they form teams, prioritize common planning blocks in the school schedule, provide professional development on the skills necessary for effective and efficient collaborative planning, and secure space for team meetings.

❏ Define inclusive roles and responsibilities for all team members.

❏ Shift the role of the special education teacher to an inclusion facilitator.

❏ Ensure that the inclusion facilitator has no more than five to eight students with complex support needs on his or her caseload.

❏ Create a weekly schedule for the inclusion facilitator that includes time in each student's general education class, time for making adapted materials, time to facilitate a team instructional planning meeting, and time to communicate with families.

❏ Schedule related services primarily within the context of general education lessons and other inclusive school activities and environments.

❏ Schedule weekly instructional planning meetings that incorporate information from the general educator about upcoming lessons and units and input from all other service providers regarding supports the student will need to fully participate in general education instruction.

❏ Identify times for service providers to work together to support student participation.

❏ Use an instructional planning meeting template to record team discussion and decisions.

❏ Share participation plans with all team members, including parents.

Figure 6.5.   Inclusive team roles and responsibilities and collaboration checklist.

Ensuring protected time for common planning is a particularly important administrative role, often requiring scheduling by hand and even becoming involved in contract negotiations. Stetson (2015) and Villa and Thousand (2005) identified many creative solutions for finding or creating common planning time.

- Develop the school schedule with common planning time scheduled first.

- Hire a permanent substitute teacher for half days, and hold team planning meetings on those days.

- Ask a principal, assistant principal, or other non-teaching staff member to cover a class.

- Hold planning meetings during recess or lunch time, and assign coverage to a paraeducator or trained volunteer.

- Group two classes together to watch a DVD or do a special project, relieving one of the general education teachers to attend a planning meeting.

- Hold meetings before or after school, and compensate team members for their participation.

- Use Skype or Facetime to allow an itinerant provider (e.g., SLP, OT, PT, AT specialist) to join via distance technology.

- Lengthen the school day by 15 minutes a day for 4 days a week and then dismiss students early on the fifth day to provide 60 minutes of planning time for teams.

- Use portions of staff development days to give teams time to plan.

- Partner with local colleges to engage their faculty to supervise interns who teach classes while general education teachers participate in planning meetings.

- Lengthen the school year so that all staff teach 4 days a week and have a fifth full day for collaborative planning and participation in professional learning communities.

School personnel are able to find or create the time necessary to make common planning time happen when they value it and the results it produces.

CONCLUSIONS

This chapter emphasized the commitment of inclusive team members and the collaboration skills that are required to establish and facilitate the optimal supports for students (see Figure 6.5). The roles and responsibilities of each IEP team member were reviewed—realizing the positive affect that common planning time has on the successful implementation of individualized student supports.

7

Establish Valued Membership in General Education

Membership is more than simply tolerance; it comprises all the symbols and signs of belonging that are afforded to typical students in a classroom and within the larger school environment. Membership means arriving at and leaving school and the classroom at the same time as other students; having a desk situated alongside others, rather than in the back of the room; being called on in class; having a classroom job; and having a locker alphabetically arranged like everyone else rather than in the special education wing of the school.

Membership in general education falls along a continuum of "not included at all" to "having all the signs and symbols of membership afforded to classmates without disabilities." Steps along that continuum include

- Student is a full-time and valued member of a general education class with all the symbols of belonging.

- Student is a part-time member of a general education class—he or she comes and goes multiple times during a day (Schnorr, 1990).

- Student is a visitor in a general education class.

- Student attends a special education class in a regular school building.

- Student attends a segregated school.

Some students with complex support needs will enter a general education class after having been in general education the year before. Nevertheless,

127

☐ The student attends the school he or she would attend if he or she did not have a disability.

☐ The student's class and other activities in which he or she is involved have a natural proportion of students with and without disabilities (i.e., the same percentage of students with and without disabilities as are present in the school population).

☐ The student is a valued member of an age-appropriate general education class.

☐ The student's name is on all class lists, group lists put on the board, job lists, and so forth.

☐ The student participates in classroom and school routines, such as the Pledge of Allegiance, lunch count, jobs, errands, eating lunch in the cafeteria, and changing classes, in typical locations and at the same times as classmates without disabilities.

☐ The student receives accessible print and other learning materials in accessible formats at the same time those materials are provided to students without disabilities.

☐ The student participates in classroom instruction in similar ways as students without disabilities, including whole class discussion, writing on the board, small-group discussion, and projects. The student is called on by the teacher as frequently as other students in the class.

☐ The student rides the same school bus as his or her peers without disabilities, arriving and leaving at the same time.

☐ The student makes the transition between classes alongside their peers without disabilities, arriving and leaving at the same time.

☐ The student progresses through the grades according to the same pattern as students without disabilities.

☐ The student learns in outside-of-school, age-appropriate, and inclusive environments before the age of 18 only when such instruction is the norm for typical students.

☐ Related services and specialized instruction are provided within the typical routines of a school day in addition to, not in place of, core general academic instruction.

☐ Related services are delivered primarily through embedded instruction in the classroom or prior to or after the school day.

☐ The school is physically accessible so that the student and other individuals with mobility challenges have full access to all activities and environments within the school building.

☐ The school accommodates the student's sensory and health care needs.

Figure 7.1. General education classroom and school membership checklist.

their teams should still use the membership indicators checklist presented in Figure 7.1 to be sure that they have not missed any opportunities for those students to experience the same sense of belonging as typical students in the classroom.

FOLLOW STEPS FOR STUDENTS MAKING THE TRANSITION INTO A GENERAL EDUCATION CLASS

Some students may be making the transition into a general education class from a self-contained class or separate school placement. The following sections outline the steps that need to be taken to secure their membership. Use the checklist in Figure 7.2 to follow the steps for a student's transition into a general education class.

At Least 3 Months Prior to the Transition

Student teams should begin by enlisting the support of the school principal, special education administrator, and the family for the student's transition. Professional development should be provided to potential team members on presuming competence, accessible instruction materials, AT, positive behavior supports, belonging and social relationships, sensory supports, movement supports, emotional needs, the student's unique medical needs, environmental adaptations, the collaborative instructional planning process, and grading. Sending potential team members to visit other inclusive schools can help them better understand inclusive education. Finally, the school principal and special education administrator should facilitate open discussions with potential team members to address their concerns and listen to their ideas.

About 2 Months Prior to the Transition

Parents and the student's current teacher should inform the student that he or she will be going to a new classroom or school and schedule a tour. Assign the student to a classroom or select high school classes. It is helpful to schedule a transition meeting between the family and school members of the student's IEP team to write or revise the IEP to reflect inclusive goals, supports, and placements. Student team members should create common planning time and schedule special education and related services for the student. If the student requires additional equipment, curricula, or software, then teams should order materials or prepare materials for transfer when the student leaves his or her old placement.

In addition, plan and arrange for the student to get on the regular bus, and assess the bus, classroom, and other school environments for accessibility. Teams should make the necessary adaptations. Team members should visit the classroom to determine where the student will sit and observe typical instructional routines to begin creating participation plans for upcoming units. It is also essential to ensure that medical and safety procedures are in place.

At Least 3 Months Prior to the Transition

❏ Enlist the school principal and special education administrator in support of the transition.

❏ Enlist the student and family in support of the transition.

❏ Provide professional development to potential team members on presuming competence, accessible instructional materials, assistive technology, positive behavior supports, belonging and social relationships, sensory supports, movement supports, emotional needs, environmental adaptations, the collaborative instructional planning process, and grading.

❏ Send potential team members to visit other inclusive schools.

❏ Have open discussions with potential team members to address concerns.

About 2 Months Prior to the Transition

❏ Tell the student that he or she will be going to a new classroom/school and schedule a tour.

❏ Assign the student to a classroom or select high school classes.

❏ Schedule a transition meeting between family and school members of the student's IEP team.

❏ Write or revise the IEP to reflect inclusive goals, supports, and placement.

❏ Create common planning time for the team.

❏ Schedule special education and related services.

❏ Order equipment, curricula, software, or prepare for its transfer when the student leaves his or her old placement.

❏ Arrange for the student to get to school on the regular bus.

❏ Assess the classroom and other school environments for accessibility and make the necessary adaptations.

❏ Determine where the student will sit in the classroom.

❏ Visit the classroom during typical instructional routines and begin creating participation plans for upcoming units.

❏ Ensure that medical and safety procedures are in place.

❏ Continue professional development.

The Week Before the Transition

❏ Set up the student's desk and ensure that he or she has all the same materials as other students.

❏ Schedule a team meeting to discuss the first week of school and ensure that supports are ready for his or her full participation on the day he or she arrives.

❏ Tell other students that a new student will be joining their classroom and support them to welcome the student.

The Week that the Student Arrives

❏ Do a welcoming activity with young children, such as *We All Fit Together* (Friedrich, 2012).

❏ Read a book about disability, such as *Ian's Walk: A Story About Autism* (Lears, 1998), *Just Because* (Elliott, 2012), *or All Cats Have Asperger Syndrome* (Hoopmann, 2006). *The Curious Incident of the Dog in the Night-Time* (Haddon, 2003) or *No Pity: Forging a New Civil Rights Period* (Shapiro, 1993) can be read by older students.

❏ Have a brief team meeting every day at lunch or after school to discuss how things are going.

❏ Call the parents to share how the week went at school and ask how the student is adjusting at home.

Two Weeks After the Student Arrives

❏ Schedule a team meeting to discuss how well supports are working.

❏ Check in with the family to see how the student is adjusting while at home.

❏ Work with the family to set up a social gathering outside of school for the student and a few classmates.

Figure 7.2. Checklist for a student making the transition into a general education classroom.

If the student's IEP requires a one-to-one paraprofessional, hire and train that person and clarify his or her role on the team.

The Week Before the Transition

The week before transition is the time to set up the student's desk and ensure that the student has all the same materials as other students. Teams should schedule a team meeting to discuss plans for the first week of school and confirm that supports are in place for the student's full participation on the day he or she arrives. Teachers can tell the class that a new student will be joining their classroom and support them in welcoming their new classmate.

The Week That the Student Arrives

Welcoming activities with young children, such as *We All Fit Together* (Friedrich, 2012), are an effective way to welcome the student to the classroom. Teachers can also read a book about diversity, such as *Ian's Walk: A Story About Autism* (Lears, 1998), *Just Because* (Elliott, 2012), or *All Cats Have Asperger Syndrome* (Hoopmann, 2006). Older students can read *The Curious Incident of the Dog in the Night-Time* (Haddon, 2003) or *No Pity: Forging a New Civil Rights Period* (Shapiro, 1993).

Student transition teams should have a brief team meeting every day at lunch or after school to discuss the process and check in on how things are going. A team member can call the parents to share how the school week went and ask how the student is adjusting at home.

Two Weeks After the Student Arrives

Two weeks after the student made the transition to the new classroom is an opportune time to schedule a team meeting to discuss how well supports for the student are working. Team members should plan to check in with the family to learn how the student is adjusting while at home. Finally, student teams can work with the family to arrange a social gathering outside of school for the student and a few new classmates.

CREATE A WELCOMING CLASSROOM COMMUNITY

General education teachers have enormous power to create a welcoming classroom environment in which all students feel like valued members, regardless of whether a student enters a general education class along with his or her peers as a natural part of moving up to the next grade or whether a student is making the transition from a segregated classroom or school.

If the school year has not yet begun, invite the student and his or her parents to come for a school tour and classroom visit. If possible, assign the student a desk and personalize it with his or her name. Point out the different classroom areas and describe their purpose. Following the student's lead, do a short activity together, such as reading a book, watching a DVD, or doing some artwork. If you are a high school educator and know that the student will be going to several classrooms every day, then arrange the visit so that the student can do a trial run of going from class to class according to his or her schedule. If you are a preschool educator, then show the student where all the centers are, point out the bathroom, and play on the playground for a little while. If you are an educator who works with students during the transition years—when they are ages 18–21—then spend a day helping the student become acclimated to a future jobsite or practice riding public transportation.

Ask the student's parents or other IEP team members from the previous year if there are visual supports that will help outline his or her personal space (e.g., colored tape on the floor around his or her desk, color-coded signs that designate the different classroom work areas). Equipment or other tools may help the student maintain his or her focus, such as adaptive chairs, chew tools (to address the need for oral-motor stimulation), and weighted blankets to help the student regulate his or her sensory system.

Make sure the student has all the symbols of belonging that other students do, such as assigning him or her a cubby or locker and having his or her name called during attendance. Find out if your student has an area of interest, and ask the librarian to find books, web sites, or DVDs on those topics.

BUILD A CLASSROOM COMMUNITY THAT VALUES DIVERSITY

All students belong to several communities—their families, neighborhoods, places of worship, clubs and sports groups, school, and the classroom. Teachers can use specific classroom and team-building activities to promote the development of a classroom community that values diversity. A few activities that work well are listed in the text box.

We All Fit Together Puzzle Class-Building Activity (Adapted from Rachel Friedrich at Sub Hub)

1. Outline a large puzzle on poster board with enough pieces for each student in the classroom.

2. Cut them out before the activity begins.

3. Students decorate a puzzle piece and write their name and a few interesting facts about themselves. If there are nonwriters in the class, then have pictures or graphics available that illustrate different cultures, activities, and interests that they can glue on their puzzle piece.

4. Fit all the pieces together and permanently mount on poster board.

5. Gather students to look at the completed puzzle and create a list of similarities and differences.

Power Line

This activity gets students talking and learning about one another as a group. Create a visual continuum from "dislike" to "love," using tape on the floor with hash marks and descriptive words, signs on the walls, or cartoon faces depicting points on the continuum. Call out a word and ask students to quietly walk to the place on the continuum that expresses their feeling about that word. Start with easy things such as kinds of food, sports, or songs. Once movement has stopped and the line is set, let a few students talk about where they are in line and why. Switch topics. Try favorite activities, places to visit, or books. See where students stand. As the year goes on and students become more comfortable with one another, change the continuum scale from "dislike" to "love" to "strongly agree" to "strongly disagree." Ask students to take a stand on questions such as, "Should the cafeteria allow students to buy soda?" or "Should a sports figure who has been accused of using performance-enhancing drugs be stripped of his or her Olympic medals?"

GUIDELINES FOR TALKING ABOUT DISABILITY

Educators often wonder if they should talk about disability. They do not want to make students feel uncomfortable, yet they think that it helps all the students to understand one another's learning styles, strengths, and needs for support. Although there are many ways to approach this subject, the following guidelines may help educators make the best decision for their classroom, depending on the educators' levels of comfort and knowledge as well as the student's and family's preferences.

Know the Law

Laws exist to protect the privacy of students and their families, and educators should be well informed about how the policies affect their role.

Ask About and Honor Student and Parent Preferences

Some young people are reluctant to talk about their disability, some do not see their challenges as any greater than those of kids without disabilities, and others have mixed feelings. Empower all students to be proud of themselves, believe that they can achieve their goals, and advocate for themselves in social relationships, school, and adult life.

Educators Need to Explore Their Own Feelings About Disability

Educators bring their personal educational histories and earliest memories about people with disabilities into the classroom. If someone grew up with a sibling or other relative who had a disability, then that may have been a positive experience or one that left him or her with unresolved questions and feelings. Think about those early experiences and reflect on how they may be playing out in current interactions with families and students. If an educator does not currently have a collegial, familial, or professional relationship with someone who has a disability, then it could be beneficial to actively look for that opportunity.

CONCLUSIONS

The title of this book is *It's More Than "Just Being In,"* and students experiencing valued membership in general education is one of the key features of authentic inclusion.

8

Facilitate
Reciprocal Social Relationships

The best IEP in the world will not lead to desired quality-of-life outcomes unless students have friends. A sense of belonging is a necessary foundation for achieving self-actualization (Maslow, 1954).

RATIONALE FOR FACILITATING FRIENDSHIPS

People with disabilities who do not have friends are lonely, isolated, and less likely to be a part of the community. To imagine that people with disabilities could have a full life surrounded only by professionals is to categorize them as "others," rather than understand their common humanity. People's lives would be empty if they only interacted with their dentist, doctor, plumber, and boss. The author's circle of friends is depicted in Figure 8.1. The innermost circle includes her family. The next circle out includes people she considers her best friends, and they also count her in that category. The third circle includes people with whom she spends time doing shared activities. The fourth circle includes people who are paid to be in her life.

Imagine if John, a student with a significant disability, has a circle that looks like the one depicted in Figure 8.2. How might feel? How might he act?

Although paid staff may perform valuable functions and sometimes become like members of the family, they cannot take the place of people who choose to associate with people with disabilities with no expectation of payment. The following was found on a web site promoting special friendships for students with disabilities under the heading "November Buddy Pair."

135

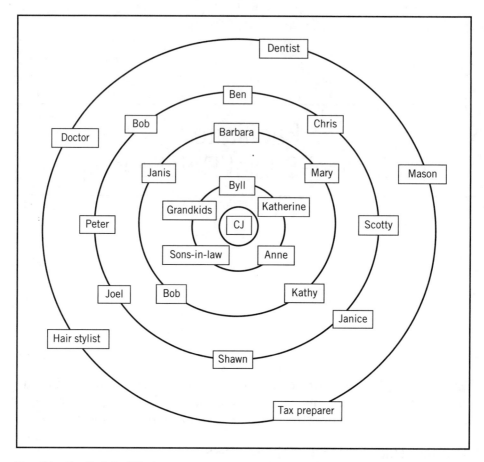

Figure 8.1. Cheryl's circle of friends.

Christine and Lesley have been friends for three years now. They share a beautiful relationship that illustrates the true meaning of friendship and serves as an example to all of us about the power of our program. When we saw the two of them at this year's Meet and Greet, it brought tears to our eyes as the two of them gave each other a real hug and asked how each other was after a summer apart. Every time I saw Lesley in the summer, all she could talk about was her "special friend" and how excited she was to see her in the fall. It is times like this that we are able to really realize the importance of true friendship and the affect it has on both the student and the special friend.

Reading this demands that the following questions are considered to help determine if these students were really friends.

- Do they spend time together when adults are not arranging or supervising?

- Do typical kids get awards for being one another's friends?

- Do real friends see each other once a year at a Meet and Greet?

- Should individuals feel good when students with disabilities get real hugs?

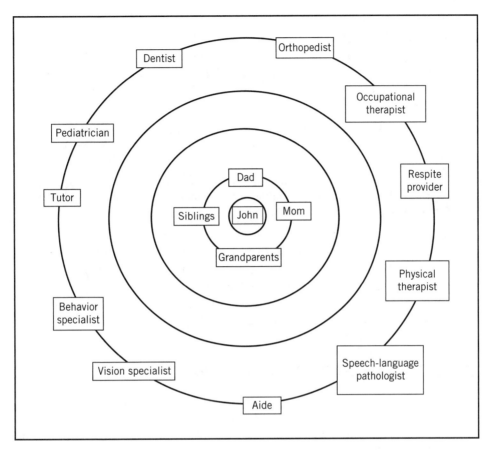

Figure 8.2. John's circle of friends.

Using this practice of arranged friendships can prevent real friendships from developing. Authentic membership in a social group defines whether students are accepted or marginalized. Supporting students to develop social relationships forces educators and parents to go to the heart of the meaning of inclusion. Carol Tashie, a former project director with the Institute on Disability at the University of New Hampshire, used to say that a person could distinguish between a non-inclusive school and an inclusive one when students with disabilities were "with" their classmates, not simply "in" a regular class (C. Tashie, personal communication, June 10, 1993).

There is no formula or checklist for helping students with disabilities make and have friends; yet there are strategies for reducing the barriers to friendships and helping students understand their commonalities as well as appreciate their differences.

POTENTIAL BARRIERS

Tashie, Shapiro-Barnard, and Rossetti (2006) argued that seemingly impenetrable barriers keep students with and without disabilities from becoming friends. They believed that reciprocal friendships may not be possible unless parents and educators address those barriers before even thinking about taking intentional steps to facilitate social relationships. The first barrier they identified is blaming a lack of friendships on some characteristics of students with disabilities, such as the way they look, the way they talk, or the way they behave.

> Now just in case you are worried, this is not the time in the book for a discussion of all the things about Liana that make it harder for her to make friends. In fact, nowhere in this book or in anything else we have written, will there be any discussion of this topic. Sure, there are things all of us could do to make ourselves more interesting, appealing, and likeable to potential friends. But despite our many "faults," we all still have friends. So this is not about "fixing" Liana to make her more desirable. Liana… is fine just the way she is. (p. 16)

Other barriers they described include students not being valued members of general education classes, making dangerous assumptions about students' intellectual capabilities, being overly reliant on one-to-one paraprofessionals, mistaking peer support as friendship, and tolerating a culture of prejudice. Although removing these barriers is often difficult, not doing so fails to address the real causes of students' lack of friends and sets up the students and their families for disappointment.

ESSENTIAL CONSIDERATIONS FOR FRIENDSHIP

Essential considerations for friendship are more easier to put into place once barriers are removed: 1) presume students are competent and have value, 2) give students a way to communicate all the time about the same things as students without disabilities, 3) fully include students in heterogeneous general education classes, 4) give students access to age-appropriate materials and activities, 5) provide support in a way that encourages interdependence and independence, 6) involve students in problem solving to remove barriers to social relationships, 7) forge a partnership between home and school to facilitate friendships and participation in social activities, and 8) position students with disabilities to give back to their school and home communities so that they are not always on the receiving end of help (Martin, Jorgensen, & Klein, 1998). Each of these considerations is explained in the next section.

Presume All Students' Value and Competence

Treating students as competent and valuable is the first essential consideration for friendship and entails challenging the concept of ableism, defined by Hehir (2002).

> The devaluation of disability that results in societal attitudes that uncritically assert that it is better for a child to walk than roll, speak than sign, read print than Braille, spell independently than use a spell-check, and hang out with nondisabled kids as opposed to other disabled kids. (p. 1)

This devaluation often takes the form of describing students with disabilities through a deficit lens rather than seeing them as people

Table 8.1. Deficit and strength-based descriptions of Anna

Deficits	Strengths, interests, talents, needs
A runner	Good fine motor skills
A biter	Loves activity and exercise
Socially awkward	Favorite musician is Taylor Swift
Does not maintain personal space	Boundless energy
IQ of 50	Likes dancing
Stims on lights	Favorite food is chicken nuggets
Lines up trucks	Artistic
Irregular sleep patterns	Enjoys order
Prompt dependent	Great smile

who have strengths, interests, talents, and needs—in other words, as whole people. Table 8.1 shows how Anna might be described in two different ways.

Speaking about and modeling the attitude that all students have gifts and talents, not just those who get 100% on their spelling tests or who score 30 points in a basketball game, is the second essential consideration. Everyday practices also give the impression that students with IDD and other disabilities are not as smart as other students. When teachers talk about students with disabilities in their presence as if they are not there, it sends a message that students are unable to speak for themselves and perhaps are unaware that others are talking about them. A lack of respect for students' identity and self-determination is communicated when staff members use exaggerated praise (e.g., saying, "Good boy" to a 15-year-old) or demand standards of behavior that are not typically required of other similar-age students (e.g., "Shake hands with Principal Smith, John"). In contrast, when teachers and parents make the least dangerous assumption about students' abilities—that they are intelligent even if they are not able to clearly communicate—this belief is modeled by students and creates an opening for students to approach one another on a more equal footing (Jorgensen, 2005). Finally, using derogatory terms such as *retard* or *low functioning* is antithetical to the notion that all students are competent. Parents and educators ought to describe students with IDD in the same way they would describe students without disabilities. For example, "Sarah is an 11th-grade student who loves English." "Seth spends lots of time on the iPad playing games such as Minecraft." "Jocelyn's friends describe her as always ready with a reassuring smile."

Provide Students With a Means to Communicate All of the Time

Although students who do not have a reliable means to communicate can make friends, those who do have a way to communicate about all of the same things as their classmates without disabilities have an easier time making and sustaining a wide variety of social relationships. Think about how communication enables friendships to be reciprocal. Expressions of empathy are comforting when a friend is down in the dumps. When one friend is looking for a job, the other friend can relate to his or her boss that the friend would be a good fit in the company. Telling a funny anecdote at a party makes a friend seem like someone the others would like to know. A friend steps up when times are tough. Communicating with classmates not only supports social closeness, but it also facilitates the discovery of shared interests related to academics or extracurricular activities. For example, students with disabilities can communicate in ways that are commensurate with their classmates without disabilities if they have the support of an AAC device programmed with age-appropriate social vocabulary, Facetime on a smart phone or tablet in which they can use sign language, or the speech-to-text feature available on most mobile phones.

Fully Include Students in Heterogeneous General Education Classes and Extracurricular Activities

Consider the following imaginary scenario to illustrate the importance of fully including students.

Imagine that you work for the Acme Widget Company. There are 100 employees in your building, which is located on four floors of the company's headquarters. You and two other employees, however, are not assigned to making widgets but rather to making gizmos. Your boss tells you that making gizmos is an honorable profession and you are a valued employee.

You are in your basement office thinking about how to get people to buy your gizmos while the marketing team is talking about the latest widget advertising campaign. Everyone is talking about the new widget marketing strategy when you come up to the employee lounge for a coffee break, but you cannot really contribute because you were not part of that discussion. They have a laugh over a mistake that the team leader made when giving her report, and you laugh along just so that you will not stand out. When you strike up a conversation with a co-worker about the latest gizmo you are working on, she looks at you blankly and says, "Good job, Henry. Sounds like you are really going to town on those gizmos," but then turns to another colleague and continues the widget discussion.

You go through the line at the company canteen during lunch to get your meal and look around for someone with whom to sit. The widget teams are scattered throughout the lunchroom, and you join the nearest table. The talk during lunch is of people's home lives, families, romances, and the baseball game that the widget team went to last weekend. You jump into the conversation to share a story about the softball game in which you played as a member of the special gizmo softball league, but your vivid description of the great catch you made falls flat because the widget makers were not at the game.

The president shows slides at the company's annual banquet of the profits that have soared because of the hard work of the widget teams. You are called up to the podium toward the end of the evening and receive an award for the most-improved gizmo maker. The audience applauds, but somehow the praise is hollow.

This scenario parallels what happens to students with disabilities when they are only partially included in general education, working on different goals, pursuing different leisure activities, and not sharing in the hidden curriculum that provides students with the opportunity to learn what it really takes to become a regular kid in the school (Apple, 1979). Students with disabilities educated in separate classrooms are outsiders for all intents and purposes because they have fewer common learning and social experiences with their classmates; they can become an "island in the mainstream" or be perceived as "a special visitor from Room 217." Conversely, students with disabilities have a common set of experiences on which to base not only conversations but also relationships when they are full-time members of general education classes and typical school social and extracurricular activities.

Strully illustrated how his commitment to the importance of social relationships grows with each passing year when he shared his worries as a parent of a young adult with complex support needs.

> I'm 55 years old now and Shawntell is 31. When I wake up in the middle of the night, wondering what will happen to Shawn when I am no longer here, I don't say to myself, "If only I had taught Shawn to tie her shoes. If only she had learned to balance her checkbook." I worry, "What if Shawn is lonely? What if she has to live in a group home with a bunch of strangers? What if she no longer sees the friends she has made who live all over the U.S.?" Then I realize that I need to spend my energy on helping Shawn become fully a part of her community and building a network of friends and acquaintances who will be there even when I am gone. (J. Strully, personal communication, September 15, 1996)

Give Students Access to Age-Appropriate Materials and Activities

Using age-appropriate and respectful materials, language, expectations, and adaptations is another essential condition for friendship. High school students with disabilities are often treated as though they are much younger than their chronological age, and this contributes to the perception that they are not friendship material. Changing the attitudes and behavior of some service providers is difficult and requires a very direct approach from those individuals' supervisors or administrators. Among the most offensive examples of infantilizing and demeaning students with disabilities are

- Talking to students in a high-pitched and loud voice as though one were speaking to an infant or young child

- Talking about students in their presence without including them in the conversation

- Dressing students in clothing that is made for much younger students, such as cartoon character T-shirts, hairstyles that are outdated, and plastic bibs, without giving them a choice of more age-appropriate wear

- Permitting students to carry school supplies intended for younger students, such as preschool cartoon character lunchboxes, book bags, pencil cases, and so forth

- Using inappropriate behavior reinforcers, such as Hello Kitty stickers

- Describing students first and foremost by their disability rather than by their educational needs. Instead of saying, "Selena is a Down syndrome student" say, "Selena is a 10th-grade student who receives direct instruction in reading." Instead of referring to Anna as "nonverbal," say "Anna is an emergent communicator." Instead of talking about James as "severely involved," describe him as a student who "needs planned supports to join his classmates in all activities."

- Making allowances for inappropriate behavior because someone thinks that it is cute that Anna runs up to a sixth-grade boy and kisses him

Yet, if all the 10th-grade girls think that Hello Kitty is cool, then by all means, support the student with the disability to join in with the fad.

Susan

Susan was a student in a self-contained educational program run by a regional collaborative housed in a local high school. Although Susan was 16 years old, she came to school wearing pigtails, ankle socks, and a sweatshirt embroidered with Minnie Mouse. The only means Susan had to demonstrate choice and control over her environment was to push a one-button switch that played "The Wheels on the Bus Go Round and Round." Is it any wonder that students and teachers alike spoke to Susan as if she were a toddler? Their voice inflections rose when they spoke to her—some even tickled her—and everyone was resistant to including Susan in age-appropriate classes and activities.

Although this description sounds like a caricature, it is all too typical of students with complex support needs who have attended segregated classes and schools or who have not been around students without disabilities. The school hired a new special education teacher to serve as an inclusion facilitator, and he met with Susan's mom, Marla, and shared some of the comments that Susan's classmates were making about her clothes and accessories. Susan's mom was very invested in Susan's successful inclusion and invited a group of girls to her house over the weekend to help redecorate her room. The Disney pictures on the walls were replaced with pictures of current music idols chosen by Susan through eye gaze. The Fisher-Price primary-colored tape player was donated to a local preschool, and Susan chose new songs to download onto her smart phone. Although Marla did not have an unlimited budget, she did ask the girls if they would like to go shopping with Susan and help pick out a new comforter set and an outfit for school that was more in line with the styles worn by other 16-year-old girls at her school. Marla purchased several bottles of nail polish, and the girls gave each other manicures.

Do people with disabilities have the right to wear whatever they want and watch their favorite television shows, even if those choices do not seem age appropriate? Of course! It is not a matter of preference for many students but, rather, of not having the opportunity to be around typical kids their own age and develop more age-appropriate interests. The girls who visited Susan were not saying that they were intolerant of Susan as a person, but they were welcoming her into their circle that was defined in part by similar clothes and interests.

Be sensitive to the age-appropriateness of materials and technologies when making adaptations to schoolwork or selecting apps to teach skills. If a student is fascinated with trains, then it is just as easy to purchase models of real trains as it is to buy Thomas the Train sets. One can easily find age-appropriate depictions of images to enhance text rather than use preschool-appropriate images.

Many strategies can be used to sensitize parents, staff, and students to issues of inappropriate language and treatment. First, openly discuss the issue. Share first-person accounts from people with disabilities about how they were once treated based solely on their IQ score. Micah Fialka-Feldman, the subject of a documentary called *Intelligent Lives* by Dan Habib (2018) (producer of *Including Samuel*), was asked how he felt when he learned that he had a 40 IQ. He responded,

> Well, I didn't know what it meant, so I Googled it. It said that people with 40 IQs could never live alone, go to college, or be employed. And I thought, "Well, I am doing all those things!"

Provide Support in a Way That Encourages Interdependence and Independence

Although many students with IDD require support from an adult at some point throughout their school day, a commitment to relying first on natural supports from classmates brings students together. Martin et al. (1998) provided numerous examples of effective natural and peer supports for 10 different activities, including transitions, teacher-directed lessons, cooperative group activities, individual seat work, personal hygiene routines, and extracurricular activities. Table 8.2 depicts these support ideas and updates them to include advances in AT since 1998.

Table 8.2. Peer and adult supports during typical instructional routines and other activities

Transitions	Peer support	Adult support
James needs assistance to hang up his coat and backpack in his cubby when he arrives at school.	Greet his bus and walk with him to the classroom. Support him at the elbow to hang up his backpack. Unzip his jacket and provide minimal physical assistance for him to remove it. Support him at the elbow to hang up his coat. Push his wheelchair to his desk cluster next to other classmates.	The regular hallway monitor watches from a distance to monitor for safety. The paraeducator gets James's home–school notebook out of the backpack and reads dad's entry. The paraeducator speaks to the general education teacher about anything he or she needs to know related to James's recent doctor's appointment.
Anna sometimes gets agitated when passing in the hallway because of the noise and crowding.	Walk arm and arm with her and whisper reassuring words.	The occupational therapist prepares Anna for the transition by giving her deep pressure on her shoulders and whispering a brief social story about successfully managing the sensory overload in the hallway.
Selena sometimes forgets whether it is an "A" or a "B" day in the high school schedule.	Classmates in Selena's first period advisory class remind her that it is an "A" day and move the arrow on her schedule board to point to the "A" column of classes.	The advisory teacher reminds all students that it is an "A" day, and as the class adjourns for second period, he or she looks at Selena's schedule board, puts his or her hand on her shoulder, and says "Yup, you have got that right Selena. It is an 'A' day today."

Teacher-led discussion or lecture	Peer support	Adult support
James needs modeling and physical support to use his augmentative and alternative communication (AAC) device to participate in whole class discussion.	Two students seated on either side of James model the use of his AAC device when they make a comment or ask a question. They put their hand under James's wrist and provide nondirectional support as he makes selections on his AAC device.	The speech-language pathologist (SLP) sits just to the side and behind James and navigates to his commenting and questions page on his AAC device.
Anna needs to hold a fidget tool during whole class instruction.	A student seated next to Anna offers her a choice of fidget tools (displayed on her iPad choice board) just as the teacher begins the discussion.	The classroom teacher validates some students' need for movement during the discussion by inviting students to sit or stand. He or she asks the students to cluster in standing groups of three every 15 minutes during a lecture to share their opinions on the topic of the day.
Selena needs visual supports to follow along with the discussion or lecture.	A classmate sitting next to her silently points to pictures/words on an aided language/topic board as vocabulary terms, important characters, or events are spoken by the teacher.	The teacher lectures and displays his or her notes on the SMART Board, enhanced with the same pictures that Selena has on her aided language/topic board.

144

Cooperative group activity	Peer support	Adult support
James needs to see enlarged text and images on a 27-inch monitor to be visually engaged in a cooperative group science activity dealing with sedimentary, metamorphic, and igneous rocks.	The students in James's group take turns narrating the features of the rock images on the 27-inch monitor, using language that describes their salient features.	James's teacher of the visually impaired works with him and his classmates during one lunch period per week to provide instruction on images that the science class will be using in upcoming lessons. The teacher models the use of salient feature descriptions and asks James's fellow students to try it out.
Anna has difficulty manipulating the small paper squares that her fellow students are using to build a tower structure in math.	The students at her table ask Anna to tell them which piece of paper she wants to be placed in which location as they build their tower structure.	The paraprofessional sits with the group and encourages them to let each person in the group have a turn to add a piece of paper to the structure or, in Anna's case, direct the rest of the group to choose a particular piece of paper and put it in a specific location. The SLP programs directional vocabulary into Anna's AAC device (e.g., UP, DOWN, LEFT, RIGHT, HERE, THERE) so that she has the words to say during this activity. Anna's team is given the choice to use a digital program to build their tower, and Anna can use the arrow keys on her iPad to move the pieces of paper around.
Selena needs visual supports to follow along with the steps in a science experiment and prepare a lab report.	Students work in pairs to complete the lab experiment, and Selena and her partner use Selena's iPad to take pictures of each step of the experiment instead of writing a summary. They both work on the lab report using a template in Explain Everything and record narration that explains their hypothesis, procedures, and results.	Selena's special education teacher creates a template for a lab report using Explain Everything and supports Selena to type captions under the pictures.

(continued)

145

Table 8.2. *(continued)*

Physical education or sports activities	Peer support	Adult support
James needs someone to push his wheelchair around the gymnasium and provide James with adapted equipment to participate in ball games.	All students do their warm-up laps in pairs. James's partner pushes his wheelchair. James hits a ball off a batting tee with assistance from a friend to help him hold the bat. A friend positions a soccer ball near James's foot so he can kick it.	The physical education teacher plans skill drills and games that embed adaptations in the rules, instruction, equipment, and environment by partnering with an adapted physical education teacher. The co-teachers use adaptations such as: Having two balls in play, with one being larger, brightly colored, and having a sound effect inside to help James locate it visually and auditorally. Ask students to do warm-ups in pairs. Provide scoops for students who have not mastered catching the ball with a mitt. Pitching distance is decreased to accommodate the needs of students with decreased strength and stamina. Students are allowed extra time to move between bases. Students are allowed to use a batting tee to push or hit the ball. Students are allowed to walk or run in a smaller area of play for basketball or soccer. Students in wheelchairs may hold the ball in their laps during periods of movement. The nets for tennis or volleyball may be lowered to accommodate students who use wheelchairs or with limited gross motor skills. Sports equipment such as larger and softer balls, lightweight racquets and clubs, and baseballs and catching mitts with Velcro are utilized.
The echo and sounds of running on the gymnasium floor make Anna anxious during physical education class.	Anna's classmates hold her hands during physical education. Her classmates take turns sitting with her when she takes a break to listen to soothing music on her smart phone for a few minutes.	The physical education teacher utilizes a small, quieter office space located just off the gymnasium floor for one of the warm-up stations. The physical education teacher spends time during each class working directly with Anna and speaks to her in a calm tone of voice.
Selena wants to join the cheerleading team but is not able to do the tumbling moves.	Two of Selena's teammates come over to Selena's house for an hour every weekend to coach her to learn the routine.	The cheerleading coach choreographs a routine that always has two girls doing something else while the rest are tumbling.

Include Students in Problem Solving Inclusion Challenges

Students who are empowered and supported to address the barriers to friendship that exist for their classmates are more likely to own the solutions that they develop than if the ideas come from adults. They are the real experts on friendship. Students can be involved in this effort through two avenues—being a member of a club or other extracurricular activity that focuses on larger issues of social justice and inclusion and being a part of an individual student's circle of belonging and support.

Selena

Selena's case manager, who served as an inclusion facilitator, worked with her to identify two extracurricular activities that she was interested in joining in the ninth grade. Selena spoke with several club advisors and chose the Key Club, and she found out that meetings included discussions of race, gender, sexual orientation, class, war, and peace, and the club chose one community service activity every year to support. Although the inclusion facilitator offered to stay during club meetings, the advisor said that it was not necessary; after all, a club focused on inclusion and social justice was a perfect situation in which to rely on natural supports. Selena is now in her second year of club membership, and the members decided that they wanted to speak out on the issue of bullying in their school. Selena joined several other club members on a panel that gave a presentation to the school board and to the student body.

Being a member of another student's circle of belonging and support is the other opportunity that students have to support friendship development (Pearpoint, Forest, & O'Brien, 1996). A circle is a group of people who are invited to get to know a student who is not yet connected in a meaningful way. The invitation that is extended is not, "Would you please become friends with Anna," but rather, "Would you like to join a group of people who are going to meet with Anna to figure out how to get her more connected with her classmates at school?" A group of other sixth-grade students were invited to be part of Anna's team when she returned to her neighborhood school after spending several years in an out-of-district program for students with ASD. Anna's team met every Thursday after school to sit around and talk, eat snacks, and play computer games together. Anna's paraeducator, Sue, provided support to the kids as they tackled issues such as Anna's difficulty participating in physical education class and loneliness on weekends. Sue asked the kids to talk about what they thought was standing in the way of Anna being just a regular kid in the school. Not one student mentioned her disabilities. They did point out, however, that Anna arrived later than her classmates, had a hard time settling into the morning routine, and had to leave early at the end of the day missing about 15 minutes of free time because she rode the special education bus. Sue spoke with Anna's parents about this issue, and they met with the principal and the director of student transportation and agreed that Anna could ride the regular bus if a harness seat belt could be installed.

Having two group members serve as Anna's "bridge builders" during the weekends was one idea mentioned in a team meeting. Tashie et al. (2006) described a bridge builder as someone who is socially connected in the school but might be outside of the student's circle. Anna's bridge builders turned out to be two students who were part of her team. Tania said that she was enrolled in a hip-hop dance group that operated out of a local community center. She asked Anna if she would like to come with her the following Saturday, and Anna enthusiastically said yes. Rashida said that she and a couple of friends were going to sell baked goods outside the local grocery story on Sunday to raise money for their end-of-sixth-grade environmental camp experience. The group developed a plan for Anna to join them, and they all worked together during the remaining meeting time to create a poster promoting the cause.

Circles of belonging and support must be organized for the right reason, with the right attitude, and, in most cases, facilitated by an adult. The facilitator's role is to 1) work with the student and his or her family to issue the initial invitation to join; 2) support the group's organizational needs such as transportation, parent permissions, and accessible meeting locations; and 3) help the group confront attitudes that stand in the way of friendship, such as peer pressure, prejudice, benevolence, and pity.

Forge Partnerships Between Home and School to Support Friendships

Barriers are more likely to be overcome when a student's family and school providers work together to support friendships, and their energies feed one another's efforts. Parents take charge of creating social opportunities for their kids through playdates, class birthday parties, and sleep-overs when students are in preschool and early elementary school. Families of students with disabilities are sometimes reluctant to reach out to parents of children without disabilities because they worry that their child will be a burden. This attitude about people with disabilities being a burden unfortunately is fueled by some charity-oriented groups (e.g., through tear-jerker telethons) and even by some disability-specific advocacy organizations who portray disability as a tragedy. Parents of children with disabilities are rarely turned away when they approach their neighbors with an open heart and a willingness to talk about the supports their sons or daughters need to attend the skating party or the sleep-over.

Students who are in middle and high school usually take control of their social lives—relying on their parents or guardians for pocket money and transportation! Some barriers to friendship need to be addressed because of teenagers' newfound freedom and self-determination, such as safety issues when students with complex health needs are out with friends, inaccessibility of students' vehicles, and harnessing teenagers' energies into productive action on behalf of their friends. Strategies that can help address these barriers include

- Making friendship a priority on students' IEPs by writing goals related to improving social-communication skills, community navigation skills, or improving students' fitness through their participation in sports

- Including classmates from a student's circle in the IEP meeting itself to advocate on his or her behalf

- Making friendship facilitation part of all providers' job descriptions

- Writing a staff member's support of a student in extracurricular activities into the service grid of the IEP

- Ensuring that students have social messages and vocabulary on their AAC devices

- Asking the OT or AT specialist to find or create adaptations for video games to provide full access to the student with the disability

- Enlisting the help of an orientation and mobility specialist in teaching a student to navigate around the local recreation center or mall

Position Students to Give Back to Their School and Home Communities

Positioning students with disabilities to serve in their school and home communities is the final essential consideration for facilitating reciprocal social relationships. If the student is a member of a club that focuses on community service, then this opportunity will naturally present itself. A student could be part of the Ecology Club and help with planting trees or tending a community garden. He or she could join a club that promotes literacy among young children by reading to them over Facetime. He or she might utilize his or her interest in and love of animals by working with a local rescue group to host an "Adopt a Pet" day at the local pet store.

Best Practices for Inclusion

Students with disabilities should be on the giving end of peer tutoring as well as being the recipients of this type of support. Many students with disabilities are proficient users of technology and might mentor a younger student in how to use a particular app. They might join a social media group for AAC users and be a role model for students who are emergent communicators. A student such as Selena might share her note-taking app with a classmate, or James could use his power wheelchair to pull friends around the roller skating rink.

❑　Create a map of the student's current circle of friends and relationships.

❑　Identify where significant gaps in the student's circle occur, and develop a plan for increasing the student's participation in shared activities with classmates or friends from community activities.

❑　Address the barriers to the student's development of reciprocal social relationships.

❑　Put into place all the essential considerations for friendship.

❑　Enlist the student's classmates in problem solving if friendships do not happen naturally.

❑　Identify a bridge builder as a strategy for getting the student more involved in social and extracurricular activities.

Figure 8.3.　Social relationships checklist.

CONCLUSIONS

This chapter focused on strategies for removing barriers to and facilitating friendships. It also examined the essential considerations for friendship and reviewed examples and case studies of these strategies and essential considerations in action in students' lives. Barbara McKenzie, a member of TASH and 30-year inclusive education advocate, wrote a book in memory of her daughter, Erin, who was fully included throughout her educational career. Her classmates contributed many memories of their friendship in *Reflections of Erin* (2006).

> Throughout elementary school we all experienced things together such as being "letter people." We all had a blast at the haunted gym and helped Erin master the monkey bars and swings. Everyone knew Erin and she was without a doubt "just one of the girls." (p. 52)
>
> In middle school, we all went through a change of environment. Erin was always there to pick up your spirits. She also joined the drama club with me and Kristin. (p. 53)
>
> I had the privilege of meeting Erin my freshman year when we both took choir, junior year I had history with Erin. I sat next to her and got to know her a lot better. I am thankful for her acceptance and her willingness to include me in the traditions that were already made. (pp. 53–54)

Being included did not guarantee that Erin would develop these deep and reciprocal friendships, but it was a necessary condition for her relationships to be much more than a "special friend." The checklist depicted in Figure 8.3 reflects the things that teams need to do and undo to create the conditions for reciprocal friendships to develop and sustain over time.

9

Develop Learning and Participation Plans and Assess Their Fidelity of Implementation

This chapter describes a collaborative team process for planning students' full participation in typical instructional routines in the general education classroom, and other inclusive activities throughout the school, for the purpose of learning general education academic content as well as meeting students' IEP goals and objectives (Jorgensen & Lambert, 2012). A process is also described for assessing the fidelity of implementation of planned supports (Jorgensen et al., 2010). The planning process brings together all of the core elements of inclusive education, including presuming students' competence, their valued membership in a general education class, full participation in general education instruction with supplementary aids and services, collaborative teaming, and opportunities for students with and without disabilities to learn together.

DETERMINE WHAT STUDENTS SHOULD BE LEARNING

With the right supports, all students have the potential to master standards aligned with the general education curriculum in the general education classroom, as well as achieve goals from other domains of learning that may be reflected in their IEPs. Some examples of these inclusive goals include the following (performance criteria not specified for the sake of brevity).

- Peter will demonstrate enduring understanding of three big ideas, five important people and events, and five vocabulary words within each social studies unit and make connections between the big ideas of the unit to his life.

- Nelson will increase his sight word vocabulary to the 1.5 grade level within the context of word study lessons in the second-grade classroom.

- Susan will demonstrate one-to-one correspondence by pointing to each word as she reads during buddy reading activities in the fourth-grade classroom.

- Anna will listen to an informational text passage and will participate in answering questions by activating a speech-generating AAC device when several possible right answers are provided.

- Peter will learn to set the table during culinary arts class by using a template to guide the placement of silverware, dishes, glassware, and napkin.

These goals reflect students who are already learning grade-level content, students who are learning lower than grade-level skills in order for them to master grade-level content, students who are emergent communicators but are not yet proficient at using their communication systems, and students whose teams have prioritized some functional skills for their educational program. The goals are written in a way that presumes participation in general education instruction, and students will be learning academic skills, not just so-called life skills.

RECOGNIZE FULL PARTICIPATION INDICATORS

Understanding the meaning of full participation is as easy as going into a school and observing where typical students spend their day and what they do. These indicators reflect the actions that students take to move through the classroom and school environment; participate in various instructional routines in the classroom, such as doing seat work, writing on the board, and talking in large and small groups; and interact with instructional materials. The indicators of full participation are depicted in Figure 9.1.

OVERVIEW: THE LEARNING AND PARTICIPATION PLANNING PROCESS

Certain guidelines should be followed for the learning and participation planning process to be successful. Planning for students' learning and participation must

- Be done by a collaborative team

- Be grounded in the general education curriculum learning standards or alternate standards aligned to general education standards

- Utilize the participation of typical students as a reference point for the participation of the student with complex support needs

☐ The student participates in classroom and school routines in typical locations (e.g., the Pledge of Allegiance, lunch count, jobs, errands, eating lunch in the cafeteria).

☐ The student participates in school plays, field trips, and community service activities.

☐ The student participates in classroom instruction in similar routines as students without disabilities, for example

• Whole class instruction

• Whole class discussion

• At the board

• Small-group discussion and projects

• By raising his or her hand and then being called on by the teacher

☐ The student has a way to communicate the same academic messages that are expected of other students in the previously mentioned instructional routines. For example

• Giving answers

• Asking questions

• Making comments

• Taking notes

• Writing

• Drawing figures

☐ The student completes assignments and other work products (with adaptations and modifications) as students without disabilities.

☐ A high school student engages in outside-of-school, age-appropriate, and inclusive activities (e.g., service learning) alongside and in natural proportion with classmates without disabilities.

☐ Students in the transition years (ages 18–21) attend postsecondary education, work, make connections to community activities and social groups, and learn to live away from their childhood home.

Figure 9.1.   General education participation indicators.

- Provide regular communication to families so that they can be involved in pre-teaching, reviewing for tests, and monitoring homework

- Occur frequently enough to keep pace with the changing curriculum

- Be done far enough ahead of time so that accessible instructional materials are available in a timely manner

- Include an assessment of the fidelity of implementation of planned supports

Teams representing elementary students with complex support needs should meet for at least 60 minutes a week to plan for the student's participation in the following week's lessons or meet for an extended period of time to plan for a future unit. Team member roles are described fully in Chapter 6. Adapting the planning process for middle and high school students is addressed later in this chapter. Teams should be able to answer four questions once they have completed learning and participation plans for each general education academic subject or class in which the student is enrolled.

1.   What should the student know and be able to do at the end of this week or unit?

2.   How will the student be assessed on whether he or she has achieved the identified learning objectives?

3.   What supports does the student need to fully participate in frequently occurring general education instructional routines taught by the general education teacher in the general education classroom?

4.   Which team member is responsible for preparing each support so they are ready when the student needs them?

Figure 9.2 depicts the learning and participation support plan template that teams use during their planning meetings. This blank form can be customized to fit individual student's needs. Completed plans for James, Anna, and Selena based on this template are included in the chapter appendix. Inclusion in a general education classroom means more than just being physically present. It means presuming students' competence, welcoming them as valued class members, and supporting their full participation in general education instruction based on the core curriculum, supported by effective collaborative teaming and administrative leadership.

Section 1: Weekly or Unit Learning Plan

Completing Section 1 of the form answers four questions.

1.   What should this student know and be able to do at the end of this week or unit?

Develop Learning and Participation Plans

Section 1: Weekly or Unit Learning Plan	
Student: _____	Subject: _____
Unit: _____	Week of: _____

Part A: Learning Objectives, Homework, and Assessment

Learning objectives from general education standards	Learning objectives for the focus student	Homework and assessments for typical students	Homework and assessments for focus student
Big ideas			
Knowledge			
Vocabulary			
Skills			

Part B. Daily Instructional Routines

Monday	Tuesday	Wednesday	Thursday	Friday
❐ Whole class instruction	❐ Whole class instruction	❐ Whole class instruction	❐ Whole class instruction	❐ Whole class instruction
❐ Whole class discussion	❐ Whole class discussion	❐ Whole class discussion	❐ Whole class discussion	❐ Whole class discussion
❐ Small-group discussion/ problem solving	❐ Small-group discussion/ problem solving	❐ Small-group discussion/ problem solving	❐ Small-group discussion/ problem solving	❐ Small-group discussion/ problem solving
❐ Individual seat work	❐ Individual seat work	❐ Individual seat work	❐ Individual seat work	❐ Individual seat work
❐ Presentation	❐ Presentation	❐ Presentation	❐ Presentation	❐ Lab experiment
❐ Lab experiment	❐ Lab experiment	❐ Lab experiment	❐ Lab experiment	❐ Reading
❐ Reading	❐ Reading	❐ Reading	❐ Reading	❐ Writing
❐ Writing	❐ Writing	❐ Writing	❐ Writing	❐ Math problem-solving
❐ Math problem-solving	❐ Math problem-solving	❐ Math problem-solving	❐ Math problem-solving	

Other Information about Daily Lessons

(continued)

Figure 9.2. Learning and participation planning form with fidelity of implementation scale. (Adapted with permission from Jorgensen, C.M., & Lambert, L. (2012). Inclusion means more than just being "in": Planning full participation of students with intellectual and other developmental disabilities in the general education classroom. *International Journal of Whole Schooling,* 8[2], 21–35.)

Figure 9.2.   *(continued)*

Part C. Vocabulary for Augmentative and Alternative Communication						
Target vocabulary words	Is it already on the device? Where is it?	Will student use this vocabulary for general communication after the unit?	What existing words can be used to describe the target vocabulary word? Can these words be used for other activities?	Should target word be programmed on to device? If yes, where should it go?	Sentence starters	Light tech format

Part D. Accessible Instructional Materials				
	Text	Worksheets	Tools/equipment/technology/software	Graphic organizers
Class/typical students				
Focus student				

Part E: CVI Supports	
❏ Color	❏ Light
❏ Movement	❏ Distance
❏ Latency	❏ Visual novelty
❏ Visual fields	❏ Visual motor
❏ Complexity	❏ Visual reflexes

Section 2: Participation Support Plan for _____ Routine				
Student: _____		Subject: _____		
What are typical students doing to participate in this routine?	Supports for the student's participation in the instructional routine			
	Communication supports	Peer supports	Assistive technology	Sensory supports

2. How will he or she be assessed?

3. What instructional routines will be used by the teacher during the following week or unit?

4. What materials, technology and communication supports, and vision adaptations will need to be provided to support his or her full participation and learning?

Section 2: Routines-Based Participation Plan

Completing Section 2 of the form answers the question: What supports does the student need to fully participate in frequently occurring general education instructional routines taught by the general education teacher in the general education classroom?

This form needs to be completed for each recurring instructional routine that the student's teacher uses, such as whole class discussion, whole class lecture with notetaking, and so forth. General education teachers describe what participation in each routine looks like for the typical students on this part of the form. This information goes in column 1 and is the reference point for what the focus student's participation should look like. Then the rest of the columns in Section 2 represent the supports the student needs to fully participate and learn in that routine. Customize the columns for the most important supports your student needs.

Assessing Fidelity of Implementation of Supports

The team uses the following scale to assess the fidelity of implementation of their planned supports at the end of the week or the time period for which learning and participation plans were developed.

1 = Supports provided accurately and consistently 75% to virtually 100% of the time

2 = Supports provided accurately and consistently 50%–75% of the time

3 = Supports provided accurately and consistently 25%–50% of the time

4 = Supports provided accurately and consistently less than 25% of the time

Rate each planned support by entering the appropriate number next to the support on the form, such as, "Position the AAC device no more than 25% to the left or right of midline and between the student's eyes and chin."

FOLLOW STEPS TO COMPLETE THE LEARNING AND PARTICIPATION PLAN

A few preplanning steps are necessary to use this planning process effectively and efficiently. First, team members need to have a good understanding of their roles in supporting a student's inclusion. The team should edit the roles and responsibilities descriptions presented in Figure 6.1 and use the new document as a guide for collaborative planning, instruction, and assessment. Second, the team needs to establish a common planning time. Third, team members should read this chapter to understand how the process works. Fourth, the team should edit the form to reflect their student's unique learning and support needs. Fifth, the team should establish a way to share the completed forms with one another, such as Google Drive, a secure folder in the school's intranet, or via secure e-mail.

Section 1: Weekly or Unit Learning Plan

Section 1 of the form is the backbone of the learning and participation plan. The team completes this section for each subject or class in which the student is enrolled. Planning can be done for a week of instruction or for a unit.

Step 1   The general education teacher should complete the following parts of Section 1 of the form prior to the team meeting.

- Part A: Columns 1 and 3 that describe the learning objectives for the class and the assessments that they will complete

- Part B: The instructional routines that will be used each day of the week in that subject

- Part D: The instructional materials, tools, and equipment that will be used by the teacher and by typical students

It will be difficult to accomplish the goals of planning if the general education teacher has not filled in these sections prior to the meeting because the bulk of the planning meeting will be used to get this information rather than for planning supports for participation.

Step 2   Identify who will type notes into the form. Open the form to the version that has been partially completed by the general education teacher. If the team uses Google Drive, then all team members can view the planning form as they are completing it during or outside of the meeting. Another option is for the notetaker to project the form on to a screen via an LCD projector or SMART board.

Step 3   Fill in the top portion of the form including the student's name, subject area, unit (if appropriate), and the dates for which the team is planning.

Part A: Learning Objectives and Assessments

Part A identifies the individualized learning objectives of the focus student and how his or her learning will be assessed. It consists of two steps.

Step 4   Determine what the focus student's learning objectives will be in this subject for the week. Enter these in column 2. These learning objectives should reflect learning objectives from the general education curriculum and may reflect annual goals or objectives from the student's IEP. If the student is participating in the state's general assessment (with or without accommodations) and striving to get credit that will count toward receipt of a regular high school diploma, then his or her learning objectives should be the same as those of the other students in the class. If the student participates in the state's alternate assessment or is not trying to get a regular high school diploma, then these learning objectives can be modified or taken from the state's alternate achievement standards.

Step 5 Describe how the student's achievement toward his or her learning objectives will be evaluated and what homework he or she will be assigned. Enter this information in column 4 along with the initials of the team member responsible for making homework and assessment adaptations.

Part B: Instructional Routines

Part B of the form describes what instructional routines the teacher will use. It consists of one step.

Step 6 Put a check mark next to the instructional routines that will be used by the teacher each day of the week in the next part of Section 1. Knowing what instructional routines will be used will help the team determine what routines need to be planned. It may be helpful for the general education teacher to provide additional information about each day's lessons during the meeting. These details should be typed into the form just below Part B.

Part C: Vocabulary for Augmentative and Alternative Communication

If the student has AAC needs, then Part C of the form guides the team to make decisions about how best to provide the student with vocabulary for communication during the following week's lessons or during the unit. If the student does not have AAC needs, the team can simply delete this section of the form for this student or leave it blank.

Step 7 Put the initials of the team member responsible for programming the AAC device or creating light-tech communication materials next to each entry.

Part D: Accessible Instructional Materials

For Part D the team identifies the accessible instructional materials needed by the student and who will prepare them. This part consists of one step.

Step 8 Virtually all students with complex support needs need to have the regular classroom materials made accessible through individualized adaptations. Most IEP forms have a box that says, in effect, "The student needs accessible instructional materials," and/or "The student needs assistive technology." Based on the information that the general education teacher has provided about what instructional materials will be used with the class (row 1), specify the adaptations that will be made to ensure accessibility for the focus student (row 2). Put the initials of the team member responsible for finding or creating these accessible materials next to each entry.

Part E: Cortical Visual Impairment Supports

The support needs by students with CVI are more extensive than those needed by students with other vision-related disabilities and Part E of the form describes how each CVI characteristic will be addressed.

Step 9   Under the leadership of the teacher of the visually impaired (TVI), record the supports needed by the student in each CVI characteristic area with the initial of the team member responsible.

Section 2: Participation Support Plan for Routines

Instructional routines are defined by the configurations of the students, teaching practices of the teacher, and behaviors of the students that show they are engaged in learning. Common routines in core academic classes include

- Teacher-led whole class instruction

- Teacher-led whole class discussion

- Students working in small groups on a common task

- Students having small-group discussions

- Students working independently at their desks

- Laboratory experiments

- Student presentations of their work

Other routines common in physical education, the arts, and electives include

- Team-based games and sports—throwing, catching, hitting balls

- Individual games and sports—running, swimming, hitting balls

- Warm-up activities—running laps, doing calisthenics

- Cooking—cutting, measuring ingredients, stirring

- Making art—drawing, painting, sculpting

- Singing and acting

- Planting

The benefit of creating support plans for the most common routines in which the focus student is engaged is that the support plan will serve the student for the entire year as long as the routine remains relatively the same (Jorgensen et al., 2010). For example, if students in kindergarten participate in calendar time every day, then the supports for the focus student's engagement will be virtually the same whether the calendar activity is done in September or June. If students write on a computer every day, then the supports for the student's writing will be the same. The only things that might change in a participation plan over time is the specific vocabulary the student will use or the adapted materials that need to be made. Planning for routines will save time for the team so that they do not have to start from scratch each week.

Managing the Planning Process

The student's special education teacher or inclusion facilitator should begin the process of completing the relevant instructional routines participation plans and then gather input from other team members by using part of the team's weekly planning meeting time or having the SLP, OT, PT, or other team members add to a Google Drive document. The first step for each routine is to ask the general education teacher (or observe in the classroom) to identify the behaviors of the students that indicate they are fully engaged in the routine. Teams can customize the plan once they have determined the routines in which the.focus student will be engaged.

Follow these steps to complete an instructional routine participation plan.

- Step 1: Enter the name of the routine in the heading of the form, the student's name, and subject area (if it is a subject-specific routine such as cooking or science). Many routines are common to all subject areas, which is one benefit of developing routines-based participation plans.

- Step 2: Use brief bullet points in column 1 to enter what students without disabilities do to participate in the instructional routine. Do not describe what the teacher is doing as he or she teaches, but rather what an observer might see students doing to indicate they are fully engaged in instruction.

- Step 3: Enter into the relevant columns the supports that the focus student needs to participate in a way that is commensurate with the participation of his or her classmates without disabilities. These supports columns should be customized to meet the student's priority support needs. For example, some students do not need sensory supports, but they may need physical supports.

These supports should be the same as those found in the section on supplementary aids and services or accommodations and modifications on the student's IEP. Sometimes teams discover additional items to add to those sections of the student's IEP as they complete a few routines participation forms. They can add those items by either writing an amendment or during the next meeting to renew the IEP.

ASSESS THE FIDELITY OF IMPLEMENTATION OF SUPPORTS

At the conclusion of every week or at the end of a longer unit, assess the fidelity (i.e., the accuracy and consistency) of implementation of supports that the team planned for the student (Jorgensen et al., 2010). Fidelity consists of two parts: accuracy, defined as providing the support in the way that it was intended, according to best practices in that particular domain of educational pedagogy; and consistency, defined as the support being provided in all the relevant activities in which it is needed by every team member who interacts with the student. Use the 1–4 rating codes explained on the planning form in Figure 9.2. If teams find that their fidelity ratings are consistently less than a 4, then they need to determine if extra professional development, cotreatment by two providers, or team coaching is necessary. The fidelity with which supports are provided is directly related to the quality of student performance and learning. Students will only do as well as the adults who teach and support them.

HOW TO USE THE PLANNING PROCESS IN MIDDLE AND HIGH SCHOOL

Students who are included in middle and high school may have many general education teachers, and the team planning process may be different than it is with one general education teacher on the elementary school IEP team. It is most efficient for the special education teacher or inclusion facilitator to schedule short weekly meetings with each general education teacher to gather the information needed to complete Section 1 of the form. Together they can identify the student's priority learning objectives for each subject for the following week or unit, discuss how assessments might be adapted or modified, and describe the instructional routines that will be used. That information is then used during a weekly 60-minute team meeting attended by the special educator or inclusion facilitator, paraeducator, SLP, OT, PT, or others who represent special education and related services on the student's IEP team. They discuss and complete the rest of Section 1 and review the routines-based participation plans that have already been drafted. They revise the participation plans to reflect any changes in the supports that the student needs during the following week or unit.

After both Sections 1 and 2 are complete, the forms are shared with all the student's general education teachers and other team members who may not have attended the planning meeting. Make sure to include students' families in the dissemination loop as well. Sample plans for James's, Anna's, and Selena's learning and participation are included in the chapter appendix. Refer to the checklist in Figure 9.3 as a quick reference guide for developing inclusive learning and participation plans for students.

☐ Make sure that the student's IEP follows the guidelines in Chapter 4 for writing an inclusive standards-based plan.

☐ Complete the membership checklist in Figure 7.1 and take steps to ensure that the student is a welcome member of a general education class.

☐ Complete the participation checklist in Figure 9.1 to identify instructional routines and classes in which the student is participating the least actively.

☐ Prioritize those routines and classes for the development of participation plans.

☐ Establish weekly common planning time for the team to develop participation plans.

☐ Complete Section 2 of the participation planning form for all the most commonly occurring instructional routines.

☐ Complete Section 1 of the form on a weekly basis or for each unit to identify the student's learning objectives, assessment, and support needs.

☐ Share participation plans with all team members.

☐ Refine the participation plans as the year progresses to reflect new supports and strategies that have been found useful for the student.

☐ Check the fidelity of implementation of supports on at least a monthly basis.

Figure 9.3. Checklist for developing inclusive learning and participation plans.

CONCLUSIONS

Creating learning and participation plans for students with complex support needs is the bridge between the student's IEP and his or her learning in the classroom. These plans serve as a good source of information that shows the team is following the student's IEP. Finally, they are an effective way to ensure that all team members, including the student's parents, are involved in supporting accessible learning opportunities for the student.

9.1

Appendix: Sample Learning and Participation Plans

Section 1: Weekly or Unit Learning Plan	
Student: James	**Subject:** Math
Unit: Numbers and operations: Using place value to add and subtract	**Week of:** September 15

Part A: Learning Objectives, Homework, and Assessment			
Learning Objectives from General Education Standards	**Learning Objectives for the Focus Student**	**Homework & Assessments for Typical Students**	**Homework & Assessments for Focus Student**
Vocabulary: Operations Unknown Estimate Rounding	Vocabulary: Add More Subtract Less Equals Unknown	Twenty multiplication facts and three word problems per night End-of-week test: five word problems; written explanation of how student used mental computations and estimation to test for reasonableness of answer	Five addition and five subtraction problems per night One word problem using addition End-of-week test: five addition and five subtraction problems; one word problem using addition
Knowledge:	Knowledge:		
Skills: Solve two-step word problems using the four operations. Represent these problems using equations with a letter standing for the unknown quantity. Assess the reasonableness of answers using mental computation and estimation strategies, including rounding.	Skills: Solve one-step real-world problems using addition or subtraction within 20.		

Part B. Daily Instructional Routines				
Monday	**Tuesday**	**Wednesday**	**Thursday**	**Friday**
☑ Whole class instruction	☑ Whole class instruction	☐ Whole class instruction	☑ Whole class instruction	☑ Whole class instruction
☑ Whole class discussion	☑ Whole class discussion	☑ Whole class discussion	☑ Whole class discussion	☐ Whole class discussion
☑ Small group discussion/ problem solving	☑ Small group discussion/ problem solving	☑ Small group discussion/ problem solving	☐ Small group discussion/ problem solving	☐ Small group discussion/ problem solving
☑ Individual seatwork	☑ Individual seatwork	☐ Individual seatwork	☑ Individual seatwork	☐ Individual seatwork
☐ Presentation	☐ Presentation	☐ Presentation	☐ Presentation	☐ Presentation
☐ Lab experiment	☐ Lab experiment	☐ Lab experiment	☐ Lab experiment	☐ Lab experiment
☐ Reading	☐ Reading	☐ Reading	☐ Reading	☐ Reading
☐ Writing	☐ Writing	☐ Writing	☐ Writing	☐ Writing
☑ Math problem-solving	☑ Math problem-solving	☑ Math problem-solving	☑ Math problem-solving	☐ Math problem-solving
				☑ Test

Other Information about Daily Lessons				
Monday	**Tuesday**	**Wednesday**	**Thursday**	**Friday**
Introduce unit Guided practice with whole class Individual practice at seat	Guided practice with whole class Math stations	Cooperative group activities	Individual practice Test prep game	Test Discussion of incorrect and correct answers

Part C. Vocabulary for Augmentative Communication						
Target vocabulary words	Is it already on the device? Where is it?	Will student use this vocabulary for general communication after the unit?	What existing words can be used to describe the target vocabulary word? Can these words be used for other activities?	Should target word be programmed on to device? If yes, where should it go?	Sentence starters?	Light tech format?
Add More Subtract Less Equals Unknown	All are on the math page sets	Yes	n/a	n/a	The operation I need to use is . . .	n/a

Part D. Accessible Instructional Materials				
	Text	Worksheets	Tools/Equipment/ Technology/Software	Graphic Organizers
Class/Typical Students	Chapter 4 in math book	Math problems	Pencils	n/a
Focus Student	Digital version text to speech on iPad	Scan into GoWorksheet and adapt to reflect addition and subtraction problems only	Unifix cubes AAC device	Math schema for solving word problem using addition and subtraction

(page 3 of 5)

Part E: CVI Supports	
1. Color	Use neon Unifix cubes against black background on felt board.
2. Movement	Use movement of teacher's hand or pointing wand to get visual attention.
3. Latency	Allow wait time between presentation of materials and expected attention and response.
4. Visual fields	Present material no more than 45 degrees from midline on a plane from his eyes to his chin but not higher or lower.
5. Complexity	Remove extraneous objects from James's desk except for black felt board and AAC device. All numbers and operations must be no less than 1-inch tall, written in black, and outlined in red.
6. Light	Use lighted wand to draw James's attention to the Unifix cubes against the black felt board.
7. Distance	Ensure that all math materials are within 12 inches of James's face.
8. Visual novelty	Subtraction sign is new to James, so it must be explicitly taught.
9. Visual motor	Provide hand-under-hand support when James is reaching for the Unifix cubes or his AAC device within his visual field.

(page 4 of 5)

Section 2: Participation Support Plan for Whole Class Instruction				
Student: James			**Subject:** Math	
What are Typical Students Doing to Participate in this Routine?	**Supports for the Student's Participation in Whole Class Instruction**			
	Communication Supports	**Vision Supports**	**Assistive Technology**	**Physical Supports**
Sitting in seats Looking at SmartBoard Writing on note-taking forms Asking questions Making comments	Model using AAC device Ten seconds of wait time before expecting response Teacher asks James an individualized question Teacher asks James, "Do you have a question or comment?" twice during lesson	Dim classroom lights while teacher is writing on SmartBoard iPad background is yellow All numbers and operations signs are at least 1-inch tall, written in black, and outlined in red	SmartBoard is mirrored to James's iPad GoWorksheet adapted note-taking form BigKeys to enter numbers into worksheet	Prone stander for 20 minutes Hand-under-hand support from adult for gaining access to AAC device and BigKeys

Section 1: Weekly or Unit Learning Plan	
Student: Anna	**Subject:** English language arts
Unit: Writing informative essay	**Week of:** September 15

Part A: Learning Objectives, Homework, and Assessment			
Learning Objectives from General Education Standards	**Learning Objectives for the Focus Student**	**Homework & Assessments for Typical Students**	**Homework & Assessments for Focus Student**
Vocabulary: Informative text Explanatory text Rubric	Vocabulary: Informative text Explanatory text Rubric	Read examples of informative essays and critique according to rubric Work on sections of essay Final essay with self-assessment using rubric	Read examples of informative essays and critique according to rubric Work on sections of essay Final essay with self-assessment using rubric
Knowledge: Informative/explanatory essays do not contain personal opinion Informative/explanatory essays are informed by research	Knowledge: Informative/explanatory essays do not contain personal opinion Informative/explanatory essays are informed by research		
Skills: Write informative/ explanatory texts to examine a topic and convey ideas, concepts, and information through the selection, organization, and analysis of relevant content.	Skills: Write informative/ explanatory texts to examine a topic and convey ideas, concepts, and information through the selection, organization, and analysis of relevant content.		

(page 1 of 4)

Part B. Daily Instructional Routines				
Monday	**Tuesday**	**Wednesday**	**Thursday**	**Friday**
☑ Whole class instruction	☑ Whole class instruction	☑ Whole class instruction	☑ Whole class instruction	☑ Whole class instruction
☑ Whole class discussion	☐ Whole class discussion	☐ Whole class discussion	☐ Whole class discussion	☐ Whole class discussion
☐ Small group discussion/ problem solving	☐ Small group discussion/ problem solving	☐ Small group discussion/ problem solving	☐ Small group discussion/ problem solving	☑ Small group discussion/ problem solving
☐ Individual seatwork	☑ Individual seatwork	☑ Individual seatwork	☐ Individual seatwork	☐ Individual seatwork
☐ Presentation	☐ Presentation	☐ Presentation	☐ Presentation	☑ Presentation
☐ Lab experiment	☐ Lab experiment	☐ Lab experiment	☐ Lab experiment	☐ Lab experiment
☑ Reading	☑ Reading	☑ Reading	☑ Reading	☐ Reading
☑ Writing	☑ Writing	☑ Writing	☑ Writing	☑ Writing
☐ Math problem-solving	☐ Math problem-solving	☐ Math problem-solving	☐ Math problem-solving	☐ Math problem-solving
				☐ Test

Other Information about Daily Lessons				
Monday	**Tuesday**	**Wednesday**	**Thursday**	**Friday**
Introduce unit Read example of informative essay Discuss rubric	Guided practice with whole class Write introduction of essay	Write paragraphs two and three	Write conclusion	Share essay with classmate and critique using rubric

Part C. Vocabulary for Augmentative Communication						
Target vocabulary words	Is it already on the device? Where is it?	Will student use this vocabulary for general communication after the unit?	What existing words can be used to describe the target vocabulary word? Can these words be used for other activities?	Should target word be programmed on to device? If yes, where should it go?	Sentence starters?	Light tech format?
Informative Explanatory Rubric	n/a	Yes	n/a	n/a	n/a	n/a

Part D. Accessible Instructional Materials[a]					
		Text	Worksheets	Tools/Equipment/ Technology/Software	Graphic Organizers
Class/Typical Students		Examples of informative essays		Pencils, pens, Chromebooks	Essay evaluation rubric
Focus Student		Digital version text to speech on iPad		AAC device Read & Write Gold on laptop	Same

[a]Because Anna does not have CVI needs, that part of the standard planning form is not used.

Section 2: Participation Support Plan for Writing Informative Essay				
Student: Anna		**Subject:** English language arts/writing		
What are Typical Students Doing to Participate in this Routine?	**Supports for the Student's Participation in ELA essay writing**			
	Communication Supports	**Peer Supports**	**Assistive Technology**	**Sensory Supports**
Sit in seats Listen to teacher during whole class instruction Write on paper or type using Chromebook Listen to classmate read essay Read own essay to classmate Make comments on classmate's essay	Use TouchChat on iPad for communication Encourage Anna through positive feedback Assist Anna to use combination of preprogrammed social vocabulary and letter-by-letter generative writing Provide hand-under-hand support to bring Anna's hand back to midline after selection	Peers provide verbal encouragement Peer and Anna take turns reading and making comments on their essays	Use Read&Write for writing essay Activate text to speech for Anna to read her essay to classmate	Provide movement break every 15 minutes Provide choice of fidget tools Give deep pressure on shoulders during breaks Do not require eye contact during lecture

Section 1: Weekly or Unit Learning Plan	
Student: Selena	**Subject:** Biology
Unit: Conducting exercise and the heart lab experiment	**Week of:** September 15

Part A: Learning Objectives, Homework, and Assessment			
Learning Objectives from General Education Standards	**Learning Objectives for the Focus Student**	**Homework & Assessments for Typical Students**	**Homework & Assessments for Focus Student**
Vocabulary: Feedback Organ systems Homeostasis	Vocabulary: Organ Heart Blood vessels Heart rate Blood pressure Homeostasis	Read Chapter 10 in biology text Watch Kahn Academy lesson on homeostasis Write lab report Present an oral lab report Complete end-of-week test	Read Attainment Company modified text on structure and function of the heart Watch BrainPop video on how the heart and lungs work Oral and video lab report presentation using Explain Everything End-of-week test on vocabulary and diagram of blood flow through heart and lungs
Knowledge: Feedback mechanisms between organ systems regulate the actions of other organ systems	Knowledge: Exercise results in changes to heart rate and blood pressure		
Skills: Plan and conduct an investigation to provide evidence that feedback mechanisms maintain homeostasis.	Skills: Collect data from an investigation to show how different organisms react to changes.		

(page 1 of 3)

Part B. Daily Instructional Routines

Monday	Tuesday	Wednesday	Thursday	Friday
☑ Whole class instruction	☑ Whole class instruction	☐ Whole class instruction	☐ Whole class instruction	☐ Whole class instruction
☐ Whole class discussion	☐ Whole class discussion	☐ Whole class discussion	☐ Whole class discussion	☐ Whole class discussion
☐ Small group discussion/ problem solving	☑ Small group discussion/ problem solving	☐ Small group discussion/ problem solving	☐ Small group discussion/ problem solving	☐ Small group discussion/ problem solving
☐ Individual seatwork	☐ Individual seatwork	☐ Individual seatwork	☐ Individual seatwork	☐ Individual seatwork
☐ Presentation	☐ Presentation	☐ Presentation	☐ Presentation	☑ Presentation
☐ Lab experiment	☑ Lab experiment	☑ Lab experiment	☐ Lab experiment	☐ Lab experiment
☐ Reading	☐ Reading	☐ Reading	☐ Reading	☐ Reading
☑ Writing	☐ Writing	☑ Writing	☑ Writing	☐ Writing
☐ Math problem-solving	☐ Math problem-solving	☐ Math problem-solving	☐ Math problem-solving	☐ Math problem-solving
				☑ Test

Other Information about Daily Lessons

Monday	Tuesday	Wednesday	Thursday	Friday
Introduce unit Lecture with notetaking	Lecture with notetaking Demonstration of exercise and effects on heart rate and blood pressure	Lab experiment with notetaking and plotting of experiment data	Write lab report	Present lab report to members of the other lab group Test on the heart and exercise

(page 2 of 3)

Part C. Accessible Instructional Materials[b]

	Text	Worksheets	Tools/Equipment/ Technology/Software	Graphic Organizers
Class/Typical Students	Chapter 10 in biology text	Study guide for tests	Lab equipment Kahn Academy video	Lab report template
Focus Student	Attainment Company text on structure and function of the heart	Adapted study guide with picture and graphic supports	Same lab equipment BrainPop video	Explain Everything for lab report with pictures and video

Section 2: Participation Support Plan for Biology Lab

Student: Selena | **Subject:** Biology

What are Typical Students Doing to Participate in this Routine?	Supports for the Student's Participation in Biology class and lab experiment			
	Communication Supports	**Peer Supports**	**Assistive Technology**	
Sit in seats Listen to teacher during whole class instruction Write on paper or type using Chromebook Walk on treadmill Write on data collection form Write lab report using template Present lab report orally	Encourage Selena to speak slowly and clearly	Peers provide verbal encouragement Peer reads lab experiment instructions to Selena and other members of group	iPad to take photographs and video during lab experiment Explain Everything for lab report	

[b]Because Selena does not have augmentative communication or CVI needs, those parts of the standard planning form are not used.

(page 3 of 3)

10

Plan and Prepare
for an Inclusive Life After High School

High school students in towns and cities across the United States are thinking, dreaming, and worrying about their futures. They are pondering their options regarding college, discussing their career choices, and hoping for futures of financial independence and personal satisfaction. Students are preparing for the future by choosing the necessary coursework, pursuing extracurricular interests, making connections with classmates, working at after-school jobs, and making contacts with school and community members. All high schools have a variety of systematic processes to help students plan and prepare for their lives after high school. They help students identify their interests and strengths, help them develop a portfolio of their best work and a high-quality résumé, and counsel them on postsecondary education, employment, or military enlistment options.

A distinct division remains in many schools about the ways in which students with and without disabilities are supported to both dream about and plan their futures. High school students with disabilities often miss out on typical future planning activities because they are often separated from their classmates during the school day (e.g., taking special education classes, engaging in separate, community-based instruction). Although students with disabilities are required by IDEA 2004 to have individualized transition plans (ITPs), these plans are often disconnected from the typical graduation planning activities in the school.

This chapter describes several options for students with complex support needs after their senior year of high school. Each option can be pursued exclusively or in combination with others. Students with complex support needs might continue to work on getting a regular high school diploma, take some college classes, work full or part time, do volunteer work, travel, move out of one's childhood home, become active in one's community, and so forth. Whichever path a student takes should be guided by an individualized personal futures plan.

RATIONALE: THE PROBLEM WITH TRADITIONAL TRANSITION

The traditional view of transition for students with disabilities poses several problems (Tashie, Malloy, & Lichtenstein, 1998). Why is the process of leaving high school and going on to adult life called *transition* rather than *graduation* when considering students with disabilities? It is almost as if special education was created with the expectation that students would not actually graduate but just age-out of their educational entitlement to a FAPE and go immediately into the developmental service system. This assumption and the practices that result from it are based on the reality that many high school students with disabilities are not included in the typical school experience (i.e., participation in general education classes, extracurricular activities, and graduation planning that can assist them in the development of their future goals). Many students with more significant disabilities progress through their school careers spending less time in the school building with their peers and more time in the community. This not only prevents students with disabilities from taking a full schedule of general education classes, but it also isolates them from the very peer group by which they need to be accepted to be successful in school and as they enter into the world of adulthood. It also serves to remove students from the valuable learning opportunities that occur for all students in these general education classes and activities (e.g., academic, life skills, and social) (Tashie & Schuh, 1993).

Traditional transition plans often describe a need for students with complex support needs to engage in community-based instruction outside of the school building, in congregate groups of other students with complex support needs. Shopping in a grocery store, eating at a fast-food restaurant, and part-time employment are common events in a teenager's life. Unfortunately, teenagers with disabilities are often doing these things when their peers are involved with English, math, or history. Community-based instruction serves to accentuate the differences rather than the similarities among students because it removes students with disabilities from their peers.

The idea of community-based instruction arose in the 1970s and early 1980s when students with complex support needs did not have opportunities to take general education classes; learning community-living skills was an improvement over the contrived life skills learning environments that were created within the school building (Brown et al., 1976). Life skills classes during those years included pretend grocery stores set up in storage rooms and simulated apartments created in separate special education classrooms.

Learning those skills in artificial environments does not translate to performing them in natural environments, and the postschool outcomes for students in life skills programs are worse than the outcomes of students who have been included in general education classes. This fact bears repeating: the postschool outcomes of students with disabilities—regardless of their disability label or the judged severity of their disability—is positively correlated with the amount of time they spend in general education classes (White & Weiner, 2004).

The traditional transition process perpetuates the notion that paid professionals are the only ones who can support students in school, at home, in the community, or on the job. Many professionals see transition as something that happens to students with disabilities to help them move from special education into the world of categorical adult services. If there are entrenched school and community traditions of segregation, then this can mean moving from a self-contained life skills class to sheltered work, "day-wasting" programs (Ringer & Lovett, 1987), or a waiting list for services.

The traditional view of transition is too often grounded in low expectations for students' futures. Rarely are students with complex support needs counseled to consider college as a postsecondary option. Rather than capitalizing on students' interests and strengths, traditional transition planning too often shuttles students with complex support needs into a limited number of work options, such as "The Four F's:" flowers (horticulture), filth (cleaning), folding (laundry), and food (prep work in a fast-food outlet kitchen or nursing home).

Although the intent of transition is a positive one—to prevent young adults from sitting at home doing nothing after they leave school—the practices are often segregating and not effective. The following changes must occur to move beyond separate planning processes for students with and without disabilities.

- Full inclusion of all students in the typical school community
- Changes in the roles of professionals and paraprofessionals
- Adoption of the typical educational timetable
- Graduation as an outcome for all students
- Postsecondary education as an option for all students
- Individualizing supports beyond graduation with a preference for natural supports

PLAN AN INCLUSIVE TRANSITION PROCESS

An inclusive transition process is focused on the goals and wishes of the students. Following is an example of the advanced planning involved and how an inclusive transition process works.

SELENA

Selena is 16 years old and will enter her junior year in the fall. Her family worked with the school when Selena was younger to use the MAPS process (Pearpoint et al., 1996) (described in Chapter 2) to design her inclusive educational experience. Selena and her family used a personal futures planning process immediately after her eighth-grade year and again in 10th grade to think about and plan what she wants to do after her senior year. She knows that she wants to go on to postsecondary education. Selena wants to work part time while she is in college and prepare to move out of her childhood home once she gets out of college and has a steady job. She hopes to get married someday and have children. Selena will continue her enrollment in general education classes, have a job every summer, and be a member of extracurricular clubs and sports to reach those goals. She will visit several college campuses that are recognized as comprehensive transition programs for students with intellectual disability and send in her applications during her junior year (Grigal & Hart, 2012). Selena will take part in all senior year graduation rites and ceremonies and then go on to postsecondary education the following fall.

Person-Centered Planning

How did Selena move from having dreams to a concrete plan for achieving them?

Selena, with the help of her guidance counselor and parents, invited a small group of people to meet several times at her house to develop a person-centered plan for her life after high school. Many models for person-centered planning are applicable to high school students. Selena and her family adapted their process from the work of Mount and Zwernik (1994), and it is briefly summarized next.

Step 1: Choose a Facilitator   Selena's family found a facilitator trained in person-centered planning through their state's Down syndrome association. They interviewed three people and chose a young woman who spoke Spanish and English, was a good listener, had a commitment to work creatively to shape Selena's dreams into realities, was committed to discovering the capacities within Selena and her community, and had a history of successful planning and community building for individuals with significant support needs.

Step 2: Design the Planning Process   At an initial meeting with Selena and her family, the facilitator described the goals of the planning process and how it would unfold over the course of two initial meetings and beyond. They developed an invitation list that included Selena's siblings, grandparents, extended family, parish priest, her developmental service agency family support liaison, five high school friends, two church friends, her computer science teacher, and her special education case manager. They identified two meeting days and times, decided to hold the meetings in a community meeting room at their church, and sent out invitations.

Step 3: Hold the First Meeting   The participants learned about the personal futures planning process during the first meeting and made a commitment to attend both meetings and support Selena over the course of the next several years to reach her dreams and goals. Selena, her family, and the facilitator completed some advanced work, and Selena read a short description of her strengths, interests, and future goals. The facilitator encouraged people in the group to ask Selena follow-up questions, and Selena became more comfortable in her role as the person in charge of her future as the meeting progressed. No one made comments such as, "Well, Selena, I am not sure that you have the grades to go to college" or "We know you like to play computer games, but that is not a way to make a living." The group was committed to figuring out ways to make Selena's dream job of working in the tourism or computer industry a reality.

For each of the main parts of Selena's dream life—going to college, living on her own, getting a job, and getting married—the group brainstormed ideas about 1) what experiences Selena would need to have during her last years in high school to get closer to her dreams, 2) what obstacles might stand in her way, 3) strategies for overcoming those obstacles, and 4) who she needed to sustain or make new connections with in order to further her plans.

Step 4: Hold a Second Meeting to Design Action Steps, People Responsible, and Time Lines   The best futures plan will fail without a concrete plan of action. Selena and her team developed a 5-year time line for implementation of her plan during the second group meeting, with the most detail given to her last 2 years in high school. They recognized that they would have to update the plan annually—particularly as Selena decided whether working in tourism or with computers was her immediate goal—so that each year's action steps reflected any change in Selena's wishes or in the opportunities and resources available to her and her family.

Step 5: Follow the Plan   Following the plan requires that key people on Selena's team follow through on their commitment to support her and her choices. Although they know there will be challenges to overcome, they are confident that Selena will be able to reach her goals. They keep their commitment to meet as part of Selena's support team and invite others into the circle as they get to know Selena through other shared experiences.

They make sure to celebrate both the small and big successes along the way. Strategies and resources related to each major aspect of Selena's plan are described next.

TRANSITION SERVICES ON THE IEP

Some requirements of transition goals and services to be reflected on the IEP were enacted in IDEA 2004. Check special education law and regulations in the student's specific state to see if there are additional regulations that apply to him or her. The requirements include

- Beginning no later than the first IEP to be in effect when the student turns 16, or younger if determined appropriate by the IEP team, and updated annually thereafter, the IEP must include

  o Appropriate measurable postsecondary goals based on age-appropriate transition assessments related to training, education, employment and, where appropriate, independent living skills

  o The transition services (including courses of study) needed to assist the student in reaching those goals

- Beginning no later than 1 year before the student reaches the age of majority under state law, a statement that the student has been informed of the his or her rights under Part B, if any, that will transfer to the student on reaching the age of majority.

- The school must invite a student with a disability to attend the student's IEP team meeting if a purpose of the meeting will be the consideration of postsecondary goals for the student and the transition services needed to assist the student in reaching those goals.

Measureable transition goals might be written the following way.

- Upon completion of high school, Selena will enroll in at least two courses at Ocean County Community College through the comprehensive transition program.

- Selena will work approximately 10 hours a week in an on-campus part-time job while in college.

- Upon completion of high school, Selena will learn to use public transportation, including the public bus and uptown trolley.

By definition, transition services can include instruction, related services, community experiences, the development of employment and other post-school adult living objectives, acquisition of daily living skills, and a functional vocational evaluation. Appropriate transition services related to Selena's transition goals might include instruction in reading, math, word processing, budgeting, and hygiene; teaching self-monitoring, goal-setting, and problem-solving skills; and instruction in community travel and safety skills. The key to making these transition services inclusive is to identify opportunities to teach those skills alongside students without disabilities within the regular school day, within Selena's participation in extracurricular activities, and while she is working at a summer job alongside classmates and adults without disabilities.

Additional resources related to the transition requirements of IDEA 2004, including sample transition plans and templates, are available from the National Center on Secondary Education and Transition at the University of Minnesota and from many state departments of education web sites.

PREPARE FOR GRADUATION AND A SUCCESSFUL TRANSITION

Selena's personal futures plan laid out several steps she and her family will need to take in order to accomplish her goals. Strategies and resources related to the successful implementation of these steps are presented next. A graduation planning checklist summarizing these steps is depicted in Figure 10.1.

Enroll in General Education Courses

Selena will continue to take general education classes during her final 2 years of high school even though she is not on track to receive a regular high school diploma. Her learning goals in these classes are consistent with her state's alternate achievement standards that are closely aligned with the state's general learning standards. She receives grades in each of her classes based on modified performance expectations. Junior and senior year she will enroll in advisory, English, French, math, science, history, computer technology, wellness, art, and band.

Participate in Inclusive Extracurricular Activities

Inclusive extracurricular activities are just as important as Selena's academic classes. She has been in French Club and the Spirit Club since ninth grade and will join the Computer Tech Club her junior and senior year, based on the results of her personal futures planning meeting. Selena does not need specialized supports to participate in these extracurricular activities. If she did, however, then her school would be required to provide those supports (including staff, transportation, AT, or others, depending on her individualized needs).

Enhance Self-Determination Skills

Decisions about which classes to choose, which interests to pursue, and which career path to follow were made far too long by people other than

188 Jorgensen

☐ Enroll the student in age-appropriate, general education classes and provide supports to enable him or her to be successful.

☐ Design the student's education plan so that he or she moves through the grades in a typical fashion and participates in all typical graduation planning and senior year activities.

☐ Teach the student to use natural supports from people and services available to typical students in the high school (e.g., study halls, nurse, guidance counselor, college fairs).

☐ Provide supports for the student's participation in extracurricular activities.

☐ Support the student to have friends and meaningful relationships in and out of school.

☐ Support the student to have a paying job after school, on weekends, or during the summer.

☐ Support the student's participation in community-based instruction only during times when other students are engaged in such activities (e.g., during school community service, after school, weekends, summers, after senior year).

☐ Support the student to develop typical connections within the community.

☐ Include the student in typical career and futures planning courses and activities.

☐ Teach and support the student to be the leader in making current and future choices by selecting classes, extracurricular activities and career paths and leading his or her person-centered planning team.

☐ Confirm that the student is eligible to continue to receive supports in the community via the school system if he or she has not received a regular high school diploma at the time of the graduation ceremony.

☐ Support the student to pursue inclusive career and postsecondary education, housing, and recreation choices after completion of senior year in high school.

Figure 10.1. Graduation planning checklist.

students with disabilities (Powers, Singer, & Sowers, 1996). Well-intentioned special educators, transition counselors, and even family members often made decisions about a student's present and future life without his or her knowledge, input, or consent. It is now clear that no one except the student should take the lead in planning his or her life. Only he or she truly understands his or her dreams, hopes, and aspirations.

Countless opportunities are available in every high school for students to learn leadership and decision-making skills. Students are learning the fundamentals of personal responsibility and decision making when they decide which classes they will take, which extracurricular activities they will join, and even which topic they will research in science class. Students are practicing self-determination skills when they take an active role in determining which supports they need and which adaptations may be necessary. Students are engaged in the principles of community leadership when they are encouraged to take active roles in schoolwide governance activities such as student councils, peer outreach, and advocacy organizations.

Wehmeyer (2002) stated,

> Promoting self-determination involves addressing the knowledge, skills, and attitudes students will need to take more control over and responsibility for their lives, and self-determined people are causal agents; they make things happen in their lives. They are goal oriented and apply problem-solving and decision-making skills to guide their actions. They know what they do well and where they need assistance. Self-determined people are actors in their own lives instead of being acted upon by others. (pp. 1–2)

Fortunately, Selena has had many opportunities to develop self-determination skills. She has always attended at least part of her IEP meetings. She described her favorite animals and picture books and said that she wanted to take dance lessons when she was in kindergarten. She told her team that she wanted to learn French when she was in sixth grade. She attends all IEP and transition planning meetings for the entire time now that she is in high school and brings flip chart paper to these meetings that reflect the discussions she has had with her personal futures planning team.

Resources for parents and educators about teaching self-determination skills—formal curricula, assessments, and even an iPad app that is a minicourse in self-determination for individuals with IDD—are available from the National Gateway to Self-Determination, a multi-university effort and web site.

Work at Summer Jobs

Selena served as a counselor in training at a local Boys and Girls Club when she was in middle school. She had increasing responsibilities at home for which she received an allowance. She opened a bank account and became proficient at using her ATM card for making purchases at convenience stores. Selena got her working papers when she turned 16, and she will work at a computer store owned by a family friend after her junior year. Research shows that a positive correlation exists between students with disabilities having paid jobs during high school and having a paid job after high school (White & Weiner, 2004). Another student working at the computer store, who is a member of the same Technology Club as Selena, will serve as her mentor, and all the employees will pitch in to provide natural supports. She will ride a city bus to and from the store each day, go out to lunch a couple of times a week with her co-workers, and happily deposit part of her paycheck into her bank account every 2 weeks.

These work experiences not only provide her with opportunities to learn valuable job skills—being on time, working with emerging technologies, and running credit card purchases—but also offer opportunities to learn some of the soft skills needed by all workers, such as talking about shared interests, inviting people to go out for coffee after work, and dealing with feedback from supervisors. All the colleges that Selena is considering have faculty and student technology centers and offer possible part-time work opportunities while she is enrolled in a comprehensive transition program.

Acquire Knowledge and Skills
for Successful Relationships and Sexual Well-Being

Contrary to some antiquated beliefs, people with disabilities have the same sexual needs as those without disabilities; not more and not less. Selena's family wanted her to develop a positive body image, good hygiene, an awareness of sexually dangerous situations, and the knowledge and skills she needs to establish healthy emotional and sexual relationships now and in the future. They are aware that many adults with Down syndrome do get married and validate Selena's wishes to do so in the future.

Selena and her classmates learned about puberty in the fifth grade from the school's health educator, but Selena's family supplemented those lessons using curriculum materials that were developed by Planned Parenthood of Northern New England and recommended by many disability organizations, such as United Cerebral Palsy and the ARC. Those materials were specifically designed for youth and adults with IDD and offered the same information that Selena was learning in school but with additional visual supports, videos, and role-playing exercises.

Selena took a wellness class in her sophomore year that also addressed sexual health issues, including sexually transmitted diseases, contraception, sexual victimization, and other heady topics. Again, Selena's parents enriched her learning by enrolling her in an empowerment group for young women sponsored by a local women's health clinic.

Participate in Senior Year Rites of Passage

IDEA 2004 states that a student's eligibility for special education services and supports ends with the receipt of a standard high school diploma. For this and other reasons, many schools have presented students with disabilities with alternative diplomas or certificates of completion during the formal graduation ceremony to maintain their eligibility for special education services through age 21. Students who are on track to receive a regular high school diploma often delay taking one required course—perhaps a health or physical education credit—until just before they turn 21. Selena will participate in all the activities of senior year, including having her picture in the yearbook, going to prom, and marching in the graduation ceremony.

Postsecondary Education

Is college possible for students with IDD? Unequivocally yes! Although postsecondary education, with support from disability service programs, has always been available to some students with disabilities who were judged as otherwise qualified (i.e., they meet the same entrance requirements as students without disabilities), these opportunities have not traditionally been available for students with intellectual disability (Grigal & Hart, 2012).

A small number of students with complex support needs from around the United States took college courses in the late 1980s with support from their high schools, vocational rehabilitation and developmental service agencies, contributions from part-time work, and their parents. These early pioneering efforts helped promote changes in the Higher Education Opportunity Act of 2008 (PL 110-315), which prioritized expanding postsecondary opportunities for students with intellectual disability. In 2016, more than 250 such programs around the United States did not require enrolled students to have a regular high school diploma, achieve certain scores on college aptitude tests, or pursue a traditional degree (Institute for Community Inclusion, 2016). These programs

- Serve students with intellectual disability on regular 2- or 4-year college or university campuses

- Provide individual supports and services for the academic and social inclusion of students with intellectual disability in academic courses, extracurricular activities, and other aspects of the institution of higher education's regular postsecondary program

- Focus on academic enrichment; socialization; independent living skills, including self-advocacy skills; integrated work experiences; and career skills that lead to gainful employment

- Integrate person-centered planning in the development of the course of study for each student

Some of these postsecondary programs for students with intellectual disability meet the standards for being comprehensive transition programs and are able to offer financial aid to qualified students with intellectual disability. Selena's state has several of these programs, and she and her family will visit them during the fall of her junior year—just like her classmates without disabilities—and submit her applications the next spring.

Moving on to a Career

Although Selena wants to combine postsecondary education and work, some students want to go right into the workforce when they leave high school. The options for employment are as varied and unique as students themselves, and the laws governing employment for people with disabilities are often difficult to interpret and beyond the scope of this book.

Employment First is a national initiative of the U.S. Department of Labor, Office of Disability Employment Policy (n.d.) and is designed to invest in systems change efforts that result in increased community-based, integrated employment opportunities for individuals with significant disabilities. This effort is built on the premise that all citizens, including individuals with significant disabilities, are capable of full participation in integrated employment and community life.

IDEA 2004 has an expressed preference for students with disabilities to be educated in inclusive environments, including inclusive career-learning environments. The U.S. Department of Education, Office of Special Education programs, clarified IDEA's requirement that transition goals and services for students with disabilities—including the work-based learning that is part of some students' transition IEPs—must adhere to the LRE mandate of the law (Yudin & Musgrove, 2012). Thus, work-based learning opportunities must consider integrated employment, with supplementary aids and services, before considering or recommending that a student work in a segregated setting.

Supports for Employment   Some students are able to secure competitive employment with natural supports provided by their co-workers and supervisors. Learning to use natural supports rather than those provided by people paid to be with a student with disabilities begins while they are in school. A system of supports that students use to navigate their way through the maze of classes, grades, and graduation requirements is in every high school. This system is highly developed in some schools; it is less so in other schools. Students rely on course-of-study catalogs, guidance counselors, their parents, peer mentors, and friends to help them decide in which classes to enroll. They rely on grades and class standing to indicate how their teachers feel they are progressing. They rely on coaches and advisors to give advice on everything from classwork to relationships. They rely on friends and classmates for just about every-thing. Students with disabilities must also be encouraged to first utilize the natural supports that are available to any student before relying on a paraeducator assigned only to him or her. The reliance on special sup-ports in high school can lead to a dependence on special supports into adulthood (Powers et al., 1996). Far too many young adults and their fami-lies assume that they will require specially trained people all their lives to be successful. This assumption can make the transition to adult life difficult. Although supports and services are an entitlement for school-age students, they are not for adults. Adults who can garner support in the most typical fashion, via co-workers, family members, roommates, neighbors, and friends, are more likely to live full and self-determined lives and not languish on waiting lists for services, watching television, and being cared for by their aging parents.

Other students, however, may choose or need to rely on temporary, intermittent, or even long-term supports from specialized employment ser-vices. These services may be part of state or local government agencies (e.g., vocational rehabilitation, developmental services), whereas others are non-profit companies that are contracted by government agencies to provide a variety of community support services (e.g., housing, work, recreation) to individuals with disabilities. Customized employment is an underutilized strategy for supporting a young adult with significant disabilities to work. It is defined by the U.S. Department of Labor, Office of Disability Employment Policy (n.d.) as

> a process for individualizing the employment relationship between a job seeker or an employee and an employer in ways that meet the needs of both. It is based on a match between the unique strengths, needs, and interests of the job candidate with a disability, and the identified business needs of the employer or the self-employment business chosen by the candidate . . . customized employment starts with the devel-opment of an employment plan based on an individualized determination of the strengths, needs and interests of the job candidate with a disability. Once the candi-date's goals are established, one or more potential employers are identified. A pre-liminary proposal for presentation to the employer is developed. The proposal is presented to an employer who agrees to negotiate an individualized job that meets the employment needs of the applicant and real business needs of the employer. (p. 1)

Using a customized employment approach usually works in one of three ways.

1. Taking the same job responsibility from several jobs in a business (e.g., faxing, filing, brewing coffee) and creating a new job comprised of just those tasks

2. Carving a new job out of some of the responsibilities (but not all) of an existing job

3. Developing an entirely new job or service for one business or several businesses

Community Living

Moving out of one's childhood home is another rite of passage for the vast majority of young adults. If they go to college, then they try out this arrangement for 4 years. If their financial circumstances allow, then they get an apartment or buy a house. This trajectory of increasing independence is possible for youth with complex support needs too, as long as independence is not confused with a lack of supports. It is possible for a person with complex support needs to live away from his or her parents' home as long as the family and any relevant service agencies are creative in the way that they utilize natural supports and the funds to which people with disabilities are entitled once they reach adulthood.

What might this look like for Selena? She might rent an apartment with another young adult and use her salary and disability benefits to help pay her share of the rent. She might get a low-interest loan from a special program designed to help people with disabilities get a mortgage (Johnson, 2016) and provide a free room to a roommate who helps her with balancing her checkbook, getting a ride to work, or doing home maintenance. Her parents might refurbish their basement or space above their garage into a private apartment. Whichever path she chooses, her full inclusion in school and college life will contribute to her ability to clearly express her wishes, solve problems, work collaboratively with others, and live in the community, interdependent with others.

CONCLUSIONS

Schools and communities must respond to the ever-growing needs of a diverse student population—one in which every student must leave public school ready for college and a career. The old way of doing business—the school schedule based on following an agrarian calendar, tracking, and segregating students with disabilities—do not help advance that goal. Fully including all students with disabilities in the mainstream of the academic and social life of the school, and supporting them in an inclusive life in the community, must be done. Mara Sapon-Shevin (2003) said,

> Inclusion is not about disability, nor is it only about schools. Inclusion is about social justice. Inclusion demands that we ask, what kind of world do we want to create? What kinds of skills and commitment do people need to thrive in diverse society? By embracing inclusion as a model of social justice, we can create a world fit for all of us. (pp. 26, 28)

11

Solutions to Common Problems and Challenges in Achieving Inclusive Education

I have fielded hundreds of questions since the late 1980s about why inclusion makes sense, how to make it work, and how to resolve thorny problems. Here are some of those questions from family members, administrators, teachers, and related services providers as well as the advice that I provided.

QUESTION 1: FROM A HIGH SCHOOL GUIDANCE COUNSELOR

Although we have been back at school for more than a month now, one of my students is having a very difficult time adjusting to this new grade. It seems like we are back to square one, and we are all getting very discouraged. He is hiding in the bathroom, refusing to do his work, and lashing out several times a day, and we are at a loss.

ANSWER 1

I can really empathize with you, and although I do not know your student, I do know there are a lot of possibilities for what the source of the problem is—not feeling well, sensory overload, and frustration because the work is too hard or too easy. I do have two ideas and related strategies that you might consider. Your team will need to discuss them, gather some data, and decide whether one of these ideas might make sense. I would recommend that you pick a couple of strategies at first, preferably those that have the highest team agreement rather than an idea that one or two people prefer but the rest of the team does not prefer.

Relationships, Relationships, Relationships

The first strategy involves building relationships. I would put a lot of energy during the next few weeks into developing your student's social relationships. I know that you know how important it is for all students to feel welcome and secure on the social front. Otherwise, all the positive behavior support plans and curriculum modifications in the world will not help. First, make sure that there are not any things standing in the way of your student feeling like a welcome member of the school and his classes. Does he ride the regular school bus? Is he enrolled in general education classes? Is his seat in each classroom right alongside his classmates? If he is supported by a paraprofessional, does he or she give your student a lot of space to get to the next class, choose where to sit at lunchtime, and hang out with other students of his own choosing? Does he have reciprocal friendships and not only relationships with peers who are his helpers?

Second, find out your student's interests and then support him to join an extracurricular activity that matches those interests. If you are not sure what might really get him excited, then pick an activity in which a lot of his classmates are members as a place to start. Have a chat with the advisor of that club or activity, describe your student in a holistic way (e.g., is shy, is keen on computers, loves music, uses a communication device, can be stubborn, likes being "just one of the guys"), and then figure out how the other students in the activity can provide any supports that the student needs before thinking about whether he needs an adult to attend the activity too.

Third, if social relationships are not happening after working on these ideas and your student still seems unhappy, then he may need you to take some intentional steps to help create community for him. I worked with a student some years ago who sounds much like your student. We asked a group of students if they would like to come together with Brandon to help figure out what was standing in the way of him really being part of the social fabric of the school. We got an energetic student teacher to advise the group, and they used a wonderful book called *Seeing the Charade* (Tashie et al., 2006) to guide them. In my experience that group really does require an adult facilitator. They could do "getting to know you" activities, participate in activities exploring various aspects of diversity (How are we alike? How are we different?), and help figure out what seems to be standing in the way. Brandon's group told us that his paraprofessional was a big barrier to natural interactions with his classmates. Your student's group could also plan outside-of-school activities for the weekends. It is important not to frame this as "we are recruiting people to be Brandon's buddies" but rather "Brandon would like to invite students to join this group because he and other students we know are interested in how to build better connections and friendships based on shared interests for all students in your school."

Functional Behavioral Assessment and Positive Behavior Supports Plan

If the strategies previously described are not helping your student, then it may be time to conduct (or update) an FBA. IDEA 2004 does not require FBAs but encourages schools to do them when students have challenging behavior that has not responded to the schoolwide prosocial behavioral supports that are implemented with all students.

The nice thing about the principles behind FBAs and humanistic and positive behavior support plans is that they do not place the behavior problem solely within the student (e.g., "He is just doing it on purpose") but rather acknowledge the interplay between the complexities within each one of us, the environment, and the difficulties that so many of our most vulnerable students have at school.

In summary, be sure that your student is experiencing a welcoming school environment, support him to join some student activities, consider intentional social relationship facilitation, and think about doing a comprehensive FBA to delve more deeply into the factors that might be at play in your student's difficulties with school.

QUESTION 2: FROM A SPECIAL EDUCATION DIRECTOR

We offer a 4-week summer program for our high school students with ASD and other developmental disabilities. It consists of tutoring in reading, writing, and math as well as working on some community living skills such as making store purchases and using public transportation. Some of our parents are not happy with this and want a more typical summer experience. I am not sure what would be appropriate and affordable for these students given our tight resources. Do you have any ideas?

ANSWER 2

When students with disabilities are included in general education classes and other typical activities during the school year, the way to extend those experiences to the summer is to ask yourself this question, "What do students without disabilities typically do during the summer, and how might I support students with disabilities to do the same thing?" Although there are some differences depending on where students live (rural versus suburban, suburban versus urban), high school students work, hang out with their friends, go to the beach, and may attend a camp related to one of their special interests. I have worked with many schools that partnered students with and without disabilities to work at jobs such as house painting, babysitting, scooping ice cream, performing light maintenance at a health club, and doing farm work. Many typical camps, town recreation departments, and community agencies are eager to offer work and leadership development opportunities to the youth in their communities.

In many cases, the school special education personnel provide some initial support to the student, but the goal should be to rely on natural supports in the environment. These summer learning opportunities are not only fun for students but can also help them maintain their reading, writing, math, communication, cooperation, and self-advocacy skills in the most natural environments possible.

QUESTION 3: FROM A MIDDLE SCHOOL TEACHER

I am concerned about the effect that students with more significant disabilities will have on my general education students. Do they draw resources and attention away from the rest of the class?

ANSWER 3

This is a common question, and I can answer it in three ways. First, let me reassure you that the research—and there is more than 40 years of it—shows that the learning of students without disabilities is not adversely affected by having students with disabilities as part of a heterogeneous general education classroom. It is important to focus on the word *heterogeneous*. A truly inclusive classroom is one in which there is a natural proportion of students with and without disabilities. There should be about three or four students with disabilities in a class of 25 students and certainly no more than one student with IDD or other complex support needs such as ASD. If the ratios are heavily weighted toward children with disabilities, then that is not really an inclusive classroom, and I have seen the negative academic and behavioral consequences of that arrangement. Furthermore, the research shows that students without disabilities have more positive attitudes toward people with disabilities when they grow up with and go to school with students who have disabilities.

Second, numerous research studies show that the academic achievement of all students rise when schools or districts embrace inclusive education as a schoolwide effort—with strong leadership from the principal, a lot of professional development for teachers, and the availability of common planning time for teams.

Third, your question about students with disabilities taking attention and resources away from the other students really makes me wonder if you and the whole class are getting the support that you need. Students with disabilities educated in general education classes are entitled to supplementary aids and services to enable them to learn, and those aids and services also include resources for the classroom teacher, such as training; special education personnel who come into the classroom to share the teaching load; AT for students who have difficulties reading, writing, and communicating; behavioral support; and common planning time. I also recommend that the IEP teams of students with complex support needs have 1 hour of common planning time per week.

I hope that you will sit down with the other members of your students' IEP teams and your administrators and have an honest discussion about what supports you need to teach all the students in your classroom well. You deserve no less and neither do they.

QUESTION 4: FROM A SPECIAL EDUCATION CASE MANAGER

We have a sixth-grade student with Down syndrome on our team and are wondering about her long-term goals. We are not sure that a continued focus on academics makes sense for this student. Should she be focusing more on life skills?

ANSWER 4

The long-term goal for any student, including one with Down syndrome, is to be college and career ready by the time he or she leaves school. Your team should develop your student's yearly IEP goals based on those long-term goals and remind yourselves of them frequently. Desired educational outcomes for students with Down syndrome include

- Becoming literate—read, write, communicate, and compute
- Acquiring lifetime wellness habits (e.g., hygiene, nutrition, exercise, stress management, sexual health, drug/alcohol awareness)
- Developing work habits and earning and managing money
- Learning about the world, including science, social studies, and technology
- Developing artistic talents (e.g., music, art, drama, dance)
- Being proud of being a person with Down syndrome and advocating for him- or herself
- Learning to cooperate
- Acquiring and sustaining friendships
- Developing ethics, caring, and responsible citizenship
- Learning to drive or getting around the community

The possibilities for people with Down syndrome were severely limited years ago—congregate living, sheltered work or day habilitation activities, and social relationships only with other people with disabilities. The possibilities for people with Down syndrome today are limited only by our expectations for them and our creativity in providing them with the support they need to gain access to those opportunities. Going to college is one of the most exciting possibilities for students with Down syndrome.

How do we realize these goals for students with Down syndrome? Forty years of research shows that students' academic achievement, communication skills, social relationships, and postschool outcomes (e.g., living in the community, being maximally independent, being financially secure) are positively correlated to the amount of time that they spend in a general education classroom. I recommend that your student be enrolled in a full complement of general education classes with the supports she needs to be successful, and the goals of gainful employment, postsecondary education, and community living serve as your "north star" until she graduates from high school.

QUESTION 5: FROM A HEAD START TEACHER

I teach in a program with 4-year-old kids who are high risk. I have a sweet little friend who has a developmental delay and is served by a resource teacher daily. He is very affectionate and has recently begun trying to touch my breasts when he hugs me. It turns into an awful meltdown when I try to stop him. I have mentioned it to the parents, but nothing has changed. Is there a better way to redirect my little guy without causing him to be upset? I made him a social story book at the beginning of the year. Do you think a page about appropriate touching would be a good idea? Do you have any other ideas?

ANSWER 5

I think using a social story is a great idea. Try it out and see what happens. Working together with his parents is a must in this situation, so try to schedule a meeting that is at a convenient time for parents to attend and create an atmosphere of "we are all in this together" rather than one that parents might interpret as blaming them.

Ask yourselves why you think he is doing it. Having a hypothesis about the causes and functions of this behavior will help you tailor supports and interventions in a more precise way. Some questions you might ask or discuss are

- Is there a new infant at home that mom is breastfeeding?

- Are there certain times of the day when he does this? During certain activities? Before or after certain activities?

- What need is being met by this behavior? Curiosity about anatomy/bodies? Seeking comfort and closeness? Fatigue? Attention?

- What kind of response does he get when he does this? Do you unintentionally give him a lot of attention when it happens? Do his peers also give him attention for the behavior, such as laughing or pointing?

I think that all children should be given age-appropriate information about their bodies and issues of good and bad touching. I would make sure to include your friend in these lessons and partner with his family so that you both are providing the same information and responding in the same way.

Although I would hate to think that this is the cause, there is always the possibility that this child has witnessed or experienced some inappropriate sexual conduct or contact. If he does not respond to your efforts at discouraging his behavior or shows any other age-inappropriate interest or actions, then be sure to follow your state's requirements regarding reporting such incidents.

QUESTION 6: FROM A KINDERGARTEN TEACHER AND PARENT

I am a kindergarten teacher in our local elementary school who is also the parent of a child with disabilities. Our administration pays lip service to inclusion but really is not committed to following through. What can I do to help them see that this issue is so important?

ANSWER 6

Inclusion is much more than students "just being in" a regular education classroom—it is welcoming all children into our classrooms and schools and providing students and staff with the supports they need to be successful. Here are two ideas for engaging everyone in the conversation about why and how inclusion works best for all students.

Idea 1: Establish an Inclusive Education Implementation Team

This team is comprised of key stakeholders, such as the principal, the special education coordinator, general and special education teachers, related services providers, a parent/guardian, and a student representative. The team's role and responsibilities include

- Modeling inclusive values and practices

- Identifying key issues and concerns

- Developing a plan for building consensus by researching options, reading literature together, engaging in critical dialogue, and visiting inclusive schools

- Drafting, vetting, finalizing, and sharing a mission statement on inclusive education with the whole faculty and school community

- Creating needed infrastructure and overseeing an implementation plan for inclusive education

- Identifying and using data management systems to evaluate the quality of student and team supports and student learning

- Planning and providing job-embedded professional development

- Actively communicating with staff members, families, the school board, and community stakeholders regarding inclusive education

Idea 2: Start an Inclusive Education Professional Learning Community

Everybody in your school probably has a different idea of what inclusion is, the effects on students with and without disabilities, and the resources needed to make it work. A professional learning community (PLC) is a small group of people who commit to learning about an issue together. Members of a PLC might pick a book to read and discuss it together; they might do a literature search on inclusive education to find out what the research says; and they might watch a video about inclusive education and discuss their beliefs and values about disability and diversity. Developing shared understanding about and commitment to inclusion is the first step to move from lip service to being a school that welcomes all children. This does not happen overnight, but these suggestions might help get you there.

QUESTION 7: FROM A MIDDLE SCHOOL PRINCIPAL

We have a student with Down syndrome whose parents want her included in all seventh-grade general education classes. How can we determine if this student will benefit from inclusion, and how will we measure that benefit?

ANSWER 7

Let me share with you what Ashley's mom said at a recent team meeting:

> Ashley started school as a guided learning [self-contained] student and remained in that class until fifth grade. She did get to experience some time in class with her typical peers through morning meetings and specials. Ashley's Dad and I were often asked about our vision for her and what we wanted her school program to look like during IEP meetings. We knew we wanted something different than what she was experiencing. We know Ashley does not have to earn being included, prove herself worthy of it, or demonstrate skills before being given the opportunity. She deserves to be educated alongside her typical peers as well as those with disabilities and have high expectations for her academic achievement and social involvement. She deserves to be perceived as competent with knowledge, skills, talents, aptitudes, and dreams. It is her legal right, and it is her civil right.

So there are many different ways of accessing benefit. One way is to assess teachers' progress in implementing appropriately differentiated instruction which can be measured by looking for the principles of universal design for learning (UDL) in teachers' lessons plans and observing their classroom instruction.

Another way to assess benefit is to take a look at the school administration's progress in supporting inclusive education practices, looking at professional development opportunities, resource acquisition, protected planning time, the number of special educators per grade, and caseloads. The culture and social norms of the school can be measured by looking at the progress being made toward a desegregated school community that embraces diversity of all kinds, values students of all abilities, and creates equal opportunities.

If you are asking about Ashley's academic progress, then look at goals and objectives derived from the core curriculum and her successful attainment of them. Looking at her alternate assessment portfolio would provide additional information.

The number and quality of Ashley's social relationships with her peers is also an important measure of success. If she is not only spending time with them during school hours but also after school and on weekends, then you can be confident that your efforts are bearing fruit.

So in conclusion, the question of benefit and progress has to be considered not only for the student but for the whole school.

QUESTION 8: FROM A SPEECH-LANGUAGE PATHOLOGIST

We are working with a student with Down syndrome who will be making the transition from fourth to fifth grade next year. He is a beginning reader and does not have any writing skills. He does talk, but 50% of it is not understandable. Does it really make sense to include him in the regular English language arts class?

ANSWER 8

I would say unequivocally, "Yes! It does make sense to include him." Here are some suggestions for supporting his participation and learning.

1. Make sure that he has a way to communicate about what will be going on in the general education class—academic and social subjects. He should have a way to fulfill the following communicative functions or purposes.

    • Expressing feelings and sensory states

    • Establishing social closeness with peers and adults

    • Requesting

    • Making choices

    • Asking questions

    • Providing information

    • Answering questions

    • Making comments

    • Refusing

2. If your student does not communicate in ways that are commensurate with his same-age classmates without disabilities, then you ought to have an AAC evaluation done. Reassure your team that providing him with augmented ways to communicate will not decrease his verbal communication, but it may increase it.

3. Provide him with books and other text materials that are fully accessible. Conduct an Internet search before creating an accessible book or other text to see if someone else has already created it. Enter these words into the browser's search box and you might find appropriately adapted materials.

   • Title of book + adapted

   • Title of book + modified

   • Title of book + accessible

4. Read Chapter 5 to learn about sources for adapted books and creating your own from scratch.

5. Take the time to plan the supports he will need in class. Use Part 2 of the planning form in Chapter 9 to identify the supports your student will need during the recurring routines that repeatedly happen in language arts, such as whole class discussion, partner reading, vocabulary study, spelling, journal writing, and guided reading. Use Part 1 of the form to think about what your student's priority learning objectives will be for each unit of study or book.

6. Figure out the supports that the student needs for writing. Some possibilities include

   • Having someone scribe for him

   • Using speech-to-text software, such as Dragon Naturally Speaking

   • Having him plan what he wants to write using graphic organizer software, such as Inspiration, convert the completed graphic organizer to the outline format, and support him to build sentences from there

   • Using software or apps, such as Abilipad, First Author, Co:Writer Universal, Clicker Connect, or Read&Write

7. He should have one-to-one or small-group reading instruction to build his fundamentals. Schedule this supplemental instruction at a time when he will not miss out on core academic instruction. I know that is a real challenge because everything is important. A student I am working with gets this instruction during the first half hour of the day when all students go to different classrooms for reading instruction. Another student gets supplemental special education services after school that are focused on "closing the gap" instruction in literacy and math so that he does not have to miss even one period of being with his classmates during the day.

8. An SLP should begin to plan for how he or she will "push in" to the language arts (or any other) class to support the student. Pull-out

language therapy has some serious drawbacks, so he can be supported in the classroom to ask questions, read with fluency, identify main ideas from a story, and expand his vocabulary.

Learning to read and enjoying reading is a functional life skill for every student and justifies this student's participation in English class.

QUESTION 9: FROM A PRINCIPAL

This spring our school is beginning to plan for including students with ASD in general education classrooms. We have 10 students with ASD in kindergarten through fifth grade. Where do we start?

ANSWER 9

I am so glad to hear that you are committed to including students with ASD in general education classrooms. This is the perfect time of year to begin taking steps toward having all students with ASD as welcome members of age-appropriate general education classes next fall.

Step 1: Bring together a team that represents your key stakeholders and designate them as your inclusive education leadership team. Include a general education teacher from each grade level; all special education case managers; the SLP, OT, and PT who provide services to students with ASD; a couple of paraprofessionals; your reading specialist (or a Title I teacher); your building or district special education administrator; several parents; and at least one student with ASD.

Step 2: Develop a plan for keeping all parents of children with and without disabilities informed of your plans as they evolve. This might include giving a monthly update at a PTA meeting, holding information sessions for parents, and talking with the parents of the children with ASD about the "why" and "how" of inclusive education.

Step 3: Identify a few key books, research articles, and videos that everyone on the leadership team will read and watch together. I would suggest the book *You're Going to Love This Kid!* by Paula Kluth (2010), the videos *Including Samuel* (Habib, 2007) and *We Thought You'd Never Ask* (Hussman, 2008) and a manual I wrote for the National Education Association called *Including Students with Autism* (Jorgensen, 2014).

Step 4: Visit an inclusive school. There is no substitute for seeing inclusion in action. Contact the Fox Prairie Elementary School in Stoughton because you live in Wisconsin. It was designated as a knowledge development school by the Schoolwide Integrated Framework for Transformation (SWIFT) project (University of Kansas, 2016), which was funded by the U.S. Department of Education, as a school in which all students are included in general education and all resources from general and special education and Title I are deployed to support all students' academic and behavioral success.

The SWIFT Center has a lot of great resources on their web site as well (http://www.swiftschools.org).

Step 5: Identify which general education classroom each student will join in September. Provide monthly professional development workshops for those general education teachers and other members of your students' education teams. The workshops should focus on seven key topics: 1) the rationale for inclusion, 2) inclusive education best practices, 3) collaborative teaming and new roles for special educators and related services providers as supporters of students' participation in general education instruction, 4) peer supports and cooperative learning, 5) UDL and ensuring access to all instructional materials, 6) planning the curricular and instructional adaptations that students with complex support needs require to encourage their full participation, and 7) positive behavior supports. If you have students who use AAC, then workshops on that topic for those students' teams would be important as well. Look for online webinars or conferences (e.g., an annual conference sponsored by the PEAK Parent Center, workshops offered by the Wisconsin Department of Education or the Wisconsin TASH).

Step 6: Plan next year's school calendar so that each student's education team has 1 hour of common planning time per week. During these meetings the teams will talk about upcoming lessons and units and discuss the supports that the students will need to fully participate and learn. You might use the instructional planning forms discussed in Chapter 9.

Step 7: Give each student's team a couple of days of planning time during the summer to get a head start on instructional planning. It will help all the students start the year off positively if the team feels as if they can "hit the ground running" with a couple of week's work of materials and other supports already planned.

Step 8: Write each student's IEP so that his or her goals and objectives are aligned with the state's learning standards and special education and related services are delivered primarily within the context of general education instruction in the general education classroom. Chapters 4 and 5 describe how to write an inclusive standards-based IEP.

Step 9: Create your staffing schedule to maximize the time that special education teachers and related services providers are in general education classrooms co-teaching whole group lessons, working with small groups, or providing side-by-side support to individual students.

Step 10: Encourage each student's parents to host at least one summer get-together for a few children who will be in their child's classroom. A low-key playdate in the backyard with one structured group activity goes a long way to help children feel as if they are part of the group even before the new school year begins.

The first few weeks and months will be filled with challenges and daily questions from staff, so be sure that you are a daily presence in those classrooms providing leadership, encouragement, and tangible supports so that everyone can have a successful year.

QUESTION 10: FROM A PARENT

Although my son is fully included in a fifth-grade general education class, I am not happy with his lack of access to what is being taught. His team seems to have a good handle on how he can work on things such as managing his belongings, moving around the classroom and school, and communicating about social things, but I do not really see him learning academics. Can you help?

ANSWER 10

Your concerns are very common and not only felt by parents but also by educators. People seem to understand the social benefits of inclusion for students with complex support needs but are unsure about how they can learn academics. Here are a few thoughts and suggestions for how his team can make his inclusion meaningful in all ways.

1. Presume his competence to learn. One of the barriers to students' participation in academic instruction in the general education classroom is that some members of their educational teams do not think that students can learn academics. If a student cannot yet communicate that he or she is learning some of the general education content, then the least dangerous assumption is that he or she is or can learn it! Donnellan (1984) said, "The criterion or standard asserts that in the absence of conclusive data, educational decisions ought to be based on assumptions which, if incorrect, will have the least dangerous effect on student" (p. 142). The least dangerous assumption is to presume competence for the following reasons.

    *   When we expect students to learn, they are more likely to do so.

    *   Traditional assessments of the intelligence of people with complex support needs—particularly those who do not use natural speech to communicate—are very flawed and often tell more about what people cannot do than what they might be able to do with support. If someone has assessed your child and told you his or her IQ is low, then ignore that information and ask what needs to be done to ensure that your child has full access to high-quality instruction in the general education classroom.

    *   More than 40 years of research has shown that an increasing number of people with intellectual disability show they are more competent than ever thought possible when they have a means to communicate and are provided with good instruction. If just one person whose IQ was measured at 40 (or 50 or 20) shows that he or she is smarter than that number would indicate, then the validity of IQ measurements should be questioned for everyone.

- A terrible disservice is done to a person if we assume that he or she cannot learn x, y, or z, and we are wrong about that assumption.

- Even if we are wrong about someone's ability to learn, that is not as dangerous as the alternative.

2. Your son's IEP team should read Chapter 9 because it describes a participation planning process that determines the supports needed by a student to fully participate in general education instruction based on general education learning standards taught by a general education teacher in a general education classroom.

3. Your son's team should read the guidelines for creating accessible instructional materials in Chapter 5. There are many links to already adapted or modified books and other texts, descriptions of apps and software that can be used to make instructional materials (both literary and informational text) accessible to students, and instructions for making adapted books and other materials. Making instructional materials accessible for students with disabilities is required by IDEA 2004.

QUESTION 11: FROM A SPECIAL EDUCATION TEACHER

We have a student who is included in all general education classes in 10th grade. So far she has not shown that she understands anything we are teaching her. Would it be in her best interest to attend the life skills class instead?

ANSWER 11

I understand your concern. When students do not show progress, we wonder if we should make a big change in their educational program. I would like to offer my point of view, developed since I began my inclusive education work in the 1980s.

I think all teachers have had students who led them to that "ah-ha" experience that helped them realize why they got into teaching in the first place. The students were eager, curious, funny, stubborn, persistent, or just plain nice kids. It happened for me in 1992. I was doing some school reform and inclusive education work with a newly built high school in southern New Hampshire. I met two incoming ninth graders on my first day of school, both of whom had pretty significant disabilities. Let's call them John and Rob. John looked terrified as he made his way down the busy hallways. He did not use his voice to communicate, but he cobbled together some gestures and signs to try to make himself understood. He seemed unable to read, and his most recent 3-year reevaluation revealed an IQ of 42. He had some compulsive behaviors and was very anxious most of the time. He was shy, withdrawn, clumsy, and overweight. The second student I met that day could not have been more different. Rob appeared to be thriving in ninth grade, giving high-fives to just about everyone he met as he walked through the busy hallways between classes. He was cooperative and was a real jokester. He had recently learned to use a communication board and was a whiz at spelling; although, he also did not use his voice to communicate. In fact, I heard a classmate tell him, "Hey, slow down, slow down, I cannot keep up with you!" I learned that he was an assistant manager of the football team, and he proudly wore his team jersey.

When I looked through John's cumulative file, I saw a typical educational history for a student with his IDD profile. He had been in all self-contained classes through eighth grade, except for art and physical education. His IEP goals focused on preacademic skills (e.g., matching, one-to-one correspondence, letter identification) as well as self-care, vocational, and life skills. He spent most of every day with other students who had significant disabilities and participated in Special Olympics. Rob's educational program was quite different. He was included in all general education classes. His IEP contained goals and objectives that reflected the essential elements of the general education curriculum, as well as objectives related to reading, managing his belongings, participating in extracurricular activities, and improving his communication skills.

I saw starkly different future expectations for these young men when I spoke with their parents. John's parents thought he would live in a group home, work in a sheltered workshop, and spend most of his time with other people who had significant disabilities. Rob's parents expected him to eventually live away from home, perhaps with roommates who might receive free rent to provide some support to him. They thought Rob might work in the family pizza business or in a fitness facility because he liked sports and was so gregarious. They hoped that the friendships he developed in school would continue into adult life and that those friends who stayed in the area would hang out together doing what other 20-somethings did in their spare time.

When I talk about these two students in workshops, I ask people to come up with a hypothesis about why their educational programs and futures look so different. Several people always say, "Well, it looks like John is a lot lower functioning than Rob." And there it is. Only 16% of students who are diagnosed with intellectual disability are included in general education classes for most of their school day across the United States. More than 50% of students taking alternate assessments do not have the AT (including AAC) they need to demonstrate what they really know. Judgments about students' intellectual capacity affect every decision made about their educational programs, communication systems and supports, social activities, and futures.

Okay, time to fess up. There actually were not two students at the high school. Just one, and his name was Amro Diab. Amro had been in self-contained classes his whole life before moving into ninth grade. A key special education teacher who served as the inclusion facilitator at his new high school developed Amro's educational program based on the idea of presuming his competence. He believed Amro could learn the essential elements of the general education curriculum, communicate effectively, have a full social life based on shared interests with his classmates, and graduate to an inclusive adult life in the community if he were given the right supports.

This notion of presuming competence tends to be a deeply held belief, and those who hold it do not need IQ or other test scores to back them up. For them, and for me, it is the least dangerous assumption I can make about any student or any person.

You should presume that your student will be able to learn in her general education classes with the right instruction and supports. Take to heart what Anne Donnellan (1984) said in her paper on the least dangerous assumption: If students are not learning, we should assume that it is because of instructional inadequacy rather than some inherent deficit within the student.

Convene your student's team and look at what the data are telling you—the data on your student's performance and the data about the fidelity with which you are providing the student with supports. Reflect on the following questions.

- Can she see and hear what is going on in the classroom?

- Is she learning right alongside her classmates rather than being taught in the back of the classroom by a paraprofessional?

- Does she need to have different adapted materials with additional visual supports or schema, such as those described in Chapter 5?

- Is there an underlying health issue that is getting in the way of learning?

- Is she generally happy throughout her school day, or are there emotional issues interfering with her learning?

- Does she have friends and a vibrant social life?

- Does she need supplemental instruction in reading or math that will help close the gap between her skills and those required of her general education classes?

- Are there assistive technologies that could enhance her reading comprehension and writing abilities?

- Does the team need additional professional development, planning time, or other resources for them to do their best work?

- Are school and home communicating regularly and working together on appropriate homework assignments?

When the problem-solving process is grounded in the question, *"How* can we make this work?" rather than, *"Why* should the student be in this class?" then new ideas and the team members' creativity will flourish.

CONCLUSIONS

Joe Petner (2004), the former principal of an inclusive elementary school in Cambridge, Massachusetts, once said that "inclusion is an easy thing to do poorly." The responses to the questions in this chapter and, in fact, this entire book, endeavors to help families and educators "do inclusion well" for the benefit of students with complex support needs and also for their classmates without disabilities who will grow up alongside them and ultimately share their lives with a commitment to inclusion of everyone.

References

American Occupational Therapy Association. (2006). *Transforming caseload to workload in school-based and early intervention occupational therapy services.* Retrieved from https://www.aota.org/-/media/Corporate/Files/Practice/Children/Resources/Transforming%20Caseload.ashx

American Occupational Therapy Association. (2013). *Guidance for performance evaluation of school occupational therapists.* Retrieved from https://www.aota.org/-/media/corporate/files/practice/children/performance-evaluation-school-based-therapists10-31-13.pdf

American Physical Therapy Association. (n.d.). *Physical therapy in school settings.* Retrieved from https://www.apta.org/uploadedFiles/APTAorg/Advocacy/Federal/Legislative_Issues/IDEA_ESEA/PhysicalTherapyintheSchoolSystem.pdf

American Speech-Language-Hearing Association. (2012). *Roles and responsibilities of speech-language pathologists (SLPs) in schools.* Retrieved from http://www.asha.org/uploadedFiles/Roles-Responsibilities-SLP-Schools-DOs-and-DONTs.pdf

American Speech-Language-Hearing Association. (2010). *2010 Schools Survey report: SLP caseload characteristics.* Retrieved from http://www.asha.org/uploadedFiles/Schools10Caseload.pdf

American Speech-Language-Hearing Association. (2016a). *Augmentative and alternate communication decisions.* Retrieved from http://www.asha.org/public/speech/disorders/CommunicationDecisions/

American Speech-Language-Hearing Association. (2016b). *Code of ethics.* Retrieved from http://www.asha.org/Code-of-Ethics/

Americans with Disabilities Amendments Act (ADA) of 2008, PL 110-325, 42 U.S.C. §§ 12101 et seq.

Anastasiou, D., & Kauffman, J. (2011). A social constructionist approach to disability: Implications for special education. *Exceptional Children, 3,* 367–384.

Apple, M. (1979). *Ideology and curriculum.* Boston, MA: Routledge & Kegan Paul.

Barnes, C. (2003). What a difference a decade makes: Reflections on doing emancipatory disability research. *Disability and Society, 18,* 3–17.

Bauer, M. D. (1986). *On my honor.* New York, NY: Clarion Books.

Beukelman, D., & Mirenda, P. (2005). *Augmentative and alternative communication: Supporting children and adults with complex communication needs* (3rd ed.) Baltimore, MD: Paul H. Brookes Publishing Co.

Beukelman, D., & Mirenda, P. (2013). *Augmentative and alternative communication: Supporting children and adults with complex communication needs* (4th ed.) Baltimore, MD: Paul H. Brookes Publishing Co.

Biklen, D. (1985). *Achieving the complete school: Strategies for effective mainstreaming.* New York, NY: Teachers College Press.

Biklen, D. E., & Cardinal, D. N. (1997). *Contested words, contested science: Unraveling the facilitated communication controversy.* New York, NY: Teachers College Press.

Binet, A. (1909). *Les idees moderne sur les enfants.* Paris, France: E. Flammarion.

Blind Babies Foundation. (2010). *Cortical visual impairment pediatric visual diagnosis fact sheet.* Retrieved from http://www.tsbvi.edu/seehear/fall98/cortical.htm

Brady, N. C., Bruce, S., Goldman, A., Erickson, K., Mineo, B., Ogletree, B. T., Paul, D., Romski, M., Sevcik, R., Siegel, E., Schoonover, J., Snell, M., Sylvester, L., & Wilkinson, K. (2016). Communication services and supports for individuals with severe disabilities: Guidance for assessment and intervention. *American Journal on Intellectual and Developmental Disabilities, 121*(2), 121–138.

Brinker, R. P., & Thorpe, M. E. (1984). Integration of severely handicapped students and the proportion of IEP objectives achieved. *Exceptional Children, 51,* 168–175.

Broderick, A., & Kasa-Hendrickson, C. (2001). "Say just one word at first": The emergence of reliable speech in a student labelled with autism. *Journal of The Association for Persons with Severe Handicaps, 26,* 13–24.

Browder, D. M., & Spooner, F. (2014). More content, more learning, more inclusion. In D. M. Browder & F. Spooner (Eds.), *More language arts, math, and science for students with severe disabilities* (pp. 3–14). Baltimore, MD: Paul H. Brookes Publishing Co.

Browder, D. M., Wood, L., Thompson, J., & Ribuffo, C. (2014). *Evidence-based practices for students with severe disabilities.* Retrieved from http://ceedar.education.ufl.edu/tools/innovation-configurations

Brown, L., Nietupski, J., & Hamre-Nietupski, S. (1976). The criterion of ultimate functioning and public school services for severely handicapped students. In T. M. Angele (Ed.), *Hey, don't forget about me: Education's investment in the severely, profoundly and multiply handicapped* (pp. 2–15). Reston, VA: Council for Exceptional Children.

Burkhart, L. (2016). *Simplified technology.* Retrieved from http://lindaburkhart.com/

Calculator, S., & Black, T. (2009). Validation of an inventory of best practices in the provision of augmentative and alternative communication services to students with severe disabilities in general education classrooms. *American Journal of Speech-Language Pathology, 18*(4), 329–342.

Calculator, S. N., & Jorgensen, C. M. (1991). Integrating AAC instruction into regular education settings: Expounding on best practices. *Augmentative and Alternative Communication, 7,* 204–220.

Casenhiser, D. M., Binns, A., McGill, F., Morderer, O., & Shanker, S. G. (2015). Measuring and supporting language function for children with autism: Evidence from a randomized control trial of a social-interaction-based therapy. *Journal of Autism and Developmental Disorders, 45*(3), 846–857.

Causton, J., & Tracy-Bronson, C. P. (2014a). *The occupational therapist's handbook for inclusive school practices.* Baltimore, MD: Paul H. Brookes Publishing Co.

Causton, J., & Tracy-Bronson, C. P. (2014b). *The speech-language pathologist's handbook for inclusive school practices.* Baltimore, MD: Paul H. Brookes Publishing Co.

Causton, J., & Tracy-Bronson, C. P. (2015). *The educator's handbook for inclusive school practices.* Baltimore, MD: Paul H. Brookes Publishing Co.

Causton, J., Tracy-Bronson, C. P., & MacLeod, K. (2015). Beyond treats and timeouts: Humanistic behavioral supports in inclusive classrooms. *International Journal of Whole Schooling, 11*(1), 68–84.

Causton-Theoharis, J., Theoharis, G., Orsati, F., & Cosier, M. (2011). Does self-contained special education deliver on its promises? A critical inquiry into research and practice. *Journal of Special Education Leadership, 24*(2), 61–78.

Center for Parent Information and Resources. (2010). *A checklist for IEP teams: Considering limited English proficiency.* Retrieved from http://www.parentcenterhub.org/wp-content/uploads/repo_items/legacy/d4.pdf

Civil Service Reform Act of 1978, PL 95-454, 92 Stat. 1111.

Cole, C. M., Waldron, N., & Majd, M. (2004). Academic progress of students across inclusive and traditional settings. *Mental Retardation, 42,* 136–144.

Cosier, M., Causton-Theoharis, J., & Theoharis, G. (2013). Does access matter? Time in general education and achievement for students with disabilities. *Remedial and Special Education, 34*(6), 323–332.

Couwenhoven, T. (2007). *Teaching children with Down syndrome about their bodies, boundaries, and sexuality.* Bethesda, MD: Woodbine House.

Cox, A. L., Gast, D. L., Luscre, D., & Ayres, D. M. (2009). The effect of weighted vests on appropriate in seat behaviors of elementary school students with autism and severe to profound intellectual disabilities. *Journal of Autism and Other Developmental Disorders, 24*(1), 17–26.

Cox-Lindenbaum, D., & Watson, S. L. (2002). Sexual assault against individuals who have a developmental disability. In D. M. Griffiths, D. Richards, P. Fedoroff, & S. L. Watson (Eds.), *Ethical dilemmas: Sexuality and developmental disability* (pp. 293–329). Kingston, NY: NADD Press.

Cress, C., & Marvin, C. (2003). Common questions about AAC services in early intervention. *Augmentative and Alternative Communication, 19*(4), 254–272.

Crossley, R. (1990). *Not being able to speak* [Poster]. Syracuse, NY: Syracuse University Center on Human Policy Press.

Cushing, L. S., & Kennedy, C. H. (1997). Academic effects of providing peer support in general education classrooms on students without disabilities. *Journal of Applied Behavior Analysis, 30*(1), 139–151.

Dessemontet, R. S., Bless, G., & Morin, D. (2012). Effects of inclusion on the academic achievement and adaptive behavior of children with intellectual disability. *Journal of Intellectual Disability Research, 56*(6), 579–587.

Donnellan, A. (1984). The criterion of the least dangerous assumption. *Behavioral Disorders, 9*, 141–150.

Dunn, W. (1997). The impact of sensory processing abilities on the daily lives of young children and their families: A conceptual model. *Infants and Young Children, 9*(4), 23–35.

Dynamic Learning Maps. (2015). *First grade English language arts: Reading.* Retrieved from https://www.dropbox.com/sh/j76szm5hvlwg7ok/AABqeve5BXB5cOl4607Xk8L1a/DLM%20Essential%20Elements%20ELA%20Unpacking%20%201st%20Grade.pdf?dl=0

Edelson, M. G. (2006). Are the majority of children with autism mentally retarded? A systematic evaluation of the data. *Focus on Autism and Other Developmental Disabilities, 21*, 66–83.

Elliott, R. (2012). *Just because.* Oxford, United Kingdom: Lion Hudson.

Erickson, K., Koppenhaver, D., & Yoder, D. (2002). *Waves of words: Augmented communicators read and write* (Vol. 3). Toronto, Canada: International Society for Augmentative and Alternative Communication.

Erickson, K., Koppenhaver, D., Yoder, D., & Nance, J. (1997). Integrated communication and literacy instruction for a child with multiple disabilities. *Focus on Autism and Other Developmental Disabilities, 12*(3), 142–150.

Every Student Succeeds Act of 2015, PL 114-95,§ 114 Stat.

Fach, B. (1994). The gift of believing. *Equity & Excellence, 2, 9.*

Fallon, A., & Katz, L. A. (2008). Augmentative and alternative communication and literacy teams: Facing the challenges, forging ahead. *Seminars in Speech and Language, 29*, 112–119.

Fallon, A., Light, J., McNaughton, D., Drager, K., & Hammer, C. (2004). The effects of direct instruction on the single-word reading skills of children who require augmentative and alternative communication. *Journal of Speech, Language, and Hearing Research, 47*, 1424–1439.

Falvey, M. (2004). Towards realizing the influence of "Toward realization of the least restrictive environments for severely disabled students." *Research and Practice for Persons with Severe Disabilities, 29*(1), 9–10.

Finke, E. H., McNaughton, D. B., & Drager, K. D. (2009). All children can and should have the opportunity to learn: General education teachers' perspectives on including children with autism spectrum disorder who require AAC. *Augmentative and Alternative Communication, 25*(2), 110–122.

Fisher, D. (1999). According to their peers: Inclusion as high school students see it. *Mental Retardation, 37*(6), 458–467.

Fisher, D., Sax, C., & Jorgensen, C. M. (1998). Philosophical foundations of inclusive, restructuring schools. In C. M. Jorgensen (Ed.), *Restructuring high schools for all students: Taking inclusion to the next level* (pp. 29–47). Baltimore, MD: Paul H. Brookes Publishing Co.

Fisher, D., Sax, C., Rodifer, K., & Pumpian, I. (1999). Teachers' perspectives of curriculum and climate changes: Benefits of inclusive education. *Journal for a Just and Caring Education, 5*, 256–268.

Fisher, M., & Meyer, L. (2002). Development and social competence after two years for students enrolled in inclusive and self-contained educational programs. *Research and Practice for Persons with Severe Disabilities, 27*, 165–174.

Forest, M. (1987). *Inclusive education.* Workshop sponsored by the Institute on Disability, University of New Hampshire, Concord.

Friedrich, R. (2012). *We all fit together.* Retrieved from http://subhubonline.blogspot. com/2012/07/we-all-fit-together.html

Giangreco, M. F. (1986). Effects of integrated therapy: A pilot study. *Journal of The Association for Persons with Severe Handicaps, 11,* 205–208.

Giangreco, M. F., Cloninger, C. J., & Iverson, V. S. (2011). *Choosing outcomes and accommodations for children (COACH)* (3rd ed.). Baltimore, MD: Paul H. Brookes Publishing Co.

Gold, M. (1980). *Try another way training manual.* Austin, TX: Marc Gold & Associates.

Goossens', C. (1989). Aided communication intervention before assessment: A case study of a child with cerebral palsy. *AAC: Augmentative and Alternative Communication, 5,* 14–26.

Grandin, T. (2009). Visual abilities and sensory differences in a person with autism. *Biological Psychology, 65*(1), 15–16.

Grigal, M., & Hart, D. (Eds.). (2012). Post-secondary education and young adults with intellectual disabilities [Special issue]. *Journal of Policy and Practice in Intellectual Disabilities, 9*(4), 221–312.

Guralnick, M. J., Connor, R., Hammond, M., Gottman, J. M., & Kinnish, K. (1996). Immediate effects of mainstreamed settings on the social interactions and social integration of preschool children. *American Journal on Mental Retardation, 100,* 359–377.

Habib, D. (2007). *Including Samuel.* Durham: University of New Hampshire Institute on Disability.

Habib, D. (2016). *Intelligent lives* [DVD.] Durham: University of New Hampshire Institute on Disability.

Haddon, M. (2003). *The curious incident of the dog in the night-time.* New York, NY: Doubleday.

Hehir, T. (2002). Eliminating ableism in education. *Harvard Educational Review, 72*(1), 1–32.

Helmstetter, E., Curry, C. A., Brennan, M., & Sampson-Saul, M. (1998). Comparison of general and special education classrooms of students with severe disabilities. *Education and Training in Mental Retardation and Developmental Disabilities, 33,* 216–227.

Higher Education Opportunity Act, PL 110-315 112 STAT.2075.

Hoopmann, K. (2006). *All cats have Asperger syndrome.* Philadelphia, PA: Jessica Kingsley.

Huefner, D. S. (1994). The mainstreaming cases: Tensions and trends for school administrators. *Educational Administration Quarterly, 30,* 27–55.

Hunt, P., & Farron-Davis, F. (1992). A preliminary investigation of IEP quality and content associated with placement in general education versus special education classes. *Journal of The Association for Persons with Severe Handicaps, 17,* 247–253.

Hunt, P., Farron-Davis, F., Beckstead, S., Curtis, D., & Goetz, L. (1994). Evaluating the effects of placement of students with severe disabilities in general education versus special classes. *Journal of The Association for Persons with Severe Handicaps, 19,* 200–214.

Hunt, P., Soto, G., Maier, J., Muller, E., & Goetz, L. (2002). Collaborative teaming to support students with augmentative and alternative communication needs in general education classrooms. *Augmentative and Alternative Communication, 18*(1), 20–35.

Hussman, J. (2008). *We thought you'd never ask: Voices of people with autism.* Boulder, CO: Landlocked Films.

Individuals with Disabilities Education Act (IDEA) of 1990, PL 101-476, 20 U.S.C. §§ 1400 *et seq.*

Individuals with Disabilities Education Improvement Act (IDEA) of 2004, PL 108-446, 20 U.S.C. §§1400 *et seq.*

Institute for Community Inclusion. (2016). *College options for people with intellectual disabilities.* Retrieved from http://www.thinkcollege.net/

Jackson, L., Ryndak, D., & Billingsley, F. (2000). Useful practices in inclusive education: A preliminary view of what experts in moderate to severe disabilities are saying. *Journal of The Association for Persons with Severe Handicaps, 25,* 129–141.

Jackson, L. B., Ryndak, D. L., & Wehmeyer, M. L. (2008/2009). The dynamic relationship between context, curriculum, and student learning: A case for inclusive education as a research-based practice. *Research and Practice for Persons with Severe Disabilities, 33–34*(4-1), 175–195.

Johnson, H. (2016). *Home ownership for people with disabilities.* Retrieved from http://www .thesimpledollar.com/home-ownership-for-people-with-disabilities

Jordan, K. A. (n.d.). *FAQ about sensory diets. Are sensory diets evidence-based?* Retrieved from https://www.iidc.indiana.edu/styles/iidc/defiles/IRCA/SensoryDietsFAQAreSensory DietsEvidenceBased.pdf

Jorgensen, C. (2005). The least dangerous assumption: A challenge to create a new paradigm. *Disability Solutions, 6*(3), 1, 5–9.

Jorgensen, C. M. (2014). *Teaching students with autism.* Washington, DC: National Education Association.

Jorgensen, C. M., & Calculator, S. N. (1994). The evolution of best practices in educating students with severe disabilities. In S. Calculator & C. Jorgensen (Eds.), *Including students with severe disabilities in schools: Fostering communication, interaction, and participation* (pp. 1–26). San Diego CA,: Singular Publishing Group.

Jorgensen, C. M., & Lambert, L. (2012). Inclusion means more than just being "in:" Planning full participation of students with intellectual and other developmental disabilities in the general education classroom. *International Journal of Whole Schooling, 8*(2), 21–35.

Jorgensen, C. M., McSheehan, M., & Sonnenmeier, R. (2007). Presumed competence reflected in the educational programs of students with IDD before and after the Beyond Access professional development intervention. *Journal of Intellectual and Developmental Disabilities, 32*(4), 248–262.

Jorgensen, C. M., McSheehan, M., & Sonnenmeier, R. M. (2010). *The Beyond Access Model: Promoting membership, participation, and learning for students with disabilities in the general education classroom.* Baltimore, MD: Paul H. Brookes Publishing Co.

Jorgensen, C. M., Mroczka, M. M., & Williams, S. (1997). *Class of '96: An inclusive community of learners* [Videotape]. Durham: Institute on Disability University of New Hampshire.

Jorgensen, C. M., Schuh, M., & Nisbet, J. (2006). *The inclusion facilitator's guide.* Baltimore, MD: Paul H. Brookes Publishing Co.

Kalambouka, A., Farrell, P., Dyson, A., & Kaplan, I. (2007). The impact of placing pupils with special educational needs in mainstream schools on the achievement of their peers. *Educational Research, 49*(4), 365–382.

Karger, J. (2004). *Access to the general curriculum for students with disabilities: A discussion of the interrelationship between IDEA '97 and NCLB.* Wakefield, MA: National Center on Accessing the General Curriculum. Retrieved from http://aem.cast.org/about/publications/2004/ ncac-curriculum-access-idea97-nclb.html

Kearns, J., Towles-Reeves, E., Kleinert, H., Kleinert, J., & Thomas, M. (2011). Characteristics of and implications for students participating in alternate assessment based on alternate academic achievement standards. *Journal of Special Education, 45*(1), 3–14.

Kleinert, H., Garrett, B., Towels, E., Garrett, M., Nowak-Drabik, K., Waddell, C., & Kearns, J.F. (2002). Alternate assessment scores and life outcomes for students with significant disabilities: Are they related? *Assessment for Effective Intervention, 28,* 19–30.

Kleinert, J., Holman, A., McSheehan, M., & Kearns, J. F. (2010). *The importance of developing communicative competence.* Retrieved from http://www.naacpartners.org/publications/20 10KlienertHolmanMcSheehanKearns.pdf

Kluth, P. (2010). *You're going to love this kid! Teaching children with autism in the inclusive classroom* (2nd ed.). Baltimore, MD: Paul H. Brookes Publishing Co.

Kunc, N. (1995). *The right to be disabled.* Nanaimo, British Columbia, Canada: Axis Consultation.

Kurth, J., & Mastergeorge, A. M. (2010). Academic and cognitive profiles of students with autism: Implications for classroom practice and placement. *International Journal of Special Education, 25*(2), 8–14.

Lears, L. (1998). *Ian's walk: A story about autism.* Park Ridge, IL: Albert Whitman and Company.

Leary, M. R., & Hill, D. A. (1996). Moving on: Autism and movement disturbance. *Mental Retardation, 34*(1), 39–53.

Leslie, L., & Caldwell, J. S. (2017). *Qualitative Reading Inventory-6.* Hoboken, NJ: Pearson.

Light, J., & Drager, K. (2007). AAC technologies for young children with complex communication needs: State of the science and future research directions. *Augmentative and Alternative Communication, 23*(3), 204–216.

Light, J., & McNaughton, D. (1993). Literacy and augmentative and alternative communication (AAC): The expectations and priorities of parents and teachers. *Topics in Language Disorders, 13,* 33–46.

Light, J., McNaughton, D., Weyer, M., & Karg, L. (2008). Evidence-based literacy instruction for individuals who require augmentative and alternative communication: A case study of a student with multiple disabilities. *Seminars in Speech and Language, 20,* 119–132.

Light, J. C. (1997). Communication is the essence of human life: Reflections on communicative competence. *Augmentative and Alternative Communication, 13*(2), 61–70.

Lovett, H. (1996). *Learning to listen: Positive approaches and people with difficult behavior.* Baltimore, MD: Paul H. Brookes Publishing Co.

Martin, J., Jorgensen, C. M., & Klein, J. (1998). The promise of friendship for students with disabilities. In C. Jorgensen (Ed.), *Restructuring high schools for all students: Taking inclusion to the next level* (pp. 145–182). Baltimore, MD: Paul H. Brookes Publishing Co.

Maslow, A. H. (1954). *Motivation and personality.* New York, NY: Harper & Row.

McDonnell, J., Jameson, J. M., Riesen, T., & Polychronis, S. (2014). Embedded instruction in inclusive settings. In D. M. Browder & F. Spooner (Eds.), *More language arts, math, and science for students with severe disabilities* (pp. 15–36). Baltimore, MD: Paul H. Brookes Publishing Co.

McGrew, K. S., & Evans, J. (2004). *Expectations for students with cognitive disabilities: Is the cup half empty or half full? Can the cup overflow?* Minneapolis: University of Minnesota, National Center on Educational Outcomes.

McKenzie, B. (2006). *Reflections of Erin: The importance of belonging, relationships, and learning with each other.* Seaman, OH: The Art of Possibility Press.

McLaughlin, S. (1985). *Sarah, plain and tall.* New York, NY: Harper & Row.

McSheehan, M., Sonnenmeier, R. M., & Jorgensen, C. M. (2009). Membership, participation, and learning in general education classrooms for students with autism spectrum disorders who use AAC. In P. Mirenda & T. Iacono (Eds.), *Autism spectrum disorders and AAC* (pp. 413–442). Baltimore, MD: Paul H. Brookes Publishing Co.

Meyer, A., Rose, D. H., & Gordon, D. (2014). *Universal design for learning: Theory and practice.* Wakefield, MA: CAST Professional Publishing.

Millar, D. C., Light, J., & McNaughton, D.B. (2004). The effect of direct instruction and writer's workshop on the early writing skills of children who use augmentative and alternative communication. *Augmentative and Alternative Communication, 20,* 164–178.

Morse, M. (1999, Spring). Cortical visual impairment: Some words of caution. *Review, 31,* 21–26.

Mount, B., & Zwernik, K. (1994). *Making futures happen: A manual for facilitators of personal futures planning.* St. Paul: Minnesota Governor's Council on Developmental Disabilities.

Musselwhite, C. (2016). *AAC intervention.* Retrieved from http://www.aacintervention.com/default.asp?sec_id=180009852

National Center for Learning Disabilities. (2008). *Executive function fact sheet.* Retrieved from http://www.ldonline.org/article/24880/

National Joint Committee for the Communication Needs of Persons with Severe Disabilities. (2003). *Position statement on access to communication services and supports: Concerns regarding the application of restrictive "eligibility" policies.* Retrieved from http://www.asha.org/policy/PS2003-00227/

National Professional Development Center on Autism Spectrum Disorders. (2016). Chapel Hill: University of North Carolina.

No Child Left Behind Act of 2001, PL 107-110, 115 Stat. 1425, 20 U.S.C. §§ 6301 *et seq.*

Oberti v. Board of Education, 995 F.2d 1204 (1993).

O'Brien, J., & Forest, M. (1989): *Action for inclusion.* Toronto, Canada: Inclusion Press.

Pearpoint, J., Forest, M., & O'Brien, J. (1996). MAPS, circles of friends and PATH: Powerful tools to help build caring communities. In S. Stainback & W. Stainback (Eds.), *Inclusion: A guide for educators* (pp. 67–86). Baltimore, MD: Paul H. Brookes Publishing Co.

Pennsylvania Training and Technical Assistance Network. (2008). *Supplementary aids and services (SaS) consideration toolkit.* Harrisburg, PA: Author.

Petner, J. (2004). *Administrative support for inclusive education.* Presentation sponsored by the Institute on Disability at the University of New Hampshire, Concord.

Pitonyak, D. (2005). *10 things you can do to support a person with difficult behaviors.* Retrieved from http://www.dimagine.com/10things.pdf

Powers, L. E., Singer, G. H. S., & Sowers, J.-A. (Eds.). (1996). *On the road to autonomy: Promoting self-competence in children and youth with disabilities.* Baltimore, MD: Paul H. Brookes Publishing Co.

Prizant, B. M., Wetherby, A. M., Rubin, E., Laurent, A. C., & Rydell, P. J. (2006). *The SCERTS Model: A comprehensive educational approach for children with autism spectrum disorders.* Baltimore, MD: Paul H. Brookes Publishing Co.

Pufpaff, L. A., Blischak, D. M., & Lloyd, L. L. (2000). Effects of modified orthography on the identification of printed words. *American Journal on Mental Retardation, 105*(1), 14–24.

Rainforth, B., York, J., & MacDonald, C. (1997). *Collaborative teams for students with severe disabilities: Integrating therapy and educational services* (2nd ed.). Baltimore, MD: Paul H. Brookes Publishing Co.

Rehabilitation Act of 1973, PL 93-112, 29 U.S.C. §§ 701 *et seq.*

Ringer, L., & Lovett, H. (1987). *Positive behavior supports* [Interview transcript]. Retrieved from http://mn.gov/mnddc/positive_behavior_supports/herbLovett.html

Roman-Lantzy, C. (2007). *Cortical visual impairment: An approach to assessment and intervention.* New York, NY: American Foundation for the Blind.

Romski, M. A., & Sevcik, R. A. (1997). Augmentative and alternative communication for children with developmental disabilities. Mental Retardation and Developmental Disabilities Research Reviews, 3, 363–368.

Romski, M., & Sevcik, R. (2005a). Augmentative and alternative communication for children with developmental disabilities. *Mental Retardation and Developmental Disabilities Research Reviews, 3,* 363–368.

Romski, M., & Sevcik, R. (2005b). Augmentative communication and early intervention: Myths and realities. *Infants and Young Children: An Interdisciplinary Journal of Special Care Practices, 18*(3), 174–185.

Rosenthal, R., & Jacobson, L. (1968). *Pygmalion in the classroom.* Austin, TX: Holt, Rinehart & Winston.

Rowland, C., & Schweigert, P. (2000). Tangible symbols, tangible outcomes. *Augmentative and Alternative Communication, 16*(2), 61–78.

Ryndak, D. L., Alper, S., Ward, T., Storch, J. F., & Montgomery, J. W. (2010). Long-term outcomes of services in inclusive and self-contained settings for siblings with comparable significant disabilities. *Education and Training in Autism and Developmental Disabilities, 45,* 38–53.

Ryndak, D. L., Morrison, A., & Sommerstein, L. (1999). Literacy before and after inclusion in general education settings: A case study. *Journal of The Association for Persons with Severe Handicaps, 24,* 5–22.

Sapon-Shevin, M. (2003). Inclusion: A matter of social justice. *Educational Leadership, 61*(2), 25–28.

Schnorr, R. F. (1990). Peter? He comes and goes: First graders' perspectives on a part-time mainstream student. *Journal of The Association for Persons with Severe Handicaps, 15*(4), 231–240.

Schuster, J., & Erickson, K. (2014). *Text complexity in the Dynamic Learning Maps Alternate Assessment System.* Lawrence: University of Kansas Center for Educational Testing and Evaluation.

Sexual Information and Education Council of the U.S. (2004). *Guidelines for comprehensive sexuality education: Kindergarten–12th grade.* Washington, DC: S.I.E.C.U.S. National Guidelines Task Force.

Shapiro, J. (1993). *No pity: Forging a new civil rights movement.* New York, NY: Crown.

Shogren, K. A., Wehmeyer, M. L., Burke, K. M., & Palmer, S. B. (2017). *The self-determination learning model of instruction: Teacher's guide.* Lawrence: Kansas University Center on Developmental Disabilities.

Snell, M., Brady, N., McLean, L., Ogletree, B., Siegel, E., Sylvester, L., Mineo, B., Paul, D., Romski, M., & Sevcik, R. (2010). Twenty years of communication intervention research with individuals who have severe intellectual and developmental disabilities. *American Journal on Intellectual and Developmental Disabilities, 115*(5), 364–380.

Sonnenmeier, R., McSheehan, M., & Jorgensen, C. M. (2005). A case study of team supports for a student with autism's communication and engagement within the general education curriculum: Preliminary report of the beyond access model. *Augmentative and Alternative Communication, 21*(2), 101–115.

Soto, G., Muller, E., Hunt, P., & Goetz, L. (2001). Critical issues in the inclusion of students who use augmentative and alternative communication: An educational team perspective. *Augmentative and Alternative Communication, 17,* 62–72.

South Dakota Department of Education. (2012). *Primer on the provision of extended year services in special education.* Retrieved from http://doe.sd.gov/oess/documents/SE_ExtScYr.pdf

South Dakota Department of Education. (2013). *Justification for placement.* Retrieved from https://doe.sd.gov/oess/documents/JustPlacE.pdf

Stetson & Associates. (2015). *Finding time for collaboration and using it well.* Retrieved from http://inclusiveschools.org/finding-time-for-collaboration-and-using-it-well/

Stimmel, K. (2010). *Supporting sensory needs in the classroom* [PowerPoint slides]. Durham, NH: National Center on Inclusive Education.

Sturm, J. A., & Clendon, S. A. (2004). Augmentative and alternative communication, language, and literacy. Fostering the relationship. *Topics in Language Disorders, 24*(1), 76–91.

Strum, J., Spadorcia, S., Cunningham, J., Cali, K., Staples, A., Erickson, K., Koppenhaver, D. (2006). What happens to reading between first and third grade? Implications for students who use AAC. *Augmentative and Alternative Communication, 22,* 21–36.

Szabo, J. L. (2000). Maddie's story: Inclusion through physical and occupational therapy. *Teaching Exceptional Children, 33*(2), 12–18.

TASH. (n.d.). *Inclusive education.* Retrieved from http://tash.org/advocacy-issues/inclusive-education

Tashie, C., Malloy, J. M., & Lichtenstein, S. J. (1998). Transition or graduation? Supporting all students to plan for the future. In C. M. Jorgensen (Ed.), *Restructuring high schools for all students: Taking inclusion to the next level* (pp. 233–260). Baltimore, MD: Paul H. Brookes Publishing Co.

Tashie, C., & Martin, J. (1996). *Voices of friendship* [Videotape]. Durham: Institute on Disability, University of New Hampshire.

Tashie, C., & Schuh, M. (1993, Spring). Why not community-based instruction? *Equity and Excellence,* 15–17.

Tashie, C., Shapiro-Barnard, S., & Rossetti, Z. (2006). *Seeing the charade: What we need to do and undo to make friendships happen.* Nottingham, United Kingdom: Inclusive Solutions.

Theoharis, G., & Causton-Theoharis, J. (2010). *Include, belong, learn.* Retrieved from http://www.ascd.org/publications/educational-leadership/oct10/vol68/num02/Include,-Belong,-Learn.aspx

U.S. Department of Education. (n.d.). *Building the legacy of IDEA 2004: Regulations Sec. 300.106 extended school year services(p. 46763).* Retrieved from https://sites.ed.gov/idea/regs/b/b/300.106

U.S. Department of Education. (2014). *Thirty-fifth annual report to Congress on the implementation of the Individuals with Disabilities Education Act, Parts B and C: 2013.* Retrieved from http://www2.ed.gov/about/reports/annual/osep/2013/parts-b-c/index.html

U.S. Department of Education, Office of Special Education Programs. (2006). *Assistance to the states for the education of children with disabilities and preschool grants for children with disabilities.* Federal Register, CFR Parts 300 and 301, p. 46765.

U.S. Department of Labor, Office of Disability Employment Policy. (n.d.) *Customized employment Q and A.* Retrieved from https://www.dol.gov/odep/topics/CustomizedEmployment.htm

University of Kansas. (2016). *Schoolwide Integrated Framework for Transformation.* Lawrence: Author.

Updike, C. D. (2006). The use of FM systems for children with attention deficit disorder. *Journal of Educational Audiology, 13,* 7–14.

Vietnam Era Veterans' Readjustment Assistance Act of 1974, PL 93-504, 38 U.S.C. §§ 4212.

Villa, R., & Thousand, J. (Eds.) (2005). *Creating an inclusive school* (2nd ed.). Alexandria, VA: Association for Supervision and Curriculum Development.

Walker-Hirsch, L. (2007). *The facts of life…and more: Sexuality and intimacy for people with intellectual disabilities.* Baltimore, MD: Paul H. Brookes Publishing Co.

Wehmeyer, M. L. (2002). *Self-determination and the education of students with disabilities* (Digest No. E632). Reston, VA: ERIC Clearinghouse on Disabilities and Gifted Education.

Wehmeyer, M., & Agran, M. (2006). Promoting access to the general curriculum for students with significant cognitive disabilities. In D. M. Browder, & F. Spooner (Eds.), *Teaching language arts, math, and science to students with significant cognitive disabilities* (pp. 15–37). Baltimore, MD: Paul H. Brookes Publishing Co.

White, J., & Weiner, J. S. (2004). Influence of least restrictive environment and community based training on integrated employment outcomes for transitioning students with severe disabilities. *Journal of Vocational Rehabilitation, 21*(3), 149–156.

Wong, C., Odom, S. L., Hume, K. A., Cox, C. W., Fettig, A., Kurcharczyk, S., Brock, M. E., Plavnick, J. B., Fleury, V. P., & Schultz, T. R. (2015). Evidence-based practices for children, youth, and young adults with autism spectrum disorder: A comprehensive review. *Journal of Autism and Developmental Disorders, 45*, 1951–1966.

Workforce Investment Act (WIA) of 1998, PL 105-220, 29 U.S.C. §§ 2801 *et seq.*

Wright's Law. (n.d.). *Inclusion: Answers to frequently asked questions from the NEA.* Retrieved from http://www.wrightslaw.com/info/lre.faqs.inclusion.htm

Wright's Law. (2011). *Extended school year services.* Retrieved from http://www.wrightslaw.com/info/esy.index.htm

York, J., Rainforth, B., & Giangreco, M. F. (1990). Transdisciplinary teamwork and integrated therapy: Clarifying the misconceptions. *Pediatric Physical Therapy, 2*(2), 73–79.

Yudin, M., & Musgrove, M. (2012). *Applicability of the LRE requirements under Part B of the Individuals with Disabilities Education Act (IDEA) to transition work placements.* Retrieved from https://www2.ed.gov/policy/speced/guid/idea/memosdcltrs/062212workplacelre2q2012.pdf

Zabala, J. (2005). *Using the SETT framework to level the learning field for students with disabilities.* Retrieved from http://www.joyzabala.com/uploads/Zabala_SETT_Leveling_the_Learning_Field.pdf

Zangari, C. (2012a). *Pivotal skills for AAC intervention: Aided language input.* Retrieved from http://praacticalaac.org/praactical/pivotal-skills-for-aac-intervention-aided-language-input/

Zangari, C. (2012b). *Using the AAC device/app: Getting the team onboard.* Retrieved from http://praacticalaac.org/strategy/836/

Index

Note: Page numbers followed by *f* and *t* indicate figures and tables, respectively.